E-Leader

Reinventing Leadership in a Connected Economy

Robert Hargrove

PERSEUS PUBLISHING
Cambridge, Massachusetts

Cataloging-in-Publication Data is available from the Library of Congress
ISBN: 0-7382-0264-9

Copyright © 2001 by Robert Hargrove

Perseus Publishing is a member of the Perseus Books Group.

Find us on the World Wide Web at http://www.perseuspublishing.com
Perseus Publishing books are available at special discounts for bulk purchases in the U.S. by corporations, institutions, and other organizations. For more information, please contact the Special Markets Department at HarperCollins Publishers, 10 East 53rd Street, New York, NY 10022, or call 1-212-207-7528.

Text design by Elizabeth Lahey
Set in 10-point Minion by Perseus Publishing Services

First printing, January 2001
1 2 3 4 5 6 7 8 9 10—03 02 01 00

Contents

Acknowledgments

I had wanted to write a book about leadership in business for a decade. Though I had a teachable point of view to offer about just what it is that makes one person a leader, much of what could be said about the subject had been said. There was no need to write yet another book that started with "build a shared vision," "build a team," "mobilize people." Besides, there was often no cultural clearing that *allowed for* and *pulled for* leadership in organizations.

The emergence of the e-economy not only created a context for leaders and a culture of leadership, it also created the context for a radically different kind of leader and for a radically new and different kind of business. Would it be possible to write a book that declared a bold new leadership style for the twenty-first century, while at the same time serving as a practical guide for becoming an e-leader and building an e-business? It was an intriguing challenge. Yet I knew that pulling all the pieces of business together to meet it would be a huge undertaking.

I knew that given the call for the book by CEOs and other leaders, as well as the timeliness of the subject, I would never be able to meet the challenge as a solitary individual working in isolation; it would take a great group. This book then is purely a result of a collaborative team effort. When I say team effort, I do not mean the typical case of the author working one-on-one with an Amy or a Bill and/or a Sam to review drafts and what not. I mean a team of people thinking and interacting together throughout the process—from concept to shelf.

I want to thank Robin Davis for courageously, skillfully, and undauntingly taking the book out into the world when it was not more than a germ of an idea and making its time come. There are certain people that I count on in life to help make my dreams come true and Robin is one of them. I want to thank Nick

Philipson of Perseus, not just the typical deal-a-day acquisitions editor, but also an inspired and enthusiastic roll-up-your-sleeves "working editor" who impacts a book's development. Our wonderful conversations were like an alchemical chamber that served to create focus around the original idea of the book, while at the same time creating space for creative sparks to fly that resulted in three to four new evolutionary permutations.

I also want to express my profound gratitude to the editorial team (first collectively then individually) of Steve Maas, Carl Kaestner, and of course my wife, Susan Youngquist. Steve was perhaps the brightest star on the roster with a positive, upbeat spirit, a dedicated can-do attitude, and an extraordinary level of creativity and productivity. Steve's genius was the inspiration behind the interludes, helping bring the stories of e-leaders and their business adventures to life. Together we framed them, passed drafts back and forth, noticed what was missing that would make a difference, and rendered them complete. Steve also proved to be brilliant in resolving the puzzles, dilemmas, and complex issues that you inevitably run into in a book of this kind.

Carl Kaestner, a colleague and friend, deserves a special acknowledgment for his enthusiastic networking and research efforts. Carl personally decided which e-leaders would provide us the most important insights and then personally orchestrated fifty interviews with people whose schedules were positively frenetic. Carl sometimes had to negotiate five minutes in a taxi to do an interview here, ten minutes in an airport lounge there, twenty minutes in the office or on the drive home from work. These conversations provided the basic building blocks upon which many of the chapters in the book are based. Michel Renaud, my coaching colleague, supported this research process and provided special perspectives on international e-business developments.

Then there is my wife, Susan, who acted as an anchor point for the whole project. Her editorial insights that always get to the heart of the matter and her organizational ability made it possible to transform what might otherwise be considered "a pile of papers" into a coherent and cohesive manuscript. She was also extremely skillful in transforming a group of far-flung collaborators, each with a set of diverse tasks, into a coherent team moving at Net speed toward a pressing deadline. At the same time, on a personal level, she was extremely patient with my often preoccupied mind and writer's hours.

Finally, I would like to acknowledge my daughters, Vanessa and Eva. Vanessa, my older daughter, initiated her budding career as a school teacher by providing superb child care of two-and-a-half-year-old Eva, whose vocabulary grew by leaps and bounds in the process. This gave me the experience of being personally supported in my efforts to make a qualitative difference in the world on a professional basis. Eva painted me bright-colored abstract paintings which she hung on my office walls in the morning, sang me children's songs in the evening, and introduced me to her stuffed pet dog whom she named "Bone." Her presence at my office door was just what was needed to cheer my spirits, inspire my writings, and bring me back to reality. Thanks to all.

Robert Hargrove
April 2000

Introduction:

Every Leader an E-Leader,
Every Business an E-Business

On New Year's Eve, the big illuminated white ball with 50,00 halogen bulbs dropped from atop the tower on a building in Times Square, marking the year 2000 to millions of revelers. Moments before, Peter Jennings of ABC news had been on the phone with Steve Case, CEO of AOL. He asked him, "What do you think we are witnessing now?" Case responded without a second's delay, "We are witnessing the beginning of what will probably be known as the Internet century." Whether Case's words were prophetic or wishful musings on his part remains to be seen.

However, only a few weeks later, an event occurred that in a sense validated what Case had said. I was in Europe at the time, staying at the Holiday Inn in Amsterdam. I had asked the receptionist to pass me a copy of the *International Herald Tribune* and was stunned by the eye-popping headline: "AOL buys Time Warner, an Internet triumph." To me this was an historic moment in that it represented a single event in which the new e-economy, based on electronic connections, trumped the old i-economy based on physical mass.

The $150 billion AOL paid for Time Warner was living proof that AOL's stock valuation was made of cash, not helium. As the smiling (but usually grim-faced) Gerald Levin said in a CNN interview, "I am here to attest to the power of the e-economy to transform business models in the media and other industries, as well as its financial strength." Some pundits referred to the deal as a powerful symbol of "simply the greatest business transformation ever." A perfect cairn marker for the new millennium, the deal brings home the message that the Net has moved from the remote margins to mainstream America.

The Internet Economy: Fad or Trend

To be sure, you would have had to live in a darkened cave without any contact with the outside world for the last two to three years to not know that the e-economy is real. And one of the surest signs of the new economy was the entrepreneurial explosion that resulted in a plethora of new Internet firms. This explosion of growth was fueled by venture capital infusion and an unexpected stock market run-up.

Unbridled optimism mixed with a growing pessimism resulted in crazy markets. The stock market tumbled in April 1999 by 500 points, only to recover the next day. The same thing happened on several other occasions, including April 2000, when the Dow and NASDAQ suffered their biggest single-day losses in history after months of unparalleled growth.

Even prior to this market "correction," investors saw that companies like Web-Van, CarsDirect, and Zhone Technologies, which had received record venture capital investments, weren't paying handsome returns, a growing number of voices began asking, "Is the e-economy over? Is the Internet not a trend, but just a fad? Comments that the Internet is over always remind me of what Jasper James, head of the U.S. Patent Office, said in 1875, "We should close the patent office, as all of the major inventions have already occurred and there won't be much for us to do."

It would be dangerous to assume that the e-economy "already happened" due to the fact that most Global 2000 firms now have Web sites or because of the flawed business models of a few dot-coms or their lack of solid business discipline. As John Doerr, the Silicon Valley venture capitalist of Smith, Kleiner, and Doerr, (who Scott McNealy of Sun Microsystems once likened to "the Energizer bunny on steroids, hard wired to the Hoover Dam") says, "Believe it or not, despite market corrections, the Internet is actually under-hyped."

In fact, he said that over the next ten years, "We all have the opportunity to be co-conspirators in the largest legal creation of new wealth in history." Just look at the track record of some of the more disciplined companies of the new economy. In April of 1999, Cisco Systems, the backbone of the Internet, surpassed Microsoft in its market capitalization, which to many represented the turning of the tide from the PC to the Internet era. At the same time, 3Com decided to spin off the Palm Pilot—a device that would free people from their desktops and allow them to connect to the Internet anytime, anyplace. Today, Palm Pilot is worth $40 billion more than its parent.

The E-Economy is Much Bigger Than E-Commerce

In the 19th century, if you wanted to get rich you bought the biggest and most efficient farm you could. In the 20th century, if you wanted to get rich, you went out and dug an oil well, or built a big efficient factory—an auto parts factory perhaps that turned out metal parts for one of the big three auto-makers. In this century, getting rich is about the power of ideas.

You get rich when you come up with a "game-changing" idea that creates a new market or recharges an existing one. Seth Godin, author of Permission Marketing, has pointed out that success is a matter of creating an "idea virus."[1] You create an idea virus by changing the conversation about how things are done. If you can change the conversation, you can change how people think and you can change the world. Companies like FedEx, Charles Schwab, and Enron changed the conversation by coming up with game-changing ideas, as did Amazon, Yahoo! and eBAy.

> The true impact of the Internet will be for ideas to combine and recombine in new ways so as to result in habitual, radical innovation.

One of the primary roles of leaders in the 21st century will be to be able to create a "farm" or "factory" for ideas. This has to do with leaders setting ambitious aspirations that can only be achieved by coming up with new ideas, fresh approaches, and innovative solutions that fly in the face of orthodoxy. It also has to do with being willing to stretch your definition of your business and create a culture based on creative collaboration—a culture where ideas circulate, combine, and recombine in ways that result in new knowledge, value, and wealth.

Gary Hamel, author of Leading the Revolution, has pointed out that the pace of economic evolution has always been a matter of quantity and quality of interconnections between the people, and the ideas that they possess inside their heads.[2] With the Internet connecting everyone and everything to everything else, the speed of innovation that we saw in the past century will be akin to moving in a slow train past a motionless pastoral scene, compared to what lies ahead.

As the ideas that people with different views and perspective circulate, combine, and recombine, creative sparks will be lit in every field, resulting in unprecedented levels of creativity and innovation. The world economy is about to enter high-velocity hyper-space through what Hamel calls a "dervish-like dance of intellect, imagination, and capital." The technology of the Internet is much more significant than e-commerce. Its true significance is that it allows for habitual, radical business concept innovation.

> We will see a dramatic increase in business concept innovation whether we run a 100-year-old natural gas business with hard assets or an ethereal dot-com.

One of the key challenges for leaders in every company will be to break the grip and excel beyond the notion that the purpose of a company is to do one thing. Ford made cars, Boeing made planes, ATT offered long distance, Dell made computers. The notion of "built to last" must be changed to "built to innovate." If we stick to the idea of doing one thing, today's visionary will be tomorrow's has-beens winding up marooned on an island of dead business models—Ken Olsen of Dec and John Akers of IBM and its main frame business are prime examples.

In fact, the idea won't be to fight the competition, but rather to avoid them by innovating new business models that surround and obviate the competition. Ford is no longer just in the business of selling cars, but has come up with an innovative business concept that involves selling life-time automotive services to its customers, from financing to repairs, to GPS map cartridges for the family trip. Schwabb is good example of this with its innovative e-trading initiatives, as well as its forays into private banking. So is Williams, a hundred-year-old natural gas company that cashed in on the bandwidth gold rush by stuffing ancient natural gas pipes with fiber optic cable.

Being an E-Leader is More Than Running a Dot-com

The "aha" experience every executive needs to have is that the secret to success in the Internet age lies in developing the capability for radically and habitually coming up with game changing business ideas, not just engaging in e-commerce. In the Internet age, companies must come up with cultures that mirror the Internet—cultures that are entrepreneurial, knowledge-based, collaborative, and experimental.

The Internet is generating a creative economy that will shape every industry and business in the 21st century, whether you are a dot-com or a Fortune 500. The single most profound influence of the Internet will be to move us to a "Creative Economy." The Web makes it possible for leaders to foster ever new juxtapositions of talent and perspectives around customer needs. This lights creative sparks and leads to both to radical innovation, as well as radical new business concepts. The era of working harder and harder to cut costs, for smaller and smaller returns is over. In the same sense, the Internet and the creative economy will transform what it is to be a leader in the 2lst century. The question: Is who you are as a leader today sufficient for you and your business to succeed in the years ahead?

> The e-leaders central task will be to create a dervish-like dance of imagination, intellect, and capital that results in unprecedented new knowledge, value, and wealth.

E-leaders will need to dance on the edge of a sword, creating space by offering an inspiring vision that provides opportunities for people, and contracting space in driving for results.

A Bold, New Leadership Paradigm for the 21st Century

Every time a seismic shift takes place in the economy, there are people who feel the vibrations long before the rest of us do, vibrations so strong they demand action—action that can seem rash or even stupid. Ferry owner, Cornelius Vanderbilt, jumped ship when he saw the railroads coming. Henry Ford quit his job as a shop mechanic and started Ford Motor. Jeff Bezos had a similar experience to that of Thomas Vanderbilt and Henry Ford when he peered into the maze of connected computers called the World Wide Web and realized that the future of retailing was glowing back at him.

We live in extraordinary times. We live in times in which the world is literally reinventing itself. The "big innovation regime" of the 2lst century that is spinning an extraordinary number of radical new business concepts is replacing the "big manufacturing regime" of the last century. The days of the stand-alone corporation appear to be over as business leaders scurry to get to market faster by building a virtual value chain. The management of hard assets like steel plants, oil refineries, and car production facilities is becoming less significant than the management of soft assets like intellect, imagination, and relationships.

Now, just as the corporation is being reinvented for the 21st century, leadership must also be reinvented. The prevailing leadership paradigm will not be sufficient to take us into the future. What will be required is a radically different leadership model, one that is so unlike the one inherited from the past that it is almost un-recognizable. The purpose of this book is to declare the leadership paradigm of the 20th century over and, in turn, to declare a bold, new, inventive and effective leadership paradigm that is as dynamic as the century that lies ahead.

One way of looking at a paradigm is as a conversation. The aim of this book is to inspire, empower, and enable you to change your own conversation about leadership so that you will be able to call yourself forth as the kind of leader who can succeed in the dynamic business environment unfolding around us. What we are talking about is a real transformation not just a change in form, one that ultimately impacts your ability to produce extraordinary and tangible results.

E-leaders must create a culture that mirrors the Internet—open, knowledge-based, collaborative, experimental, and boundaryless.

Changing the Conversation About Leadership

What is an e-leader? E-leaders are real entrepreneurs, who at the same time are masters of creative collaboration, sculpting new patterns of relationship and interaction to make the impossible happen. They develop a point of view about the future and the new opportunities that it holds, preferring the creative disequilibrium of creating new businesses to the tranquility of the status quo. Richard Branson, of Virgin LTD is an excellent example of an e-leader, one who not only uses a management style that mirrors the Internet (democratic, knowledge-based, experimental), but who also personally uses his imagination to create new business concepts, building a powerful, portable brand in the process.

E-leaders not only create an entrepreneurial environment for themselves, but also for e-leaders at every level of the company. They do this by setting "ambitious aspirations" that they and others can passionately engage in and by encouraging people to use their imagination to come up with non-conformist strategies to meet them. Charles Schwabb, for example, regularly challenges everyone in his company to grow the business by a minimum of 20 percent a year. The result is that every year is about creating something that never existed before rather than being a continuation of the same old story. This is what led to Schwabb's impressive foray into on-line investing.

E-leaders are willing to stretch their definitions of themselves and their business in order to realize their ambitious aspirations and are willing to put at risk the success they have become to make the impossible happen. Gary Wendt of GE Capital, for example, set a goal of 20 percent growth in earnings each year. To reach it, he created an elastic definition of the business, which was only financing household appliances when he took over. Today, GE Capital not only finances big ticket items like power plants, but works in close collaboration with GE's other product divisions, like the Jet Engines division, making it possible for them to develop innovative products faster by leasing jet engines to customers on a five year basis, rather than selling them.

> Can you concretely and holistically come up with new business concepts, rather than merely create new products or services?

Being an E-Leader is a Matter of Distinction

Generating a new conversation about leaders starts with a big idea—the e-leader—and then making some powerful new distinctions that give people a language to talk about it. Here are some of the transformations you will probably need to make to become an e-leader:

E-leaders invent their leadership style rather than inherit it from a recipe box. The fact is in today's fast paced business environment, the only way you can be effective is to adopt a dynamically "balanced" leadership style. Leaders can shift their leadership style in various situations by asking, "Who do I need to be in the matter?" and by calling themselves forth accordingly—directive, empowering, collaborative, facilitative, or whatever. As an executive coach, I often see leaders caught in a trap, one that comes from the belief that there is "the one right way to manage." Some managers get trapped in "bosship" which tends to shut creativity and initiative down. Others get trapped in empowerment, which leads to discussing everything to death. Still others get trapped in collaborating when its not needed.

E-leaders imagine the future, rather than try to predict it. When the charismatic CEO of DoCoMo, the Japanese telecom, looked at his white hot wireless telecommunications business one night in 1995, he didn't make any attempt to envision the future by predicting what his competitors would do. Instead, he made a declaration that DoCoMo would be the future of wireless telecommunications by providing customers with constant access to the Internet from their mobile phones. He then instructed his designers to create the first "I-mode phone," which in Japanese means "anywhere." Today, over 15 million subscribers have signed up, using I-mode to pay for commuter train tickets, shop for dinner by browsing the shelves of the local su-permarket on the way home, or play games like "fishing." DoCoMo has signed up over 15,000 Web sites that provide e-commerce content and are the first company in the world to offer high-speed Internet access. They are five years ahead of any North American or European competitor.

Design, build, test . . . and scale.

E-leaders focus on sourcing versus reacting. The e-leader is a generative leader who creates the future, rather than attempting to maintain the status quo. Their style is to "source" the future based on declaring powerful new possibilities, rather than to simply react to what s wrong, which is often the case with many managers. "Sourcing" the future not only means starting a lot of initiatives but bringing something into existence independently of its originator. This means standing in the future and acting from that future versus just pushing for results today or fix-ing what's wrong. E-leaders come up with innovative business concepts but also design, build, and test them and then finally scaling them until they take on a life of their own. Ask yourself, what do you spend most of your time doing, sourcing or reacting to what's wrong?

E-leaders accomplish what they need to accomplish through relationships, not re-sults-oriented doingness. Today, the three S's—strategy, structure, and systems—are being replaced by the three "P's"—purpose, processes, and people. Yet organiza-tions still often fail to accomplish what they need to accomplish. The reason is that many people in leadership positions do not know how to drive a result over the line. If we define a meaningful result as creating something new that builds knowl-edge, wealth, and value, rather than just saving nickels and dimes, what does it take to produce one? It not only requires passion and determina-tion, but also bringing far-flung collaborators together around a purpose larger than themselves to reach goals, solve problems, or discover something new.

We need passionate workers, not just knowledge workers.

E-leaders create a culture of spirits and hearts, not just heads and hands. John Burdette, a colleague in the Masterful Coaching Worldwide Network has made a brilliant observation. Great leaders have four qualities. First is spirit, which involves setting aspirational goals. Second is heart, which means in-spiring courage and compassion. Third is head, which represents knowledge. And the fourth is hand, which represents skills. The fact is that what shows up as missing with most leaders are the qualities of spirit and heart. The most obvious symptom of this is the climate of profound resignation that exists in many companies. What shows up as present is an abundance of head and hand. E-leaders need to be able to dynamically balance all of these qualities, in order to transform a climate of resignation into a climate of possibility and opportunity that brings out the best in people.

Five Clues to Doing Business in the E-Economy

Kevin Kelly, publisher, has written a book called *New Rules for a New Economy*. [3] In this book he says that in the old economy, the rules for getting wealthy were to set up a basic commodity business like cars or gasoline and be productive and efficient. Everything was done to get productivities and efficiencies. Today, the rules have changed. Your ability to amass wealth comes from the quantity and quality of economic relationships. The task is to bring far-flung collaborators together in ways that light creative sparks. These sparks can in turn be used to catalyze new innovations and new ventures.

> To succeed, e-leaders must be deeply clued into the changing shape of the new economy.

Other commentators beside Kelly have said that the new economy is still in its infancy and that it may be premature to carve a set of rules in stone. Nonetheless, I think we can find some pretty strong clues. The insights offered here were gleaned from studying hundreds of companies while writing this book—some big Fortune 500 type incumbents, others entrepreneurial e-attackers. They apply to almost any kind of business imaginable off- and on-line. They also introduce many of the key concepts you will find later in this book.

Clue 1. Shift from a management-led company to a customer-led company.   The industrial era was characterized by a push economy. Managers tapped natural resources like oil or gas, refined it and marketed it by pushing it out to as many consumers as possible. A push economy made sense in a world where most mass produced products like cars or gasoline were at best glorified commodities.

In a push economy, you tend to have management-led companies (rather than customer-led companies) where management sets the direction and everyone else follows. In most cases, these companies operate from a "me" point of view rather than a "you" point of view. They fall in love with their products and organize the company accordingly. This shows up in their product catalogues and Web site brochure-ware. When they build a Web site, it is designed around the products, not specific customers.

> The e-leader is one who creates a culture were people dream, imagine, collaborate, invent, and experiment.

These companies may have listening devices for their customers, but in most cases, there are only a very small number of people who have any contact with customers. Also these people tend to listen for filtered information in a tactical way, like what product model or product color they need to make, not soliciting feedback about the customer's real needs.

In a customer-led company, leadership takes a stand for what will differentiate the company in the marketplace. The leaders listen to their customers strategically, not tactically—not in a one-way, chest-pounding monologue, but a two-way dialogue. They are listening for answers to questions like: Who are our core customers? What are their desires, needs, dissatisfiers, and frustrations? What is our game-changing business model that will revolutionize our industry? How can we leverage the Internet to delivery great customer experience? What products and services should we be innovating with our customers? Can we change how we are organized to better serve our customer segments and do so on a one-to-one basis?

Instead of censoring or keeping a secret what customers say about their company, these leaders provide spaces for people to speak openly about what's great and what stinks. It's a good way to listen and respond to customers' real feelings. They even engage customers in supporting each other. AOL, for example, "hires" guides on a freebee basis to help new AOL users negotiate the Web portal. Cisco Systems has created a community space where its expert customers assist intermediate or beginner customers in deciding which of Cisco's products and services to buy, and more importantly, how to implement them. This not only reduces Cisco's service costs, but also serves to generate customer relationships and loyalty.

Clue 2. In a creative economy, the key is to continually come up with game changing business models.   Flashback! You are running a Global 2000 corporation, pre Internet, and working harder and harder to increase tenths of a point in market share and cutting costs for smaller and smaller financial returns. The people who work in your organization are used to having new ideas squashed and a climate of profound resignation is brewing.

Perhaps you have wondered, how do I transform this climate of resignation into a climate of possibility and opportunity? Perhaps you have told yourself that you can't shrink your way to greatness, that you have to grow your business, but the question of how do that has kept you awake at night. Given the way you have defined your business, your rigid adherence to "core competency" and your orthodox beliefs about the right way to manage growth seems like a remote possibility.

Then one day about 1990, you pick up the *Wall Street Journal* and read about these new fangled Internet companies that are reaping success through radical, new business models that satisfy customer needs by leveraging the Internet, and a light goes on. Perhaps you can grow your business exponentially and multiply your profits

> Radical new business concepts are more than improvements, they open up new possibilities.

by coming up with an innovative business concept. You decide that this insight represents an enlivening and monumental shift for you and your company and with a new spring in your step, you begin to call your team together to get going.

According to Bruce Bitler, Director of Strategy for Conoco, in American history during the time of the westward expansion, the Cherokee Strip delineated the western frontier. But not only did this prairie represent the western frontier, it represented the frontier of wide space which opened up all kinds of new opportunities and possibilities for people. Easterners who were stuck in their caste and calling packed up their wagons and drove out into the wide open space, even in the face of Indian attacks and the hardship of the wilderness, to create new lives for themselves.

The Internet is today's Cherokee Strip. The new pioneers are leaders from companies of all sizes who are escaping the limits of their current possibilities and driving themselves and their businesses out to the wild open space and the possibilities and opportunities that the Internet affords. Rather than doing more of the same, these leaders have liberated themselves and their businesses and are boldly going where no man has gone before—and in the process creating new markets, new customers, new revenue streams, and new wealth.

Clue 3. Build a power brand by getting there first with the most.   Today brands are more important than ever. The reason is that customers want to know where to shop, what to buy, and most importantly, who to trust.

At the same time, if you do not have a well-recognized brand you will find it increasingly difficult to get your message across in an economy where there are an increasing number of new business ventures, new products and services, and distribution channels.

Achieve the impossible by collaborating with colleagues, customers, and competitors.

Therefore one of the most important clues to commerce for the years ahead will be for companies to worship brand equity. The watchword will be to either build a brand fast or create a relationship with a company that already has a stranglehold on its market. In Christmas 1998, new dot-coms like e-Toys siphoned off a ton of e-commerce business. Yet by Christmas 1999, the "old reliables," Toys'R'Us, Sears, and JC Penny, began to leave the dot-coms in the dust. This was not just because they had established brands but because people prefer doing business on the Web with dot-com companies that have a brick and mortar connection somewhere and the business processes that they can count on to deliver.

It's tempting to think you can build a brand by coming up with the latest killer app, the next PC, the next Palm Pilot, or waffle iron. In fact, this is a shaky strategy due to the fact that in the e-economy there are no secrets and it may only be a few weeks or months before someone copies your idea. In fact, there are no killer apps. In the past, companies built their brands by differentiating their products. Today and in the future, companies will build their brands by differentiating their services. This involves getting there "first with the most" so as to provide incomparable customer experiences. Amazon.com is a great example of this.

Clue 4. Build capability fast through a virtual value chain and deliver through world-class processes.   Companies used to be hierarchically managed and they exercised control over the whole value web. They did everything themselves—designed, manufactured, and sold products with their own sales force—as it cost too much money to manage a series of arm's-length relationships. With the arrival of the Internet, the notion of hierarchy and corporate control has become less important, as the costs of collaboration and information have come down.

Today's leading companies don't focus on doing it all themselves. Instead, they focus on getting very good at that the one thing they can do with excellence, and then creating powerful partnerships with other firms to do the rest. Every company is part of a puzzle that provides a missing piece in a particular value web. If your piece of the puzzle fits well into the framework of another entity, you may either get bought out or get connected to another firm.

Thus, the 21st century corporation will not only have to be a hothouse for innovative business concepts, but also a coffee house where new business partnerships are formed that allow people to package the capabilities that are needed to move an idea from concept to market at the speed of the Internet. This will require leaders who not only put together a bunch of deals, but who also realize that partnerships require a culture of curiosity, openness, communication, and trust at every level of the organization.

At the same time, the bigger a business becomes, the more important it becomes to design efficient processes that can really delivery the goods and services to customers. Also the bigger the business becomes, the more costs it will generate, and the more important it is to contain those costs in order to achieve profitable growth. This is why programs like Six Sigma quality practiced by Motorola, General Electric, and other firms will play a powerful role in the coming years. The focus will be on fostering a sense of interdependency not only within companies, but also between business partners, looking for specific areas where real improvements can be made that impact customer relationships as well as the bottom-line.

Clue 5. Hire the best talent you can find, train for whatever.   One of the most influential pieces of writing that I have come across is an article called the "Talent Wars" in *Fast Company* magazine.[4] It was based on research of McKinsey & Company of 10,000 managers in fifteen or so countries. Essentially, the article said that by far the most important strategic resource over the next several decades would not be strategy or capital, but talent.

It warned leaders of companies to get ready for a protracted talent war to recruit, develop, and retain the best talent available. The emergence of e-business since the McKinsey article was written has created an additional talent squeeze on big companies and presented small ones with challenges.

Create as much opportunity for people as you possibly can.

Today, attracting, developing, and retaining talent is a strategic priority, not just a good idea. Today, with an increasing level of knowledge work and knowledge workers, and the ability to connect through phone, e-mail, and groupware, it doesn't matter where the people you hire live.

To Reinvent Your Company, Reinvent Yourself as a Leader First

The times in which we live present extraordinary challenges for executives and managers of large corporations, as well as budding entrepreneurs ready to do competitive battle. Each leader needs to ask him or herself: Is who I am as a leader today sufficient for me and my business to succeed in the years ahead?

Based on my experience as an executive coach, I assert that most business executives are only adept at a basic level of leadership that allows them to improve upon the probable. This basic level of leadership is concerned with being in a position of authority, pushing old business models to the limit without challenging the orthodoxies that underlie them, as well as with saving nickels and dimes.

What will be required is an advanced level of leadership that has to do with making the impossible happen—for example, creating game-changing business models, revolutionary process improvements, and dramatic improvements in growth and earnings. Yet, most managers do not distinguish between these two levels of leadership and, as a result, tend to create the predicable future rather than the possible future.

I often tell leaders that, if we can acknowledge that this kind of leadership is missing and see that as an opportunity rather than a threat, we can begin to call forth the leadership that is needed and wanted. Furthermore, we will be able to create inspired organizations that bring out the best in people, while creating and dominating markets on an unparalleled scale.

Let Go of the Success You Have Become To Make the Impossible Happen

You have the power to create the "impossible future" for your business or industry if you are willing to stand in the future and act from that future versus just pushing for today's results. The idea is not to redesign, for example, your Web site, but to redesign your business—and yourself—at the same time. To be sure, you will only be able to do this if you are willing to take on what looks impossible, and to do that means putting at risk everything that has defined and contributed to your success in the past.

Figure I.1 illustrates how every person and business works toward creating the future.[5] We tend to create the future by following our history and our "winning formulas." Our winning formula is what made us successful in the past. It starts with how we compensate for what we see as impossible. For example: "I will never make CEO, so I will try for production engineer or chief accountant." "We will never be able to achieve being the # 1 player in our industry, so let's settle for being a good competitor." "We will never be able to achieve 50 percent growth, so let's succeed at 10 percent growth."

> The e-Leaders of the future will be so different from the I-Leaders of the past that they will be almost unrecognizable.

A goal is something to get to; a future is something that you create from.

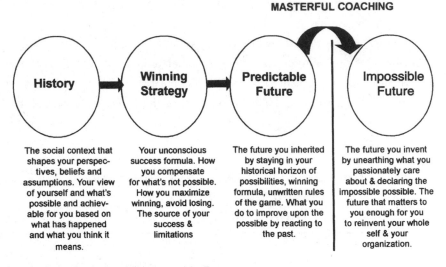

MASTERFUL COACHING

History	Winning Strategy	Predictable Future	Impossible Future
The social context that shapes your perspectives, beliefs and assumptions. Your view of yourself and what's possible and achievable for you based on what has happened and what you think it means.	Your unconscious success formula. How you compensate for what's not possible. How you maximize winning, avoid losing. The source of your success & limitations	The future you inherited by staying in your historical horizon of possibilities, winning formula, unwritten rules of the game. What you do to improve upon the possible by reacting to the past.	The future you invent by unearthing what you passionately care about & declaring the impossible possible. The future that matters to you enough for you to reinvent your whole self & your organization.

Figure I.1   Creating the Impossible Future

Our winning formula also represents what we habitually do to win and avoid losing as an individual or organization. It might involve adhering to the same old tried and true business model, coming up with better or different versions of the same strategy, following conventional wisdom and suppressing innovative ideas. On a leadership level it might involve "looking good" to please the boss, setting predictable goals, avoiding confrontation, or covering up mistakes. Ironically, the more our winning formula works to produce results, the more it inhibits us from taking on the impossible.

The key question to ask is: "Where do our winning formulas/action strategies come from?" The answer is that they come from the past, from the history that we have inherited—born from our personal, industrial, or organizational background. Another key question to ask is: "Where does our image of the future come from?" For most people and organizations, it also comes from the past—from trying to improve on the possible. Even the stretch goals that most companies create can be placed in this category. As a result, most of our actions are bent on creating the predictable future.

Declare a New Future and Step into the Reinvention Paradigm

Creating the impossible future starts with setting ambitious aspirations that you commit to passionately engaging with and then, standing in that commitment, you step into what I call the reinvention paradigm. The key is to establish expectations that take you beyond your notions of what's possible based on conventional wisdom. For example, if you declare that you will reach a growth rate of 30 percent from new, innovative ventures that create lots of opportunity for people, that possibility begins to come into existence just because you said it, whereas if you set a growth goal of 6 percent, chances are you will never achieve more than that no matter how hard or intelligently you try.

Declaring your commitment for aspirational performance creates a context for personal and organizational reinvention. One of the key premises of this book is that, in order to reinvent your organization, you must reinvent yourself as a leader first. For example, it's one thing to tell your team that you are committed to giving them the opportunity to come up with radical, new business concepts that will allow you to grow your business exponentially and multiply your profits, it's another to personally learn to care and feed new ideas when they are still in their fledgling stage, rather than squash them.

The reinvention paradigm is founded on the premise that the only way to alter history or "what is" is through the power of your declarations.[6] There are three specific declarations that move you into the reinvention paradigm.

1. **I declare that what is possible is what I say is possible.** This declaration gives you the power to determine what is possible through the power of your word rather than forfeiting this power to people, circumstances, events.

   For example: I declare as possible that our company will be the future of XYZ industry.

2. I declare that who I am is the stand that I take. This declaration gives you the power to stretch your definition of yourself, so as to become a clearing in which you can be the kind of leader you need to be in order

You invent the impossible future by declaring an ambitious aspiration and declaring that fulfilling that future is the game that you are playing in life.

FIGURE I.2   The Reinvention Paradigm

to fulfill a possibility you have declared. It also allows you to get beyond your notions of how you should or should not be, or what you can or can't do based on the past.

3. The stand that I take is . . . .   This declaration represents your commitment to transform a possibility into a reality. It gives you the power to persist in the face of difficult facts and circumstances.

Transformation Versus Change

It's important to emphasize that this book is about transformation, not change. Transformation is an alteration in who you are being, which in turns alters what is possible and not possible for you in any given situation. Change is an alteration in the process of what we are doing—and usually involves a lot of prescriptions. I have seen many people change what they are doing personally or organizationally, without necessarily changing themselves or the organization they are in.

For example, most managers espouse the notion of an inspiring, empowering, enabling management style, yet under stress and pressure revert to form—command and control. I often ask people in seminars, "How many of you are closet control junkies?" and all hands go up. In the same sense, despite years of trying to get more company collaboration and communication by putting people on teams and processes, the real barriers to collaboration and communication still remain the ones in people's heads.

I assert that becoming the kind of leader who creates a new future for your business or industry stems from an alteration in how people are being rather than a set of prescriptions designed to alter what they are doing. This alteration starts with looking at the future you and others passionately care about and asking yourself, "How can I be in the matter?", and then calling yourself forth accordingly.

Again, the only way to disentangle yourself from history is through the power of your declaration, not by psychologically trying to understand why you are the way you are. Start with declaring your commitment to new possibilities for yourself as a leader—new ways of being. For example, "I am committed to the possibility of being an extraordinary leaders who is a master of creative collaboration." Then look at what old ways of being you are committed to giving up. For example, "I am committed to giving up being a bulldozer," or "being a hero," or "always needing to impress people." The following will support you in declaring new possibilities for yourself as a leader and dismantling your winning strategy:

It is how you are being that determines what's possible in any given situation.

- I am committed to the possibility of _____. (Describe what kind of leader you need to be.)
- I am committed to giving up_____. (Describe what old ways of being, thinking, and attitudes you need to abandon.)
- What's next is_____ . (Describe what actions you can take that are consistent with the above.)

About this Book

I want to make clear that this book is not about the leadership in an Internet economy as much as it is about leadership in a connected economy that the PC, the mobile phone, the PDA and, of course, the Internet have made possible. To succeed in a connected economy, each of us needs to get to the heart of leadership and discover the difference between things like sourcing and reacting, between what's possible and what's predictable, between transformation and change. At the same time, each of us needs to develop the ways of being, mindset, and behavior for succeeding in a connected economy.

The seven chapters of the book are designed to produce seven powerful, fascinating, and distinct transformations. Each chapter is designed to provide you guiding ideas, tools and methods for being an e-leader; between these chapters are "interludes" or extended profiles of e-leaders who exemplify the qualities and principles presented in the chapters.

Chapter 1. From the CEO as Steward to the CEO as Entrepreneur

Tomorrow's CEO will be less like a steward who polishes grandma's silver to protect the past and more like an entrepreneur who creates something that never existed before. While CEOs like Jack Welch of GE and Carly Fiorina of HP who talk about "aspirational performance" provide powerful role models for the typical Fortune 500 CEOs who need to transform their business, Jim Clark and Marc Andreessen, co-founders of Netscape, are role models for stacks of Internet entrepreneurs who want to create something new. When Andreessen started his new company Loud Cloud, he immediately delegated the role of CEO saying, "I can contribute more if I am free to drive everyone crazy with new ideas and impatience and don't have to be consistent. I'm happy to push people right to the edge. I don't mind ticking people off." This chapter will show you how to be the kind of leader who can create or transform your business.

Chapter 2. From Game-Player to Game-Changer

What do Jeff Bezos of Amazon, Jerry Yang of Yahoo!, and Michael Dell of Dell all have in common besides being Internet billionaires? First of all, each was not just a game-player, but also a game-changer who stared into the future and came up with a new business model that revolutionized his industry. Second, each figured out that the Internet has everything to do with customers, nothing to do with technology. This chapter will show that while most ordinary business leaders are rule-followers, extraordinary business leaders are rule-breakers and -makers who change the paradigm of their industry over time and become incredibly successful. This chapter will inspire and empower you to be come a rule-breaker and -maker in your own right.

Chapter 3. From Top–Down to Lateral Leadership

As Avram Miller, former director of business development for Intel, points out, today's CEOs need to recognize that "no one is in command anymore" and that "they need to give up the illusion of control." The reason is that the stand-alone corporation is being replaced by something called "collaborative commerce." As a result, the old power of authority is being replaced by the new power of collaboration. Today, all top-down leaders need to reinvent themselves as lateral leaders who can lead when they are not in charge. This chapter will inspire you to make the shift from top-down to lateral leadership, from giving orders to framing issues, from a chain of command to a network of commitments, from passionately expressing your views to exploring the views of others, and from working in isolation to producing collective work products.

Chapter 4. From Production Builder in Chief to Brand Builder in Chief

Starting right now, learn to see yourself differently: as a brand builder in chief, not a production guy, as a marketing whiz, not a process improver, as a sales ace, not a manager. Today, success is about your ability to be the biggest brand owner, not the biggest production owner. Companies like Dell Computers, Cisco, and HP sell their brand, not their PC's, printers, or routers. You have to personify your brand by getting personally and directly involved in building it, not delegating it to marketing or an ad agency. For example, Richard Branson still plays songs on his guitar and serves drinks to passengers on Virgin Atlantic to show he's serious about service. This chapter will show provide you with the seven immutable laws of e-power branding.

Chapter 5. From a "Me" Point of View to a "You" Point of View

You're a business leader—of your own job. Right! Well, think about it. Do you operate from a me point of view in relationship to customers and colleagues or a you point of view? In too many cases, business leaders tend to fall in love with their company, fall in love with their advertising, fall in love with their product, and even their me-oriented customer service policies. As a result, they don't really pay attention to what the customer experiences when looking at their ads, using their products, or dealing with their customer service reps. By shifting from a me point of view to a you point of view you will learn to focus not so much on providing products or services, but on great customer experiences that win loyalty and commitment and that result in multiplying your profits and in exponential growth.

Chapter 6. From Being a Great E-Tailer to Being a Great Logistician

Fred Smith, CEO of FedEx, once complimented Sam Walton of Wal-Mart for being a great retailer. Walton shot back that the secret of being a great retailer was to be a great logistician. Competitive success is not just about getting people to shop in your on-line store, it's about winning the ground war. Sure you've got infinite shelf space to play with, but can you deliver? A friend on a trip to England tried to order on-line groceries for a party from a company called Sainsbury. Everything was perfect until he pressed the order button, and things went haywire. The next company processed his on-line grocery order with just two clicks of a mouse, but the ice cream for the party melted in the delivery truck. This chapter will show you how to not only be a great retailer, but a great logistician. You will discover how to do it yourself, as well as where you can find help.

Chapter 7. From Being a Manager/ Technician to Being a Coach/Mentor

You want to be able to call yourself an e-leader and to start or transform your own e-business. You've come up with a potentially viral idea that will spread like wildfire and drive business to your Web site or doorstep. What do you do next? If you are thinking like a manager/technician, you will concern yourself with things like buying new technological gadgetry, planning the next three years, and designing processes. If you are thinking like a coach/mentor, you will go out and recruit a talented team of people and generate a conversation for action that will make your viral idea a reality while bringing out the best in those around you. While it might not be an either-or proposition, if you are a leader you are first and foremost a coach and mentor. This chapter will provide you with a powerful, concise, five-step method for recruiting, developing, and retaining talent.

From CEO as Steward to CEO as Entrepreneur

S uppose you're Samir Gibara, a fifty-year-old Goodyear Tire and Rubber vice president with over thirty years with the company, stepping out of the elevator on the fifth floor of Goodyear's corporate offices near Akron, Ohio, and onto the blue and gold carpets. You're on your way to a meeting with the CEO, Stanley Gault. You're greeted by Mary Cheevers, Gault's secretary for the last fifteen years. "He'll just be a few minutes," she says and she ushers you into the pharaonic antechamber to the CEO's office. It was company tradition that executives would line up there, waiting for their meeting with the CEO, whose time was too precious to waste even one minute between meetings.

You're here to talk to the CEO about how you would lead the company, if you were in charge. You and Gault had been talking about the kind of leadership that would be required in the twenty-first century, how, in the past, the CEO was a *steward* whose job it was to *conserve* what had been built up over generations. Gault feels that in the future what will be needed is a shift to the CEO as *entrepreneur*, whose job would not just be to bring equilibrium to an operation but also "creative destruction" through disruptive innovation.

Gault steps out of his office and welcomes you. There are signs of "stewardship" everywhere, including a sign over the office door that says, "Protect our Good Name." Your eyes are drawn to the huge stained glass windows directly over Gault's desk that are like heraldic shields. There are four of them, each four feet long by almost three feet wide. These windows bear the same emblems as the ten-, twenty-, thirty-, and forty-year service lapel pins passed out to employees, which seem like a paternalistic anachronism in an era referred to as "free-agent nation."

"Let's continue our talk about leadership," says Gault as he invites you to sit down on a white sofa by the coffee table, "If you look at today's leading companies in every industry, it is not the *stewards* of the old Fortune 500, but rather the *entrepreneurs* that are creating most of the new wealth."

Gibara offers some examples, "Home Depot, Dell Computers, The Gap, America-OnLine, MCI Worldcom, Cisco Systems, Starbucks, Amazon.com, Southwest Airlines, Sun Microsystems." Gault adds, "If you look at these companies, most of them did not even exist more than a decade or so ago." Gibara responds, "Yet, I was just reading that, by the year 2000, the combined market capitalization of the companies I mentioned had soared to nearly $100 trillion. Furthermore, in almost every industry, aggressive upstarts are replacing incumbents."

Gault says, "Yes, in the next ten years, as e-business comes increasingly to the fore, the stewards will face increasing pressure from entrepreneurs. Frankly, I have seen a lot of companies where too many people in leadership roles are devoid of passion and imagination. They have too many stewards who spend their time saying 'no' in the name of 'company policy' and who spend their time trying to protect wealth by buying back shares, rearranging processes, and slashing costs."

Gibara responds, "The question I have often asked myself is, 'Why do companies have leaders who don't really lead, even in the face of real change?'" Gault muses, "I guess it's because leadership isn't just about having a vision or *seeing* clearly into the future and stepping up to the opportunities in front of you. It is about *seeing* where you are, challenging people to face reality and change. There's always a danger that you will be attacked, seduced, diverted, or marginalized if you do that."

"Also," says Gault, "There's a lot of pressure on you to protect the big, established legacy business and the people in it. It is very stressful to have to say, for example, 'We need to make the transition from bricks and mortar to a virtual company and to do that we are going to cut 5,000 jobs.' Maybe it's a matter of learning to dance, to shift your weight to the opposite foot, of knowing when to protect people and knowing when to unprotect them."

•   •   •

Although this is a fictitious account, the words of Gault might be the words of many business leaders around the world. If you want your company to be a leading wealth-creator, rather than just another business, hammering down costs, you have to shift the balance of leadership from stewardship to entrepreneurship.

E-leaders are radical, incessant entrepreneurs. They understand that, if they are not continually creating new markets, new customers, or new revenue streams, they may be out of business tomorrow. They develop a point of view about the future, create an idea manifesto that shows how they will create and dominate markets, and jump into action. They create a culture where people are free to dream and experiment, not just apply their knowledge and skills.

What questions should you ask yourself if your company is looking to hire a new CEO or leader? The litmus test: Can they create like a God and do they think like an artist? In the future, it will not be enough for a CEO or other top leader to be a vassal of the company board of directors, operating and maintaining its 100-year-old business in cars, computers, lightbulbs, or whatever. They must increasingly be revolutionaries and heretics who recognize that the real challenge is not thinking long-term but rather thinking unconventionally. Figure 1.1 illustrates the differences between *i-stewards* and *e-entrepreneurs*.

In Today's Economy, Stewards Have Internet Anxiety; Entrepreneurs Have Internet Opportunity

How often do you wake up in the morning, scan the headlines and see yet more stories about the Internet gold rush, and then have the gnawing feeling that the world is passing you by? Perhaps you tell yourself that it is OK for right now because your company is still relatively successful and, after all, you are secure in your job. But what if you suddenly found yourself an incumbent, facing an e-attacker?

Imagine that you're David Komansky, CEO of Merrill Lynch when Schwab.com comes along. You're Leonard Riggio, CEO of Barnes & Noble when Amazon.com hits big. You're Toys "R" Us when eToys shows up. What do you do? Do you act as a steward protecting the existing business and risk losing out on the e-revolution? Or do you take the entrepreneurial route and perhaps wind up groping in the dark? To even take the plunge means that the leaders of successful

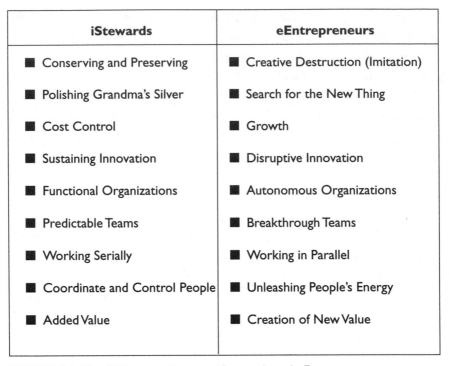

iStewards	eEntrepreneurs
■ Conserving and Preserving	■ Creative Destruction (Imitation)
■ Polishing Grandma's Silver	■ Search for the New Thing
■ Cost Control	■ Growth
■ Sustaining Innovation	■ Disruptive Innovation
■ Functional Organizations	■ Autonomous Organizations
■ Predictable Teams	■ Breakthrough Teams
■ Working Serially	■ Working in Parallel
■ Coordinate and Control People	■ Unleashing People's Energy
■ Added Value	■ Creation of New Value

FIGURE 1.1 The Difference Between iStewards and eEntrepreneurs

companies must do the very thing that is often most difficult for them to do, which is to let go.

John Steffens, vice chairman at Merrill Lynch, held out for months with the stewardship approach, arguing that Merrill Lynch's coterie of sophisticated investment advisers, market savvy, and superior services would trump budding on-line investment rivals. Then the unthinkable happened. Merrill started losing huge amounts of business to on-line brokers such as Charles Schwab, E*Trade, and Ameritrade. Merrill then announced on June 1, 1999, that it was going to have to rapidly develop an on-line business. Yet by this time, Merrill had to play catch-up.

Schwab, by contrast, decided to take the entrepreneurial route. Its co-CEOs, Charles Schwab and David Pottruck, and others saw the Web's potential long before Internet mania spread beyond Silicon Valley. Their alarm clock went off in

1995 when they learned that, for the first year, more personal computers had been sold in the United States than televisions. Although not a techie by any means, Charles Schwab jumped on the bandwagon and convinced the board that it needed to make a big investment in e-commerce, even though the new approach might temporarily threaten existing phone and brick-and-mortar operations.

Schwab had to make some tough decisions about where to invest its capital at the time. Its highly profitable international operations needed capital and looked like a sure thing, whereas on-line investing was still specula-tive. There was also the potential problem that the leaders of Schwab's investment cen-ters would be threatened by the new operation. The board decided to go the e-commerce route because it felt it would revolutionize their industry. To prepare, the senior staff sent frequent e-mails to employees telling them about the growth of on-line trading. Also it was decided to train the investor center man-agers first so that they would lead the change rather than resist it.

> **The shift from leader as steward to leader as entrepreneur requires that leaders do the thing that is most difficult for them to do—letting go.**

The staffers' backing turned out to be essential when customers rebelled against the two-tiered pricing system that Schwab.com eventually set up, where full-service customers were being charged an average of $65 a trade and Schwab.com customers were paying only $29.95. Pottruck ignored fears that a shift would cannibalize Schwab's traditional business and decided to price all Net trades at $29.95. The move initially cut $150 million from expected revenues and sent Schwab's shares tumbling from 41 to 28.

Soon, however, the risk paid off, as volume increased dramatically. By 1999, Schwab could boast that it got 76 million hits a day on its Web site. Since it started its Web business, it has added 1.3 million Internet accounts, and that number is growing daily. In 2000, Schwab conducts approximately 42 percent of their on-line trading. Even after the Internet stock rally was over, its stock price grew in 1999 by 329 percent, to around eighty-nine dollars a share.

Similar threats to those that David Komansky and others at Merrill Lynch faced led to disaster for Eckhard Pfeiffer of Compaq Computer. The once highly respected chairman, whose brilliance was touted in management books in the early '90s, was ousted in 1999 because he was unwilling to bypass his distributors and sell computers directly over the Web. Compaq's sales drifted away fast to on-line rivals like Dell and Gateway. Others responded more entrepreneurially, such as James Halpin, CEO of CompUSA, who believes you have to forge ahead and not worry about cannibalizing your existing bricks-and-mortar operation.

There are also examples of CEOs who started out as stewards when the Inter-net craze hit and who then transformed themselves into entrepreneurs. The Toys "R" Us CEO, Robert C. Nakasone, first took the stewardship approach, delaying jumping into the e-revolution with a view toward protecting his 1,486 stores. He also assumed that the real enemy was not Web-based competitors, but giant dis-counters, like Wal-Mart and Target.

Nakasone was stunned, however, when during the 1999 Christmas season a tiny on-line entrepreneurial retailer called eToys racked up $30 million in sales, leaving Toys "R" Us in the dust. Even worse, eToys scored a market cap of $7.8 bil-lion, dwarfing Toys "R" Us's $5.6 billion. Nakasone did an about-face. Realizing that Toys "R" Us had too much of a hierarchy, was too bureaucratic to move quickly, and had too many cultural ties to the brick-and-mortar world, Nakasone set up a separate e-commerce operation.

He formed a partnership with a Silicon Valley venture capital firm, Benchmark Capital, and funded his on-line operation with $80 million from Toys "R" Us's own coffers, moving the Toys "R" Us on-line operation from New Jersey to northern Cal-ifornia. Setting up a separate e-commerce operation was essential, Nakasone said. "Over time we would have gotten it right . . . but we didn't have the time."

What do these examples tell us about the future of leadership in the 21st Cen-tury? In the past, business leaders acting as stewards of their businesses attempted to produce wealth by doing one thing exceedingly well for a long time—Ford pro-duced cars, U.S. Steel produced steel, Conoco produced oil and gasoline. The In-ternet has fundamentally changed this by creating a spiraling dance of intellect, imagination, and capital that is resulting in a "creative economy" and an unprece-dented level of innovation. I am speaking of business concept innovation, not just innovative products and services.

The dot com explosion is not the cause of the creative economy, but an effect, a burst of light in the night but also part of a much larger meteor shower. Compa-nies like Schwab and Toys 'R' Us, as well as those like Enron or even Ford realize that their future lies not with the singularity of their past, but with continually coming up with new innovative business concepts. Their leaders understand that companies will increasingly be "built to create" rather than "built to last." They understand that CEOs who are today's heroes will become tomorrow's "also rans" if they ignore this.

Thus, CEOs of the future will be more like artists than MBA accountants, social architects rather than industrial engineers, and Hollywood movie directors packaging knowledge from whomever or whatever to meet unconventional customer demands. Rather than seeking to compete by doing what they do better, these entrepreneurs will see to invent what's missing that will revolutionize their industries.

Why are There So Few Entrepreneurial Leaders in Most Fortune 500 Companies?

Why didn't someone at Barnes & Noble, when Amazon.com struck, say, "Wait a minute. Knowing what we now know about e-commerce, would we even go into the brick-and-mortar bookstore business today?" Why didn't someone at Compaq, when Dell struck, say, "Instead of just putting up some brochure-ware on the Internet, why don't we do an e-business experiment?" Why didn't someone at Merrill Lynch, when Schwab struck, say, "Here's an idea? Why don't we just take one idea for the Web and run with it?"

I believe that one reason why there are so few entrepreneurial leaders in most companies is that the traditional management culture that has existed for decades is a culture of profound resignation where people's horizon of possibility is limited. As a corporate coach, I have worked with over a hundred big companies, in dozens of industries, in various kinds of "transformation" or "improvement" efforts. These programs asked people to become leaders, to shift culture, to build teams across boundaries, and so forth. While people thought that these were admirable and desirable behaviors, they didn't believe that it was really possible to act that way in their organization. They often said, "This too shall pass." Thus, they adopted an attitude of "why bother?" in which everything they did became an accommodation of their resignation.

The E-Economy Is Transforming the Prevailing Climate of Resignation into a Climate of Opportunity for Entrepreneurs

However, from the mid-'90s onward, there has been a shift in the wind. It started with eye-popping headlines about upstart companies like Amazon.com, eBay, and others going public with new IPOs and achieving greater market capitalization overnight than traditional rivals had built up over decades. Then there were the stories of Internet billionaires that stunned us. Margaret Whitman, a former senior manager at Hasbro Corporation, a midsize toy company in Rhode Island, became a billionaire, at least on paper, within three months of joining eBay, surpassing the substantial $503 million fortune that the owners of Hasbro, the Hassenfelds, had built up over forty years in business.

At the same time, what has been called the Internet Century and the Digital Revolution were causing a major shift in the business landscape. As IBM Chairman Lou Gerstner put it, "The Internet and e-business will reshape the world as fundamentally as the invention of the printing press, the light bulb, or manned flight. It will reshape every leader's approach, every business, and every institution in the world."[1]

If a CEO from the 1980s, shackled by Wall Street to short-term profits, fell asleep like Rip Van Winkle and woke up in the surging growth economy of the '90s, he would have felt he was hallucinating. He would have entered a world in which the companies that showed the most innovation and entrepreneurship, even if, like Amazon.com, they made the most losses, were the ones that were walking away with the marbles. Furthermore, he would have entered a world of the Internet gold rush where, at one point, anyone smart enough to come up with a business-building idea and put it on the Internet could attract more capital than ever dreamed of.

> If a CEO from the past woke up like Rip Van Winkle in today's economy, where growth potential often counts more than short-term profit, he would feel he was hallucinating.

And guess what, there was a new name for a company's human resources: Talent Pools. Instead of employers interviewing prospective employees for jobs, employees began interviewing employers. *Did they disavow hierarchical management in favor of a more egalitarian style? Did they guarantee fascinating, intriguing projects to work on?* And the rewards: Prospective hires were getting to write their own banquet tickets replete with the promise of hefty signing bonuses and rich stock options. Who needs a salary when your 200,000 shares shoot from eighteen cents to eighty dollars in six months? One company I heard about even offered free daily foot massages to help employees reduce stress caused by doing things at Net speed. Suddenly the climate of profound resignation that pervaded most companies during the 1980s and 1990s was being transformed into an incredible climate of opportunity.

Start Your Own Entrepreneurial Revolution

Suddenly, it no longer made any sense just to be a steward of an existing business, shrinking costs, even if you were successful at it. It made a hell of a lot more sense to become what Tom Wolfe called in his book *A Man in Full* a "budding entrepreneur."

By 1999, a growing number of corporadoes began abandoning the Fortune 500 ship of state in droves. It was as if somehow, suddenly Hans Christian Andersen's tale had come to life and the emperor (or corporation) had no clothes. There was no getting away from the fact that life in the big corporation, regardless of your position, was often a soul-deadening, mind-numbing, and enslaving experience.

Interestingly enough, the first defections more often than not came from people at higher levels, people with plum jobs—CEOs, executives, mid-managers— talented professionals of every ilk, not just the desperate. It was as if all of a sudden executives, and even middle managers, woke up and saw their jobs in the corporation in bold, stark relief, stripped of all of the pretenses and defenses, and said, "You know what, here I am at the top of this company (or maybe near it) and if this is as good as it gets, it's still insane." Plus . . . "Before I had no alternative but to pretend that everything was OK when it really was not. I don't need to do that anymore. I can follow my passion, pursue my life's ambition. Here's my resignation. See you later. Sayonara."

Let Go of the "Ma and Pa" Corporation, Seize New Opportunities That Serendipitously Arise, Challenge Orthodoxies

I can remember waking up one day and reading in the *Wall Street Journal* that George Shaheen, chairman of Andersen Consulting, had decided to leave his job as the CEO of the biggest consulting firm in the world, with over 65,000 people, a hundred different locations throughout the world, and an annual salary of $4 million plus to become part of a new entrepreneurial start-up called WebVan, a company that delivers groceries to your doorstep.

I was stunned and fascinated by the question of why Shaheen would make such a move. He had certainly had ample opportunity to spread his wings. Shaheen was an entrepreneur who in ten years pushed $1 billion in annual revenues to $10 billion. He was also a high-tech aficionado who lived in Silicon Valley and focused his company on building Enterprise Resource Planning (ERP) systems for its customers.

However, I discovered another piece of the puzzle: Shaheen, a brawler who led a civil war against the firm's older corporate sibling, Arthur Andersen, was disturbed by the political infighting involved in managing this dysfunctional situation, and began to think of a possible career change.

When David Beirne from Benchmark Venture Capital called Shaheen to talk about an interesting idea, WebVan, Shaheen told him, "David, you're nuts!" adding he might think about a career switch in a year or so. Beirne replied, "This opportunity won't be available then." It was Shaheen's continued lust for entrepreneurial freedom, in the face of the Arthur Andersen situation, and his growing intrigue with the idea that WebVan could possibly out e-tail Amazon.com, together with the pay package, that made him jump ship. "I didn't say I wanted a job where I could make a hundred million," he said, "but the money made it hard to turn down."[2]

Just to be clear, leaving a big company and going to a dot-com isn't all smooth sailing. The advice of John Doerr, a Silicon Valley VC, to Shaheen and others is to get ready for a whitewater ride. There's a moment of truth where you have to look at yourself and your team and ask: "Are these the people I want to be in trouble with for the next five to fifteen years of my life? Because, as you build a new business, one thing's for sure, you will be in trouble." Shaheen is certainly no exception. After a record-breaking initial financing of WebVan to the tune of $375 million, its post-IPO stock dropped by a half and more. The company looked shaky, although analysts believe its long-term prospects are still quite promising.

Many Executives Are Leaving the Big Traditional Corporation to Go Solo

As Harriet Rubin, the highly respected former publisher at Doubleday Currency, her own business imprint, said about her departure in her book *Soloing—Realizing Your Life's Ambition*, "People said in astonishment when I left, 'Why are you leaving? You have so much freedom and power.' In fact I had none," though she was publishing best sellers like Peter Senge's *The Fifth Discipline*. "I didn't even have the power to use paper for the book projects that was thicker than a beaver lick," meaning that, if a beaver licked the paper and it didn't dissolve, it was too thick and therefore too costly. Rubin's solution to all this: Start your own entrepreneurial revolution. And that begins with pursuing your life's ambition.[3]

It's not just the privileged few who are doing this, but also the many. What are some of the tangible signs? How did we get to be where we are today? In 1993, corporate layoffs topped 615,000, nearly six times that of 1989. An estimated 10 to 15 percent of white-collar workers retreated to home offices as entrepreneurs and consultants. In 1995, shares in Netscape Communications, a company begun as a lark by college-age geeks, doubled in their first day of trading. Suddenly thousands of indolent GenXers found direction—"Get Rich Quick." At the same time, "credit scoring" took off, a practice that involves making a computerized assessment of credit risks, allowing more banks to make loans at lower costs, stimulating competition. Also by 1995, a quarter of the large banks were mailing pre-approved credit card applications, an increase from zero in 1972.

In 1996, the number of university-endowed chairs in entrepreneurship swelled to 171, up 38 percent from 1985. The same year, a survey showed that 72 percent of American college students hoped to own their own business—up from 52 percent in 1989. In 1999, America found itself in the height of the IPO boom with 1,760 companies offering stock versus 154 in 1990. (Most of these were Web related.) With so many entrepreneurs in the environment, companies began to attract customers to their business with innovative marketing campaigns. Mail Boxes Etc., for example, launched a "see your small business on the Super Bowl" campaign in which small firms vied for a free third-quarter spot.

Entrepreneurial Leadership
Is a Matter of Distinction

Entrepreneurial zeal, new business models that change the face of things, and disruptive technologies like the Internet and wireless products will require business leaders who can reinvent their businesses overnight for the foreseeable future. Thus, I believe that entrepreneurial leadership will become the primary discipline practiced by business leaders in the twenty-first century. Furthermore, entrepreneurial leadership will not just apply to small start-ups or e-commerce, but to large and small firms, profits and nonprofits, government groups and private social agencies. Having said that, let's clarify what we mean by entrepreneurial leadership.

Around World War I, there was an entrepreneurial explosion. The practice of management started to develop to manage the rapid growth that came from the war. Yet, even by the 1930s, there were only a few big companies around—General Motors, DuPont, and Sears, Roebuck. After World War II, management as a distinct discipline played a large role in the rise of many large corporations symbolized by the Fortune 500. CEOs saw their roles not to create new resources, but to optimize existing ones.

"The entrepreneur, by contrast," said the French economist J. B. Say around 1800, "shifts economic resources out of an area of lower yield to an area of higher yield . . . " and in so doing creates new resources. Say also believed that the real entrepreneur did something to change the face of things.

Joseph Schumpeter, a German economist interested in entrepreneurs, built upon Say's definition. His view was that the entrepreneur "disrupts and disorganizes" and in the process creates new wealth. In contrast, classical economists, like John Maynard Keynes, always believed that the effective businessperson "created equilibrium" and optimized existing resources. Schumpeter also said that real entrepreneurs don't just build businesses that make money for themselves and their shareholders; they transform the values of the society that they operate in.

Finally, Michael Gerber makes a great point about entrepreneurship in his book *The E Myth Revisited*. He says that most entrepreneurs are just employees with an entrepreneurial seizure. He adds that they often get trapped in drudgery because they "work in their business, not on their business."[4] Working on their business involves improving its systems so that it becomes world-class and can operate independently of its originator—such as the McDonald's franchises.

Entrepreneurial Leaders: Either *Creators* or *Transformers*

I see two distinctly different kinds of entrepreneurs in the e-economy. First there are those who can *create* a new business or business category from scratch and build it into a substantial enterprise that generates and sustains rapid growth. The other kind of entrepreneur is one who can *transform* an existing enterprise. This usually involves transforming the strategic business model of the company, its processes, and its culture so that it is consistent with today's economy.

Jack Welch, CEO of General Electric, is a good example. Truth be told, he is much less a steward than an entrepreneurial leader. When he came to the company, he insisted that GE be number one or two in each business—not just hold onto businesses that were always there. He pushed the company into finance business services and entertainment, and then did the same with the Internet. Welch also transformed the culture, preaching and teaching new values, like boundary-less behavior, that would allow GE to respond quickly to markets and customers. Finally, he improved the processes of the company by adopting a Six Sigma Quality Program, a business process that enables companies to increase profits dramatically by streamlining operations, improving quality, and eliminating defects or mistakes in everything a company does.

Bill Gates, chairman of Microsoft, is a classic example of an entrepreneurial leader who starts from scratch and creates a big company that dominates

"Leadership not only means influencing the organization to follow your vision, it means influencing people to face reality, and mobilizing them to change." **Ron Heifetz,** *Leadership Without Easy Answers*

its industry. Yet, there is an irony here in that Microsoft next needed an entrepreneurial leader who could transform the company in terms of the products it makes and how it delivers them to the customer. In 2000, Microsoft decided to change its strategic direction from selling stand-alone products, like Windows or Office 2000, in brick-and-mortar stores to selling customerized combinations of products over the Internet. This means that Microsoft's different business units will have to become much more collaborative. According to Microsoft CEO Steve Ballmer, "Microsoft may have a grand vision, but we will be cut off at the knees if we don't transform."[5]

Two Distinct Entrepreneurial Strategies: "Be the First with the Most" and Creative Imitation

Just as there are two kinds of entrepreneurs, there are basically two entrepreneurial strategies that can result in building a powerful business. The first is to "be the first with the most." This means creating something new or different, and doing it faster than the competition. Amazon.com, Federal Express, eBay, and the Gap are all excellent examples of this.

The other entrepreneurial strategy is creative imitation. In fact, most entrepreneurs don't start by creating something revolutionary or new. Instead they identify profitable opportunities based on what another company is already doing in a field in which they have some expertise. They then "creatively imitate" by adding a different twist.

For example, while Amazon.com started e-tailing, hundreds of others have followed suit. One of them is Overstock.com, which sells at a 50 percent discount of retail consumer goods from companies that have overproduced. Overstock.com gets enormous discounts because it guarantees the makers that the goods will never be sold at retail outlets, which would destroy the manufacturers' traditional retail distribution channel.

The Best Gift Is a Good Example

The question you may be asking yourself right now is: How do I learn to be the kind of leader we have been talking about? At this point, I would like to say I look at leadership as a way of being, rather than just a set of functions. My view has always been that the best way to grasp how to be a leader is through an example, as well as by experiences. I have chosen Carly Fiorina, who took over as CEO of Hewlett-Packard (HP) in 1999, as an example of the entrepreneurial leader whose role it is to transform a business so that it is consistent with the e-economy. Interestingly enough, HP has been a creative imitator in computers and an innovator in desktop printers. One of the best examples I found of the entrepreneurial leader who creates a new business—*"the first with the most"* *school*—is Jim Clark, founder of Netscape and numerous other ventures, who said on CNN that he preferred "creating companies to running them." First, let's look at HP's Fiorina.

CEO Carly Fiorina's Revolution— Transforming Hewlett-Packard

For eight years, CEO Lew Platt's leadership of HP was a classic example of stewardship. He painstakingly upheld a culture in which people showed almost religious devotion to HP's founder's vision, values, and management culture. The results were nothing to scoff at. HP had a commanding lead in many computing products, as well as with the famous DeskJet printers. However, when the e-business revolution struck, HP was caught sleeping, allowing IBM and Sun to gain ground, which led to Platt's retirement.

Within a few weeks of Carly Fiorina's arrival on the scene as the new CEO, many people were asking whether HP—always a stodgy, quiet, kind of place—was still the same company. Her first moves, after a period of due diligence, were to sound the tone for a new HP that both insiders and outsiders would hear. TV ads carried the tag line, "The company that started as a start-up in a garage is going to act like a start-up in a garage." Newspaper ads carried the tag line, "Reinventing the New HP," and almost weekly the company declared new partnerships with Internet stalwarts, like Yahoo! and Amazon.com.

The glitz was all part of an effort to re-brand the company in the Internet age. When Fiorina took over HP, at least one of the four major product divisions came out with a new product every day, many of them consigning the HP name to small print. Fiorina recognized that the HP brand was one of the company's distinct assets and that the different divisions were acting too much like separate companies whose strengths could not be brought together and leveraged. She began touting the motto "One brand, one company" and had a flashy HP logo designed to symbolize it.

"Leadership is a performance. You have to be conscious about your behavior, because everyone else is." Carly Fiorina, CEO, Hewlett-Packard

Her efforts were equally focused on transforming HP's strategic business model, structure, and management culture. Due in large part to Fiorina's efforts, the company is well on its way to becoming as fast-paced and customer-centric as the best Silicon Valley upstarts. She was neither being intimidated by, nor disrespectful of, the HP legacy of her predecessors. Her motto, a good blend of stewardship and entrepreneurship, became, "Keep the best and reinvent the rest."

To get her message out there, Fiorina pranced around the world, descending on twenty HP sites in ten countries to enlist entrepreneurially minded rebels and to fight resistance. She told people, "As a company we need to be faster in all kinds of ways, faster to decide, faster to choose, faster to act . . . . We need to take risks and act on less information."

To counteract what she considered an almost pathologically consensus-oriented decisionmaking process, which slowed everything down, she asserted her authority, telling people, "I make the decisions now." At the same time, she also increased the level of collaboration between division heads when a real consensus was needed.

Another important action was to raise performance standards by insisting on "breakthrough goals," breaking down internal barriers, and reducing costs by a billion dollars in months without a major layoff.

Pressing the company to operate at Net speed, she instituted marathon meetings every six weeks, where all four division heads got together. When she was told at one of these sessions that it would take at least three months to do a strategic review of the company's new e-services business opportunities, she shot back, "You have the next three days." The same kind of thing happened with the company's new brand image, integrating its business processes, and transforming its archaic payroll system.

According to one insider, "We knew we needed real change, even if it meant shaking things up, and Fiorina is bringing it to us."[6] Figure 1.2 illustrates the learning we can take from the Carly Fiorina story.

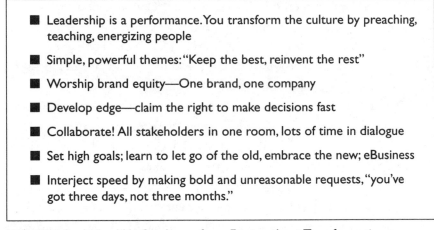

- Leadership is a performance. You transform the culture by preaching, teaching, energizing people

- Simple, powerful themes: "Keep the best, reinvent the rest"

- Worship brand equity—One brand, one company

- Develop edge—claim the right to make decisions fast

- Collaborate! All stakeholders in one room, lots of time in dialogue

- Set high goals; learn to let go of the old, embrace the new; eBusiness

- Interject speed by making bold and unreasonable requests, "you've got three days, not three months."

FIGURE 1.2   What We Can Learn from Fiorina about Transformative, Entrepreneurial Leadership

Jim Clark—Searching for That New, New Thing

According to Michael Lewis, in his book *The New New Thing*, Clark, who creates new companies the way a master chef creates recipes, has a hard time describing what he does for a living.[7] To Lewis, "When a person sets out to find a new idea or a new technology that will (a) make him rich, (b) throw entire industries into turmoil, and (c) cause ordinary people to sit up and say, 'My God something has changed,' he might be called an entrepreneur."

Clark's early life stands in contrast to how he is today. He was expelled from high school in Plainview, Texas, for prankish behavior. He proceeded to join the Navy in the '70s, was labeled a delinquent, and given a job on a ship of swabbing the mess room floor. After scoring high on a battery of tests (that the Navy officer first thought he had cheated on), the Navy decided to send Clark to the University of California. Eight years later, Clark had a Ph.D. in computer science. When he got out of the Navy, he wandered in and out of marriages and was fired from several jobs. One of his bosses referred to him as the "disorganization man."

According to Clark, "I was sitting home and I remember having the conscious thought that I have dug a big hole for myself. 'My God I am going to spend the

rest of my life in this fucking hole?'" In something like an instant the man transformed his life. He developed a maniacal passion for wanting to achieve something. This was at a time when Steve Jobs of Apple Computer and Scott McNealy
of Sun Microsystems where nurturing businesses that would give rise to Silicon
Valley.

Clark's first major innovation was a project he called the "Geometry Engine,"
which made it possible to produce computer-generated graphics. Soon people
like George Lucas and Stephen Spielberg were knocking at the door of the company he created, Silicon Graphics, asking to be one of his first customers.

Clark readily acknowledged, however, that after a few years he had no interest
in running the company and began groping around in the quest for what Michael
Lewis called that *new, new thing*—an idea just waiting to be taken for real by the
marketplace, an idea that is just a small nudge away from acceptance by the
madding crowd, and when it gets that nudge, will change the world.

Jim Clark's next project turned out to be Netscape Communications. Clark,
who considers himself a "searcher," thought about the Internet and said that what
was missing was a "gateway." He then led a team of people who invented the
Netscape browser, which transformed the Internet from a marginal medium used
by government officials, the military, and computer geeks into something that
within three years 100 million people in the United States
and elsewhere couldn't live without.

*"Jim Clark,
though 50, seemed
perpetually young. He
was totally bored to talk
about anything related to
the past. He lived totally
in the future."* Michael
Lewis, *That New
New Thing*

Clark became a billionaire, and within a few
short years again left in search of that *new new
thing*, or as I sometimes put it, "what's missing
that, if provided, could make a difference." In
1999, Clark launched Healtheon as a public
company, believing its products and services
will make it the Microsoft of the healthcare
industry. In 2000, he started an e-commerce
venture capital firm and another successful start-
up called MyCFO, whose purpose is to help wealthy
people manage their money effectively.

The curious thing is that the companies Clark has created represent only a
small fraction of the business-building ideas he has seriously considered over the
last decade. He often comes up with an idea, ponders it, talks about it as if it's the

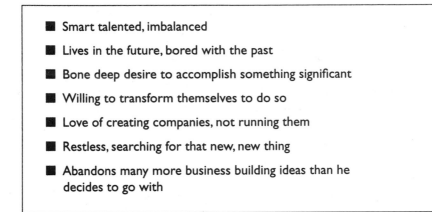

- Smart talented, imbalanced
- Lives in the future, bored with the past
- Bone deep desire to accomplish something significant
- Willing to transform themselves to do so
- Love of creating companies, not running them
- Restless, searching for that new, new thing
- Abandons many more business building ideas than he decides to go with

FIGURE 1.3 What We Can Learn from Clark about Creative, Entrepreneurial Leadership

greatest thing since sliced bread, and then mysteriously drops it. Other times, he decides to run with it. The difference: He chooses those ideas that he believes have the potential to change the world and convinces everybody else that they can. Figure 1.3 illustrates the learning from Jim Clark's story.

Creating an Entrepreneurial Culture

What we are talking about in this chapter is not limited to transforming a single individual from a steward to an entrepreneur. We are talking about something more profound. We are talking about creating a culture in companies large and small that supports entrepreneurial leadership at all levels. This sometimes appears like a daunting task. The leaders have to nourish the new opportunity and new good idea. Yet the fires in the existing business have to be put out as well. Next to the big, ongoing business, the new entrepreneurial idea always looks so puny. What are some of the things that you can do?

1. Create a growth-oriented versus a productivity- and efficiency-oriented business. In most Fortune 500 companies, I have observed, there has been very little entrepreneurship. Most of these companies are focused on hammering down costs, which doesn't create much of a climate of opportunity for testing new business models. The few exceptions are the companies that are focused on growth—either fast-growth organizations or those poised for growth. Imagine the opportunities that exist for people in companies like Amazon.com, Yahoo! or even fast-growth brick-and-mortar firms like Intel or Corning. When you are growing at 100 percent a year, you can't help but create opportunities for people to spread their wings.

2. Bring Silicon Valley inside through a special capital allocation fund. The way capital allocation happens in most businesses is hierarchical, not market-oriented. As HP's Fiorina said, almost no one person in the chain of command can say yes, and everybody can say no. One way to avoid this, Gary Hamel pointed out in a *Harvard Business Review* article, "Bringing Silicon Valley Inside,"[8] is to set aside a special capital allocation fund for new good ideas that emerge in response to sudden market changes—ideas that couldn't be predicted, planned for, or budgeted. Ask entrepreneurial leaders to take their ideas and present a business plan—not through the usual hierarchy, but to a selected group of leaders drawn from all levels and areas of the organization. This group should have funding approval for a specific dollar amount.

3. Encourage entrepreneurial leaders to set up promising e-business as a separate unit.   One of the most crucial issues facing legacy businesses in the e-economy is whether to try to start an e-business within the existing business or set it up separately. My advice is to create the space for entrepreneurial leaders to set up a separate business. It's important that the new venture not be subject to the leadership's attachment to the legacy business, the bureaucratic rigmarole found in most companies, or the glacial speed with which things usually happen. The e-commerce division of Toys "R" Us, mentioned at the outset of this chapter, is a case in point.

4. Learn to say "I'm a yes for that," instead of always saying, "I'm a no." In the year or so that I acted as a marketing consultant to Fidelity Investments, the company went from $350 billion in assets under management to $750 billion. This automatically transformed the usual "scarcity consciousness," found in most big firms, to a "consciousness of abundance." The idea was not to spend money wastefully, but to look for additional ways to create and add value for customers. I was fascinated with one manager I met, Roger Servison, EVP of retail marketing, who encouraged people to come up with innovative ideas and proposals at staff meetings. His whole way of being was to be "I'm a yes for that," unlike most managers whose whole way of being is to be a "no." Servison's way of saying yes usually involved giving people lots of encouragement and enough resources to get started.

> Transformation is an alteration in the underlying context that shapes who we are and determines what's possible. Change is an alteration in the process or prescribed actions.

To Reinvent Your Organization, You Must Reinvent Yourself First

There are many leaders who have the sincere and honest intention to reinvent their companies, but fail to do so because they don't recognize the necessity for reinventing themselves first. As I mentioned in the introduction, the *reinvention paradigm* involves declaring a new possibility—one that we are willing to passionately engage in—and then reinventing our organization and ourselves in order to transform that possibility into a reality.

The *reinvention paradigm* requires that we be able to distinguish between *transformation* and *change,* as well as between *how we are being* and *what we are doing.* Transformation is an alteration in the context that shapes how we and others are being, thinking, and acting—whether it's as a steward or entrepreneur, resigned or inspired. The context determines what's possible and not possible in any given moment. By contrast, change is an alteration in the daily process that shapes what we are doing.

It is possible to alter what we are doing without necessarily changing the organization or ourselves in any real way. As a case in point, over the years, thousands of managers have attended leadership programs. These leadership programs provided lots of good information on what to do, but little impact on people's leadership ability. In the same sense, in the last ten years, many companies shifted from functions to teams and processes, but the real barriers to communication and collaboration remained—the ones in people's heads.

To reinvent ourselves, we must alter the underlying context, not just the process. I am speaking of the history, winning formulas, or unwritten rules of the corporation that shape, limit, and define our thinking and actions at any given time. The most powerful way to alter this underlying context is through declaring powerful new possibilities, not by trying to psychologically understand all that has happened to us.

Let's review here the declarations that Tracy Goss identified and which I outlined in the introduction.[9] It is with these declarations that we begin to discover and express our power to make the impossible happen. We do this by reclaiming the power we have previously invested in our history, winning formulas, and unwritten rules.

1. *I declare that what is possible is what I say is possible, just because I said it.*
2. *I declare that who I am is the stand that I take, my commitment, not my history or winning formula.*
3. *The stand that I take is_____.*

Babe Ruth was making a declaration of what would happen, without evidence or proof, when he pointed to the right-field stadium wall, in effect telling people that he was going to hit a home run. Phil Jackson, head coach of the Los Angeles Lakers, makes a declaration every time he predicts that his team will win the NBA finals; moreover, he focuses on his commitment to the future, not to the past: "What worked with the Bulls wasn't going to work with the Lakers." This mindset has allowed him to create the space to look at who the team and he need to be and to reinvent the team and himself in the process.

Let's say that you are ready to take a stand. Start by declaring an impossibility, an ambitious aspiration: *To be the future of XYZ industry in the age of the Internet.* To accomplish this you will have to step beyond your history and your winning formula. For this to work, your declaration of possibility must be something that you are passionately committed to, something that matters to you enough that you are willing to reinvent your whole self.

Once you commit to the possibility, the next step will be to look at how you need to be, think, and act; for example, realizing your "impossibility" might require that you make a shift from being CEO as steward to CEO as entrepreneur. At that point, you make another declaration: "I am committed to the possibility of being entrepreneurial, a rule-breaker and -maker." This, in turn, requires that you be willing to excel beyond old patterns. "I am committed to giving up always needing to being in control." From that point on, acting from the future that you have declared, your thinking and behavior will begin to move into alignment with your declaration.

Masterful Coaching Will Give You the Power to Reinvent Yourself and Your Organization

The fact is that the more you seek to produce a breakthrough, by reaching results not currently possible, the more likely it is that you will hit breakdowns. When going for an impossible future, I recommend finding a masterful coach—someone who will stand with you in the face of breakdowns and support you in producing the results you intend.

The method that I have developed for coaching people to produce extraordinary results is based on triple-loop learning. (See Figure 1.4.) The notion is that when you declare a powerful new possibility and take action, and you wind up with unintended results, it tells you something. It tells you that there is a mismatch or error between your action and desired consequence. Learning occurs when we eliminate this mismatch and produce intended results for the first time.

Masterful coaches tend to start with altering the context that produces how people are being and therefore their thinking and actions, where most others try to simply alter people's behavior with tips, techniques, or prescriptions. It is predictable that if you haven't changed your way of being and thinking, that under stress and pressure, you will revert to form.

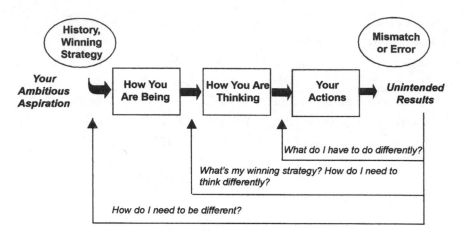

FIGURE 1.4   Triple-Loop Learning

Triple-Loop Learning

*The first question to ask is,
"How do I be?" not "What do I do?"*

Beginning first with the triple loop, ask yourself: How am I being today—a steward, manager, doer, and so forth? How is that determining what's possible or not possible in this given situation? What is the history or winning formula that shapes how I am being? Base the answer on your history and the background that has shaped you. If you can, write that down in one sentence. Writing this sentence can be a powerful act, because it allows you to become conscious of your old way of being and thereby gives you a choice to act on it or not. You can choose to abandon this way of being through a declaration: *I am committed to giving up___ from my history or winning formulas.*

Then ask yourself: How do I need to reinvent who I am based on what I want to accomplish? Write another sentence that contains a new leadership declaration: *I am committed to the possibility of_____.*

The declaration does not automatically make you a different kind of leader, but it begins to support you in seeing yourself in a new way and in acting in a new way. In other words, it begins to allow for and pull for the thinking and behavior that is consistent with who you intend to be. It also provides a mirror for when you backslide into old patterns.

In coaching senior leaders on their leadership declaration, I usually hand them a notebook and ask them to write down on a daily basis three examples of successes they have had with respect to transforming themselves into a different kind of leader. I have found that acknowledging successes in this way is essential to making real progress

Double-Loop Learning

How am I thinking about my business today?
How do I need to think about it differently?

In double-loop learning, your attention shifts from your personal attributes to the *mental models* that shape who you are and how you run your business. It is these mental models that shape your strategies and then ultimately your actions. To put it simply, *thinking drives behavior.* This kind of learning requires taking a reflective stance and then pushing yourself to bring to the surface, question, and revise underlying beliefs and assumptions.

Most people tend to think that there is one right way to run their business and, in effect, they have paradigm paralysis that keeps them from adapting to change. A typical belief might be, "We need a large field sales force to run this business." Or it could be, "Our products can't be sold on the Internet. If we do, our sales force or distributors will abandon us, and we'll be out of business." The discipline of surfacing, questioning, and revising mental models requires letting go of old ways of thinking and acting and is always an emotional process.

Write one sentence that describes your mental models about running your business as it relates to being a steward. Now write one sentence that describes new mental models about running your business as it relates to being more of an entrepreneur.

Single-Loop Learning

What do I need to do more, better, or differently?

Single-loop learning is the kind that most people are most familiar with. It usually involves coming up with a prescription about how you should alter your behav-

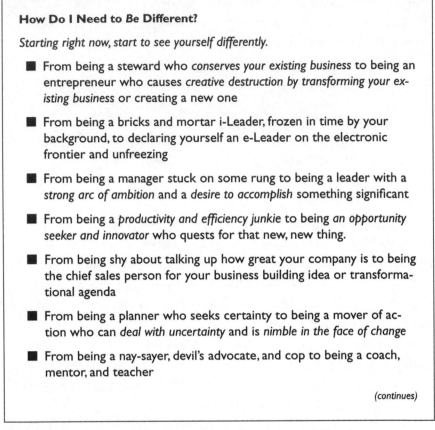

How Do I Need to *Be* Different?

Starting right now, start to see yourself differently.

■ From being a steward who *conserves your existing business* to being an entrepreneur who causes *creative destruction by transforming your existing business* or creating a new one

■ From being a bricks and mortar i-Leader, frozen in time by your background, to declaring yourself an e-Leader on the electronic frontier and unfreezing

■ From being a manager stuck on some rung to being a leader with a *strong arc of ambition* and a *desire to accomplish* something significant

■ From being a *productivity and efficiency junkie* to being *an opportunity seeker and innovator* who quests for that new, new thing.

■ From being shy about talking up how great your company is to being the chief sales person for your business building idea or transformational agenda

■ From being a planner who seeks certainty to being a mover of action who can *deal with uncertainty* and is *nimble in the face of change*

■ From being a nay-sayer, devil's advocate, and cop to being a coach, mentor, and teacher

(continues)

FIGURE 1.5   A Template for Becoming an Entrepreneurial Leader

ior. "I need to look for more entrepreneurial opportunities, focus on building an e-brand by Webifying myself or my company, and be willing to improvise." On the surface, single-loop learning would seem just fine, but it's easy to fool yourself with it. The issue is that it's who we are and our mental models that shape our behavior. If we don't reflect on these, we may find ourselves adopting a prescription for a while, yet reverting to form under stress and pressure.

I have found that single-loop learning usually results not in doing something different, but in doing the same thing better. That's why I suggest starting with triple-loop learning: *How do I need to be different?* Then double-loop: *How do I need to think differently?* Then single: *How do I need to act differently?*

(continued)

How Do I Need to *Think* Differently?

Starting to question what you take for granted

- From thinking that being a leader is about simply "improving" processes to thinking that being a leader is about creating what never existed before

- From thinking that an entrepreneur is an isolated individual to thinking that an entrepreneur is superb team builder and player

- From thinking in terms of pursuing efficiencies to thinking in terms of pursuing opportunities

- From thinking that there is one orthodox way to run your business to thinking that there are many ways—some unconventional

- From thinking about eBusiness from a narrow perspective—Web transactions—to thinking about it from a broader perspective—1:1 marketing, B2B process, HR

- From thinking in terms of building a Website to thinking in terms of building a brand

- From thinking in terms of pushing products/services to thinking in terms of branding

- From thinking in terms of planning for certainty to planning to improvise in the face of ambiguity

(continues)

Write down five things that you need to do differently to be more of an entrepreneur rather than a steward of your business. Figure 1.5 provides some guidelines that represent the new ways of being, thinking, and acting required to make the shift. It also answers the question of what makes a successful entrepreneurial leader.

In the next ten years, we will see a fundamental shift from the leader as steward who polishes grandma's silver to the leader as entrepreneur who must continually reinvent company business models in an environment of change and complexity. There has never been a better time to spread your entrepreneurial wings and exer-

---

(continued)

What Do I Need to *Do* Differently?

Jump into action—the eEconomy waits for no one:

- Read up on people who have transformed their companies—Jack Welch of GE, Roberto Goizetta of Coke, and Andy Grove of Intel

- Develop a personal leadership mission that includes soaring goals

- Develop a teachable point of view that will shape your company culture-eg. Keep the best, re-invent the rest

- Identify opportunities to create a new business with transformational potential; or look for other profitable opportunities in your own area of expertise and plagiarize

- Build your brand equity from day one-link with other existing brands

- Plan so that its 80% right, then jump into action

- break big goals into small breakthrough projects—think weeks, not months

- Achieve speed to value-iterate, iterate, iterate

---

cise your creative imagination than in the surge of the e-economy. Why not give yourself a little push to take you past the places where you stop or cling to the past? Or find someone else who will give you that push, like your boss or a coach. I'm reminded of a poem about the parent of a flock of baby eagles: "And he took them to the edge and pushed them, and they flew."

Interlude

Tony Tjan, Co-Founder, and Bill Seibel, CEO, of Zefer eConsulting

Come Up With an E-Business Idea and Run With It

Scene 1: Tony Tjan sits comfortably in the leather wingback chair. Outside, twenty floors below, workers are removing the holiday lights from the trees lining Market Street. The January cold has descended on Boston. It's time for the city to return to work. It's a new year, and a time for new opportunities. Tjan feels lucky.

The venture capitalist sitting across the mahogany desk gently lays the business plan down and pushes his glasses farther up the bridge of his nose. "Looks interesting. Let me think about it. Come back in a couple of days."

Tjan has heard these words before. Several other VCs had thought his plan interesting, had been impressed by his initial client successes, or had simply been amused by the name "Zefer." A couple had even invited him back for second meetings. But would any of them be willing to risk $20 million on a concept they thought merely interesting?

•   •   •

Scene 2: Bill Seibel paces. He is growing impatient with what he perceives as a lack of choices: "Bill, tell us what you're looking for." The venture capitalist adjusts his glasses and leans back in his chair, ready to listen.

Seibel has given this speech a dozen times. He is very focused on the opportunity he seeks, and the words tumble out with little effort. "I'm looking for a chance to bring my expertise to a truly exciting venture in the e-business landscape. That means a company with fresh ideas, fresh spirit, and a visionary plan for growth."

"I see," the VC responds slyly. He slides three folders across the desk. "You might be interested in taking a look at these." Seibel quickly flips through the papers as the VC continues with a speech of his own. "We respect your work, Bill. And you know we don't make our investment decisions lightly. Your expertise, along with our backing, would be a formula for success for any of these companies."

Seibel disagrees. "My leadership and your backing are just two pieces to the puzzle. What's missing here," he says as he waves the folders loosely in the air, "is vision." He lays the folders back on the desk. As he does, he notices another folder, perched precariously on the edge of the mahogany desk. Even upside down, he recognizes the company name: Zefer.

Seibel has recently seen Zefer's ads, which intentionally provoke CEOs with the message: "Be honest. Do you know your Internet strategy?" And he knows that its positioning runs deeper than ad copy. Zefer is committed to developing Internet strategies—and then delivering them. To Bill Seibel, recognizing the importance of strategy is a first step to being visionary.

He picks the folder up and says, "Here. This is the type of company I'd like you to introduce me to. C'mon. I feel lucky."

At first glance, Tony Tjan and Bill Seibel seem to be hopelessly mismatched. Tjan is young and effusive. Seibel is older and more reserved. Tjan is looking for the next big idea. Seibel is looking to apply his operational expertise to drive a sound business strategy. Tjan makes deals. Seibel makes decisions. What they have in common is that they both have what the other needs. Tjan must grow his start-up fast and, in order to do that, needs someone with operational skills and the credibility to attract investors. Without Tjan and Zefer, Seibel would have to build the company and brand he wants from ground zero.[1]

After meeting both men, I realized that they are anything but mismatched. Tjan had incubated dot-com companies and delivered dot-com strategy to Fortune 1000 companies. He and his team could identify six different business models on the Internet and knew the advantages and disadvantages of each. They came of age reading *Red Herring* and *Industry Standard*. They thought and talked differently. Because of that, they could attract different people. Seibel and his team, on the other hand, would have no problem running $10 million projects or attracting big investors. Together and separately, they knew what it took to get a business off the ground.

Despite their different backgrounds and experiences, Tjan and Seibel converge on the issue of wanting to create something new, different, and powerful. This is the mark of the true entrepreneur—a willingness to throw out the traditional "stewardship" rule book in order to make a real difference in revolutionizing the dot-com landscape. With the powerful combination of these two entrepreneurs at the helm, Zefer, in little more than a year, has positioned itself as one of the recognized leaders in strategy-led Internet consulting and implementation solutions for dot-com and traditional businesses. Its philosophy is simple, yet elegant and differentiating. By focusing on value-added strategy in addition to implementation, and by integrating the three disciplines of business, design, and technology, Zefer helps organizations translate their strategic objectives into tangible value in the digital world. Together, Tjan and Seibel have woven a culture of innovation and experience that breaks conventional wisdom and transforms business on the Internet.

Look at any of the many magazine articles, press releases, and company profiles written about this company and you will stumble, repeatedly, upon the word "strategic." For good reason. It's the cornerstone for Zefer's vision.

In the pre-Zefer market space, Tjan saw many companies rapidly launching Web sites that were treated as marketing tools rather than business assets. Not only did many of these sites disregard the strategic role they might have played in a business's success, but they also typically lacked either adequate function or appealing design. "There was lots of up-front building, not so much up-front thinking," said Tjan. "With Zefer, I saw an opportunity to provide 'soup-to-nuts' solutions, with a lot of energy spent on front-end strategy."

Bill Seibel saw a similar opportunity for businesses to use the Internet much more strategically. Specifically, he saw these opportunities driven by the Internet's ability to generate new business models and new business insights. This is the field of opportunity focused squarely in Zefer's sights. Just as first-wave solution providers, mostly creative design firms that posted brochure-ware on the Web, found it impossible to make the transition to second-wave opportunities that allowed business/customer interaction, Tjan and Seibel believe that it will be difficult for second-wave players to make the transition to delivering third-wave solutions. Buyers of the third wave are CEOs and the result they are seeking is business transformation. Major investors, dozens of Fortune 1000 clients, and industry analysts agree. They are all impressed with Zefer's attention to strategy—and the firm's capabilities to implement that strategy.

Bill Seibel and Tony Tjan share an entrepreneurial vision for Zefer that starts with strategy before application or Web development. Both men also appreciate the boldness of the strategy they are undertaking. They understand that they need to act quickly and deliberately in order to make the most of Zefer's new e-business idea. And they are driven by the fact that they can make a difference in their industry. That is, both men are energized–not by stewarding the growing company, but by the opportunity to create something new, exciting, and entrepreneurial. This does not mean that the men approach Zefer with an identical mindset. But it's this shared vision, and the complementary roles they play, that make them ideal partners.

The Spontaneous Entrepreneur

According to Jim Biolos, author of an article in the *Harvard Management Update* titled "Career Models for the 21st Century," one of the five career models we will be seeing is that of *spontaneous entrepreneur.*[2] This is the career model that best describes leaders like Bill Gates, Richard Branson, Michael Dell—people who know from an early age that they are destined to build a business of their own.

People who can't *not* be passionate about an idea. People who can't imagine working to create another person's dream. People like Tony Tjan.

Tjan was born in St. John's, Newfoundland, the son of immigrants who arrived in Canada from China with $200. By witnessing his parents' ability to succeed despite the significant challenges posed by a foreign culture and language, Tjan learned about determination and ambition. He also learned about hard work— not just in school, but also through a series of odd jobs as a young boy. These included the usual paper route, as well as not-so-usual gigs as grave cleaner, cod gutter, and computer technician. At the age of sixteen, Tony was running an IBM micro-center. A few years later, he launched a sports clothing business. "I have always had a relentless passion for innovation. As a boy, I considered it 'pregnancy envy.' All I wanted to do was give birth to something."

While an undergraduate at Harvard College Tjan stepped back and evaluated what he wanted to experience as an adult and where his "pregnancy envy" was leading him. "All I really knew was that I would always be passionate about the creation of something. Would I be able to create something that really fired my passions of technology, art, and strategic thinking?"

At Harvard, Tjan was self-reliant and fiercely independent. Rather than networking with fellow students (and future business leaders), Tjan focused his attention on gaining tactical knowledge not only in finance and new technology, but also in the "softer" disciplines of leadership, organizational behavior, and management. "What really fascinated me was understanding how other leaders led," he said.

Within months of arriving at Harvard, Tjan was to have unique, first-hand experience in watching leaders lead. He was selected to attend the World Economic Forum in Davos, Switzerland, where he served as aide-de-camp for the presidents of Singapore and Hungary. Not only was Tjan able to witness the interactions of the world's most powerful leaders, he was also able to observe the day-to-day idiosyncrasies with which these leaders defined their lives.

He points to experience with Lee Quan Yu, president of Singapore. "Here was the man who built Singapore. He is known to be maniacal and tyrannical about managing his schedule, which is really not too surprising when you realize that Singapore was developed through similar maniacal methodology. When I worked with him, one of my duties was to plot the number of minutes . . . the number of steps President Yu would have to take between meetings. I'd calculate the number of steps required to walk to the subway, for example, and then determine whether it would take 3.2 or 3.7 minutes. That's a lot of pressure for a college freshman, but I did have an experience of handling emotional pressure."

After graduating from Harvard College, Tjan deferred his admission to Harvard Business School and joined McKinsey & Company as a consultant. In the mid-1990s, McKinsey was one of the leading consulting firms helping clients realize the potential of the Internet. But Tjan learned much more than the practical application of Internet technology at McKinsey. He learned what it meant to be in the professional services industry. "McKinsey was a great firm that had built a wonderful philosophy, a mission, and a set of cultural values around which the firm could rally. For the first time I understood what it meant to be a professional and trusted adviser. Sometimes I had to deliver unwelcome news. At other times, I was able to suggest alternative solutions that would cost a fraction of what they had anticipated spending. But in every situation, my decisions were based on facts, and were objective and unbiased."

At McKinsey, Tjan also met Kaming Ng, who was manager of visual aids and would later serve as co-founder and creative director at Zefer. Tjan and Ng agreed that an opportunity existed for a company that combined the strength of business insights, which McKinsey was well known for, with effective interactive solutions and basic client communication. "What we realized is that you could have the best strategic insight in the world, but if you couldn't communicate it to the whole array of people who would be implementing it, you wouldn't make an impact at the end of the day. Your insight would be useless if it couldn't be communicated and implemented."

What Tjan and Ng originally saw as an opportunity quickly turned into the business model that underpinned Zefer's philosophy. "We saw the opportunity as one of combining left- and right-brain thinking. You can't approach a client with Internet solutions based solely on logic and science. It must be integrated with art and emotion. And we didn't see any companies out there bridging the left- and right-side thinking. There was no default consulting group a client could turn to for a clear understanding of what they should do on the Internet."

At the time, Tjan and Ng were envisioning their new venture as a "new media consultancy," although they admit they weren't sure what that meant. "What we did know was that we wanted to focus on building capabilities that would be needed in the future. And that meant building combined disciplines across business, design, and technology. I was, and still am, convinced that these are the three legs of a successful Internet solution. Most importantly, these three legs–these three categories of thinking—must work together."

In 1997–1998, the ideas originally proposed over coffee breaks and breakfasts took on a life of their own. Tjan returned to Harvard Business School, while Ng remained at McKinsey. They selected the name "Zefer" that same year. "*Zephyr* means 'west wind.' It can also be used to describe a transitory state, something airy. We felt that really symbolized the nature of communications. *Zefer* is not a misspelling on our part. We chose the phonetic spelling for the simple reason that the *zephyr* domain name was already taken." At HBS, Tjan recruited two classmates, Matthew Burkley and Alexandre Scherer (now respectively the managing director of Zefer's Boston office and partner/director general of France development), who shared his and Ng's vision for a new company. Together, they began developing a formal business plan.

True to form, Tjan did more than simply write a business plan. While at Harvard, he and his colleagues raised $2 million in venture capital from Mosaic Venture Partners. Vernon Lobo, Mosaic's managing director, and a former McKinsey colleague, explained, "When Tony first started, their differentiation was in the integration of the three disciplines—business, design, and technology. They were the only ones who could claim that." Lobo's decision to provide the seed money to Tjan was simple: "His abilities entrepreneurially are second to none."[3]

Buoyed by this initial investment, Zefer secured two clients, leading to $500,000 in revenues. In 1998, Zefer entered the prestigious Harvard Business School business plan competition. The competition criteria included likelihood of success, quality of people, and soundness of the strategic plan. Of thirty-two contenders, Zefer walked away with the $50,000 top prize. According to John Deighton, the group's Harvard project adviser, "The reason they won was basically they didn't need the judges. They conducted, by far, the most effective field study I've ever supervised. It was a great example of intelligence and audacity." Deighton went on to say, "That audacity may be Zefer's key. It's not an easy game to play because you have to convince companies they are not using their technology in a strategic way. That's a CEO-level conversation, and these are young guys. And they did it."[4]

According to Tjan, winning the business plan competition was well timed. "It was really the first time we got on the map." By the time he left Harvard Business

School, Tjan had assembled a group of twelve fellow students and professionals and a run rate of $1 million. Yet, he knew that to grow Zefer with the speed that was required, he would need more help. He needed someone with a name in the industry to help re-launch the company, oversee expanding operations, raise investment capital, and attract top talent.

Little did Tjan know that he would have to look no farther than across the Charles River. There, Bill Seibel was planning to leave Cambridge Technology Partners (CTP) in search of a new and exciting opportunity.

The Planful Entrepreneur

According to Jim Biolos, the second type of entrepreneur, known as the "planful entrepreneur," is also deeply committed to his or her internal passion.[5] These individuals, however, tend to be more methodical in determining their best course of action. Often they will be involved with large organizations for a number of years, acquiring the skills and leadership capabilities they need to start their own business. Some may be unsure of what they'd like to do; others are quite deliberate in taking the necessary steps toward a clearly defined business goal. Regardless of which camp they fall into, "planful entrepreneurs" are passionate and have the experience needed to bring this passion to life.

Bill Seibel walked into the venture capitalist's office in January 1999, prepared to start something new and exciting. Armed with twenty-five years of experience in leading information technology divisions at Air Products and Chemicals, Dunn & Bradstreet Software, Index, and Cambridge Technology, he was ready to make the jump.

Entrepreneurship is nothing new to Seibel. A part of the CTP's original management team and executive vice president, he not only helped turn CTP into a world leader in information technology solutions for Fortune 500 companies, but he also launched and built the company's international operation. By the time he resigned from CTP, Seibel was responsible for nine of the company's business units, including the e-business/Internet practice. "I was very proud of my work with Cambridge. But I was facing a series of dilemmas. How could I compete with firms doing one thing, when I was doing nine things in nine different cities? How could I attract the best and brightest team when they were being lured away by start-ups that guaranteed work on exciting projects and pre-IPO stock options? The business processes and infrastructure that had made Cambridge great were also making it difficult to branch out in new areas. Winston Churchill once said, 'At first, man defines his infrastructure. Then the infrastructure defines the man.' That's what I felt had happened at CTP."

This, as well as the cultural baggage that prevented the company from focusing on e-business opportunities, was Seibel's motivation to walk away from a company he had worked so hard to build. His decision to leave, while difficult, was also crystal clear. "I knew I wanted to create a successful company, a sustainable company, and a special company." Many of Seibel's colleagues, both within and outside of CTP, respected his decision. In fact, twenty of them joined him in his new venture, whatever that was going to be. This group of professionals had remarkable experience—the average was twenty years' worth—in building and scaling service delivery companies such as Gemini, Renaissance, and, of course, CTP.

Seibel knew, as well, that the company he hoped to create would have to be positioned to take advantage of the "third-wave" opportunities he saw emerging around him. Internet projects were bigger than they had been in the past. The primary customer was now an organization's CEO. And the value of these projects was measured in the ability to transform business. The company Seibel dreamed of would have to be able to implement a portfolio of solutions that was bundled in a framework of a new business strategy for a client. "Strategy was often the piece that was missing from the competitor's portfolio. Strategy is new business models, business insights, and fact-based approaches that can transform a business when it goes on-line."

Bill Seibel was thinking about the importance of strategy that day when he saw the Zefer business plan balanced on the edge of a wide desk, destined for the trash can below. . . .

Planful and Spontaneous: A Common Vision

Several things distinguished the first meeting between Tjan and Seibel from other meetings between visionary entrepreneurs and leaders. First, it lasted for four hours, ending only because Tjan had a conflicting appointment. Second, it didn't cover any of the topics one might expect. "What I liked about Bill," recalled Tjan, "is that he encouraged us to spend a great deal of time really trying to understand each other's intrinsic motivations, our passions, our ambitions."

This type of conversation was consistent with the way in which Tjan had originally formed his team. "I had an appreciation for what Bill had accomplished in his career. The heritage from which he came was no longer the right one for him, and he was open to being part of something exciting and completely different. And he was interested in hearing what my aspirations were for myself and the company."

The initial conversation was followed by another a few days later. This one, too, lasted four hours and continued the exploration of personal and professional goals. In their third meeting, another four-hour marathon session, Tjan and Seibel discussed client needs and the value that these clients sought in the Internet provider marketplace. A few days later, they met again. This was the meeting that many would have assumed occurred first. Here, they discussed how a company should be organized and whether Tjan's and Seibel's approaches to business were compatible. According to Seibel, "Often, when you have conversations about re-organizing a business, there's a lot of tension, debate and disagreement. There wasn't with Tony, I think, because we had spent so much time establishing a common platform about the things that really mattered. We had the same vision and the same values. I was confident, as was Tony, that we could work out the details."

And they did. Seibel joined Zefer as CEO in March 1999. News of his appointment was immediately followed by an investment of $100 million from GTCR Golder Rauner, the largest amount of private equity capital ever raised by an information technology startup. Obviously, Zefer and its new vision-based leadership team had caught the eyes and ears of the investment community.

Zefer: Making the Most of Planful and Spontaneous Entrepreneurship

It soon became clear that Tjan and Seibel had more in common than passion and vision. Their management styles also shared common ground. "Decisions for both of us, and all of our leadership team," said Tjan, "are based on the question, 'what's the best thing for the company overall?' And we believe that our success will not be defined by how well we have served ourselves, but by how well we've served our clients and stakeholders. And we do that at Zefer by running out and doing things."

Tjan is certainly "running out and doing things," with Seibel's blessing. "Tony has a true talent. If we put Tony in a room with a client, that client will invariably come away with an understanding and a respect for our point of view on his or her business issues. He's working seven days a week, twenty hours per day. He's traveling the world, speaking with the press and potential partners. He's building relationships for Zefer, and he's becoming the icon of the company."

Seibel is equally busy, with operational responsibility for Zefer's four offices, 500 employees, and growing list of clients. "People have asked me how I can subjugate my ego to Tony's increasing visibility. But I tell them it's not about ego. We're building a special company, and Tony is the best guy I've ever seen doing what he does. We should all learn to put our egos behind us if it means we'll be doing the right thing."

Seibel has noticed several changes in the required qualities of leadership during his tenure at Zefer. One has to do with the speed with which decisions need to be made. In the past, leaders had months to ponder alternatives. Today, those same decisions must be made overnight. Another difference is the need to evolve one's leadership style to match the evolution of an entrepreneurial organization. Because these organizations tend to evolve quickly, so too must the leader's capabilities.

According to Tjan, "Being a manager of thirty people is much different than managing 400. As the organization grows, you have to become more focused and be able to delegate responsibility." Seibel describes the evolution in the following way: "Early on, you need to be an entrepreneurial leader. Later on, you need to be a 'rainmaker.' Finally, you need to be able to bring stability to a fast-growing organization."

So, how does Seibel bring stability to a fast-growing entrepreneurial start-up without stifling the creativity and passion that launched it in the first place? The answer is "clarity of focus." According to Seibel, in an environment of rapid growth, it's more important than ever to keep people focused on the goals of the organization. "We often take a breath and say, 'remember, this is what we're trying to do here.'" To drive the importance of this message home, Seibel spent the first nine months as CEO putting together a book entitled, simply enough, "Clarity," which illustrates for all employees how all the pieces of the organization fit together.

Another important way in which Seibel and Tjan maintain stability at Zefer is through ongoing vision sessions, held every three months. "It's not that our vision is changing," said Seibel, "but as we're growing fast, we'd like to be able to take advantage of new perspectives. Our vision may remain the same, but markets are changing and our capabilities are changing. We begin each of these sessions with a statement: 'Here's who we thought we were three months ago. Who are we today?' We want to create a company that everyone feels they are a founder of. That's why their contribution to our vision is so important."

Agreeing to Disagree

Even though Seibel and Tjan share many of the same values and aspirations for Zefer, the relationship has not been one of total harmony. In fact, there was a point near the beginning of the partnership at which the deal almost fell apart. Interestingly enough, it had less to do with differences of opinion between Tjan and Seibel than it did between their respective followers.

Bill Seibel explained it this way: "The most difficult thing for me at the beginning was introducing my team of twelve people to Tony's team of twenty. The average age of Tony's team was twenty-eight. The average number of years of experience on my team was twenty-eight. As one of my colleagues put it, 'Bill, we feel like a bunch of middle-aged guys wearing tight jeans in a pickup bar.' Because Tony and I had developed a solid platform of understanding, it was easy for us to resolve issues. It was not so easy for the others. The people I brought in felt unappreciated and underutilized. They felt that we didn't really need the Zefer team. The problem was this: While my team had built numerous companies, Internet systems, and Internet practices, they simply didn't have the insights around new business models that Tony's team did. It was obvious that something needed to be done, or this venture faced unraveling."

Seibel and Tjan decided to provide a forum where these two groups could collaborate and air their concerns. "The way I looked at it," said Seibel, "if my team could appreciate the value of understanding new business models, then I was confident we could get Tony's team to appreciate their years of experience." Seibel and Tjan arranged for the entire group to spend four days on Cape Cod. There, they worked together to hammer out roles, culture, responsibilities, protocols of working together, and how each group would treat the other. When they returned to Boston, they used those discussions as the platform to build the company.

It is ironic that this dilemma faced the company, since it was this combination of skills—insights and experience—that the public was yearning for. Since that meeting on Cape Cod, the employees of Zefer no longer consider themselves part of Tony's team or Bill's team. They are part of the Zefer team, as it should be. The management team, too, reflects this. It comprises a cross-section of original founding members and new hires. In fact, the company now operates so smoothly that only one employee has left the firm since its founding. Only one. Out of four hundred. That's an amazing feat by anyone's standards.

While the Cape Cod episode is an extreme example of what can happen when two cultures clash, it also illustrates the important role that collaboration can play in "cleaning the slate." Leaders in the e-economy will face this sort of dilemma more and more, and they must be willing to collaborate with all parties for the best interest of the employees and the company.

Zefer is unique in that a spontaneous entrepreneur was opening up his business to a planful entrepreneur. It is equally unique that the planful entrepreneur realized the opportunity that Zefer presented. The relationship required give-and-take on both sides. Zefer is realizing the tremendous synergy that Tjan and Seibel (and their respective teams) bring to a client solution.

It was, and is, a powerful combination.

What Zefer Brings to Clients

Zefer's sixty-five clients—including Sears, Abbott Labs, Hallmark, Infoseek, and Kraft—are the ones ultimately benefiting from the synergy that exists at the company. They are the ones clamoring for the fresh perspective, brought to life by the capabilities of experienced talent. What, though, do they actually get when they sign on with Zefer?

First of all, Zefer clients receive solutions that are driven by business needs. This, while a simple concept, is relatively rare in information technology solutions. "We say to a CEO, 'This is how your Internet strategy and implementation plan is going to translate into profits,'" said Tjan. "They're not used to hearing that." Second, Zefer approaches client solutions with an interdisciplinary approach. Zefer tries to maintain a balance of capabilities that roughly map as follows: 30 percent business strategy, 30 percent design, and 40 percent technology. These capabilities are equally balanced on client engagements. Third, Zefer successfully marries insight and transformation. Not only can the company provide for an organization's strategic thinking, it can also handle all of the implementation, seamlessly. Fourth is Zefer's commitment to customer service, embodied in the company's philosophy of "doing the right thing for the client." Finally, Zefer clients gain access to an intellectual capital base that is second to none. Zefer has the insights to be at the forefront of Internet solutions.

"The most important thing for CEOs to acknowledge," said Tjan, "is that the Internet is going to impact them. And it's going to impact them in more than one area. What I really try to make CEOs understand is that you can't truly appreciate where your competitive Internet advantage lies unless you understand the whole portfolio of options available to you." Zefer is known for its "boot camp" approach to problem-solving with CEOs. Working together, they answer the fundamental business model questions: "What business am I in?" and "What business should I be in?"

Once the Zefer team has mapped a portfolio of opportunities based on the discovery process, it creates a blueprint for the initiatives. This includes an explicit methodology that combines business strategy, design, and technology. In conjunction with the development of blueprints, Zefer explores the organizational model and change-management issues that need to be addressed for the solution to be implemented successfully. "We talk to a lot of middle managers and the people doing the work. We usually have to develop a new organizational design, complete with governance and incentive policies. The Internet doesn't have a home in most organizations. It belongs to the entire organization. For that reason, it's vital that we build alignment throughout the organization. We try to include as many people in the process and design work as possible. At a minimum, we make sure that their concerns are heard." Finally, Zefer defines key operating and success metrics so the client will know what to measure once the organization has been changed.

The process varies slightly for Internet start-ups and traditional companies transitioning to the Internet. For the start-ups, Zefer will teach companies how to launch and manage their business—from helping them draft business plans to developing marketing plans to securing venture capital. For the traditional companies, Zefer helps them figure out how to use the Internet for the greatest advantage. According to Steve DiMarco, Zefer's head of consulting projects, "The scariest thing to a big company is, what does the Internet mean to my business? They're paralyzed by not knowing what the opportunities are and then not knowing what to do first."

Obviously, this comprehensive approach to Internet solutions is paying off. Zefer's client roster is growing quickly, as are its revenues. In 2000, the company had 750 employees, five offices across the country, and an office in Europe. *Red Herring* has named Zefer one of ten companies to watch for explosive growth. Additional articles have appeared in the *Wall Street Journal* and *Business Week*. On January 10, 2000, Zefer filed a registration statement for an initial public offering of its common stock. It is estimated that the market for Internet services will reach $35 billion to $40 billion by 2004.

Lessons of Leadership

It's clear in speaking with Tony Tjan and Bill Seibel that both men have already learned a great deal from their experience at Zefer, and from each other. For Seibel, the lessons fall into four areas. "The leadership capabilities that I need to develop in this environment are completely different. I must leverage the diversity associated with what we're trying to do. That means delegating and doing so quickly. I must also constantly build and refine our business model in order to scale this company quickly. I'm always asking the questions, 'How do we deliver? How do we sell? What's our structure? What are our values?' Finally, one of the more exciting challenges for me is to aggregate the capabilities of our people. At Zefer, we look for a great person, rather than someone to fit a particular role."

Seibel offers two additional pieces of advice for other planful entrepreneurs. "First of all, you need to accept the premise that if something has never worked before, that doesn't mean it won't work now. Conversely, something that *has* worked for twenty years is not necessarily a bad idea. Secondly, you need to make sure you leverage your experience in an enabling way. You do this by listening first. If I tell you what won't work before you tell me what you want to do, that's a very different conversation from one in which you tell me what you want to do and I offer reasons as to why it might not be feasible."

Tony Tjan thinks about leadership a lot. "It's a question I've been asking myself recently . . . . Can leadership be taught? Or are leaders born and developed? I think the answer is a combination of the two. In my mind, leaders, at the end of the day, must accomplish four things. They must be innovative. They must be able to develop people. They must be able to make change happen. And they must be able to allocate scarce resources and prioritize."

Given Tjan's belief that leadership can be developed in others, one of his goals is to provide an environment that nurtures leadership potential. "We pay competitive salaries, but people are here because we offer an environment of learning, development, fun, and high-quality work. We attract people who are intrinsically motivated, and that's the critical ingredient to leadership. With new recruits, I always ask, as Bill did of me, 'What are you passionate about? What drives you?' Then I tell them they can be leaders of their passions at Zefer. We have a host of people interested and passionate about a wide variety of things—jazz, classical composition, education, or science. There's room for all of them here, and it's a compelling case for the right type of person."

"But the most important quality of leadership," Tjan continued, "is passion. I would choose someone with high passion over someone with high skill any day."

Fortunately for Zefer, Tjan and Seibel are examples of that rare breed of leader who has both qualities.

From Game-Player
to Game-Changer

How to create a business model that
revolutionizes your industry

• • •

In Chapter 1, I looked at making the shift from the CEO as steward to the CEO as entrepreneur. In this chapter, I will look at how you can shift from being a game-player to a game-changer who reinvents your business or industry.

• • •

David Siegel, Web guru, is addressing an audience of about 2,500 business people at a meeting of the Direct Marketing Associates in Toronto. Siegel had been introduced as one of the world's leading Internet strategists. Instead of beginning his talk from the stage or showing a bedazzling array of PowerPoint slides, he prances around the room and asks to borrow a nice watch. A volunteer named Ted offers his Rolex.

"Thank you, Ted," says Siegel, taking the Rolex in his hand. "Now this watch represents your existing business model. It's finely crafted and it runs like clockwork." Siegel then takes out a Ziploc bag. "And this," says Ted, "represents your current value chain and sales distribution network. It completely surrounds the business model." Siegel places the watch in the bag and then places the bag on the stage.

Then he puts on a pair of safety glasses and takes out a sledgehammer. "And this, Ted, is the Internet." He asks Ted whether he thinks his current business model and distribution network can protect his company from the impact of the Internet. Ted hesitatingly says no. "Right!" shouts Siegel, as he brings the hammer crashing down. At that point, he removes his glasses and holds up the bag, which is now filled with hundreds of watch pieces. "Now what have we learned at Ted's expense?" Siegel asks the group.[1]

Create a Strategy of Preeminence— Breakthrough Business Models

The impact of the Internet carries a shattering message that needs to be thunderously demonstrated for many leaders to hear. The e-economy is moving with so much power and velocity that your business model, no matter how finely crafted, can be obliterated overnight.

Case in point: In the spring of 2000, the stock market went into a kind of correction and many of its prior darlings were punished. For example, Dr. Koop.com, a medical site, previously valued at seventy dollars, was crushed to two dollars. IVillage.com, a women's site, previously valued at about twenty-five dollars, was knocked down to about five dollars. Even WebVan, with venture capital funding at an historic $375 million, saw its initial IPO stock price reduced by half three months later.

As Jim Lanford, CEO of NETrageous, an Internet marketing firm, told me, many e-business leaders have not adequately thought through their business models. If you liken their business schemes to a model airplane, they have given a great deal of thought to designing a great propeller, but not enough to the engine, wings, or landing gear. "Many companies have made a total commitment to branding and customer acquisition," Lanford said, "but paid no attention whatsoever to costs and fulfillment."

He recalled CEOs of Internet firms bragging to him that they were going to spend their venture capital money on Super Bowl ads. "The idea behind this was to build brand recognition; they were thinking in terms of web hits." His challenge to them was not to place a bet on whether the $5 million to $10 million per spot would result in more "Web hits", but to place bets on things they could do that would result in "credit card hits." In other words it doesn't make any difference if you get 50 percent more Web hits if you only get 2 percent more credit card hits.

To Lanford, it was surprising that even some of the best e-leaders, with flushed high stock prices and soaring market caps, have not given due thought to such things as when they will turn a profit or to the expenses of their business. "It's a fact that it costs Amazon.com (a company he likes) 50–80 percent more to send a book out by FedEx than Barnes & Noble or Borders." There is absolutely no justification for that except that someone in the organization isn't paying attention to the numbers. "It's dumb," said Lanford, "and if you do dumb things, you will be punished," not only by the marketplace, but also by your customers.[2]

To ensure that they won't be punished, leaders need to be not only determined to win, but also determined to serve as game-changers and revolutionaries who can reinvent the rules. What most corporations tend to foster are managers and technicians who follow the rules. Today, companies must both transform their business models and their leaders at Net speed.

In today's e-economy you must have a strategy of preeminence. It is not enough to be a worthy competitor. You have to think in terms of how you can use the Internet to be the preeminent, predominant, and defining force in your field, or you may not be around for long.[3] When you think in terms of a strategy of preeminence, you suddenly begin to break the grip and excel beyond the old patterns that limit your company's possibilities and opportunities.

We Need to Transform the Legacy Mindset Around Leadership and Business Models

This isn't a matter of taking your existing legacy business and putting it on-line; it's a matter of creating something that never existed before. It's not a matter of thinking in terms of what's predictable; it's a matter of thinking in terms of what's possible and how the Internet can realize it. It isn't a matter of dreaming up new variations or new categories; it's a matter of wiping the slate clean and starting from scratch. This starts with abandoning the legacy mindset altogether. If not, you will never be able to envision and execute a business model that allows you to lead in your field.

To understand the importance of abandoning the legacy mindset, consider the following:

Was it Barnes & Noble or Borders that created the most successful bookseller on the Internet? Neither! It was Amazon!

Was it Sotheby's or Christie's that created the most successful auction on the Internet? Neither. It was Meg Whitman of eBay!

Was it AT&T, MCI, or Cablevision that created the most successful Internet service provider? None of the above. It was AOL!

What Kind of Leader Do You Need to Be?

What makes any CEO great (on or off the Web) is who they are as a leader, not just the set of strategies, implementation plans, and decisions they come up with in response to situations. So what kind of leader do you need to be to design a strategy of preeminence, to create a game-changing business model that will revolutionize your industry by leveraging the Internet? How is that different than the kind of leader you are today?

For one thing, it's not just a matter of having a vision or coming up with an "outside the box" business model that you are certain is the right answer. If you don't also possess within yourself the kind of leadership traits that can mobilize people to change, nothing will happen.

What we are talking about here is not the kind of leader who plays the game according to the standard industry practices, but who is in fact a game-changer. Most leaders and their businesses tend to be rule-followers. In every business and in every era there are usually a set of time-tested rules, and leaders who are rule-followers benefit. The rules represent the prevailing strategy, business model, and standard practices.

The rules are usually so much a part of people that they are as transparent as water is to a goldfish. In the recent past, some of the rules were: *Computers come with the operating system for the same price; Ma Bell is the only way to make a long-*

distance call; the only way for a big company to have meetings is face-to-face, which means people from different regions getting on a lot of airplanes.

Instead of Being a Rule-Follower, Be a Rule-Breaker and Rule-Maker

If you will notice, each of the rules above has been swept away by company leaders who were not rule-followers but rule-breakers. For example:

- Bill Gates decided to sell the Windows operating system of the computer separate from the computer, creating a whole new industry.
- William McGowan, who was the founder of MCI, broke the rules when he challenged Ma Bell's monopoly of the long-distance phone system.
- Companies like Placeware (Web conferencing) are challenging the rule of having to be face-to-face to have a meeting. Placeware's TV commercials show airlines falling into wastebaskets.

Yet, there is another dimension here. The leaders of today's super-successful companies are not just rule-breakers who do things differently in their companies, but are leaders who over time become rule-makers, revolutionizing their industry and creating dazzling wealth in the process. They do this by introducing new strategies, new business models, and practices that represent the new standard. They not only do the same thing better, but also create whole new categories.

> *"Usually, if everyone is going in one direction, it's wrong."*
> Hank Greenberg

Here are some examples of rule-breakers who became rule-makers:

Hank Greenberg, Chairman of AIG. When Hank Greenberg took over AIG, which started in Shanghai, China, in 1919, most insurance companies operated in their home countries and were content to break even on their underwriting insurance. They made their money by investing the premiums in the stock market. Greenberg came up with a game-changing business model by focusing on building a company that was global in scope but with a local attitude. He also insisted on lean and mean policies that resulted in hefty underwriting profits. Because of his leadership, AIG produced more shareholder value than the next two competitors combined.

Scott McNealy, CEO of Sun Microsystems. Before Sun, every computer company sold its products proprietarily, with closed operating systems. The result was that computers could not "talk" to each other or be interoperable. Scott McNealy and Sun came along and created "open systems" computers, allowing people to develop networks through Sun servers. Sun's motto, "The network is the computer" is now being followed by IBM, HP, and even Microsoft. Sun went from rule-breaker to rule-maker in a decade or so. In 1999 and the beginning of 2000, Sun's stock split twice and, at the time of this writing, was threatening to do so again.

Chris Cotsakos, CEO of E*Trade. In 1995, Cotsakos went to place a stock trade through an 800 number with a "registered rep." He noticed it cost twenty-five dollars. Ouch! There had to be a better way. When he first heard about e-tailing, Cotsakos got the idea that he could empower the customers with the free research they needed to make their own trades, as well as cut the price of a trade to five bucks. This idea has not only had a big impact on big investment companies, but also converted millions of household savers into real-time investors.

Rewrite the Rules Before Someone Else Does

What will it take to be a leader in the twenty-first century? It will take CEOs who can shift from *game-player* to *game-changer*, from following to rewriting the rules of their industry. For example, Compaq was a phenomenally successful company with a traditional distribution model. And because of Michael Dell and Dell Computers, the rules of the game changed. Compaq's sales went down, huge amounts of capital became tied up in inventory, and the CEO, previously the darling of the industry, was fired.

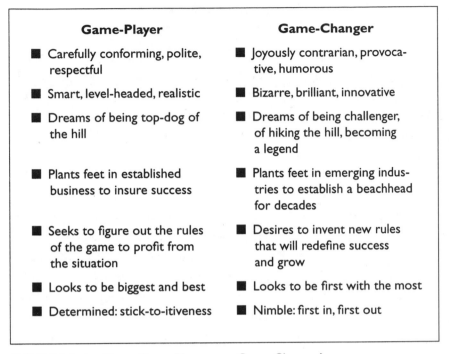

FIGURE 2.1 Are You a Game-Player or a Game-Changer?

Michael Capellas, the present CEO of Compaq, doesn't plan to make the same mistake. "The world of personal computers may cease to exist in two to three years."[4] There will be up to seven, eight, nine, or ten different devices in addition to the PC to access the Internet. Leaders are rewriting the rules again.

You may be saying to yourself that rewriting the rules is OK for leaders who were born with the necessary personal attributes to be a game-changer, rule-breaker, and rule-maker, but what if you weren't? The first step is to distinguish those attributes that you need to discover and call forth from yourself and from the people around you. (We will revisit this at the end of the chapter.) The second is to believe that transformation is possible and to begin a process of reflection-in-action. Figure 2.1 contrasts the game-player with the game-changer.

Do You Have an Internet Mindset?

> *"We may not be at the dawn of the Internet century, but it is still very early morning."*
> Steve Case, CEO, AOL

Now that we have looked at who you need to be as a leader to succeed in the e-economy, the next thing is to make sure you have an Internet mindset that allows you to respond creatively and powerfully to the changes of the e-economy, rather than resist them. According to Ken Kaplan, an e-business guru, whom many CEOs of top firms consider to be one of the best in the country, "The typical scenario with big, established legacy businesses in the face of powerful e-attackers like Dell, Amazon, or eBay always reminds me of H. G. Wells's famous book, *War of the Worlds*, a story about beings from another planet invading the earth, and threatening to subjugate all of human civilization."

The first response of the earthlings to the invaders was very much like the response of the CEOs in the mid-'90s to e-attackers: denial. They denied that these warriors from another world were real, saying the alien sightings were a "hoax," or things like "here today and gone tomorrow." They also refused to believe that anything so alien, so strange, and so small (like an e-start-up) could possess the power to conquer their world (their well-established legacy institutions). They refused to face reality and, in many cases, were subjugated by the invaders.[5]

The Four Dimensions of an Internet Mindset

I have found that the following dimensions are the foundation of an Internet mindset.

Mindset 1. The window of opportunity is still open—it's still early in the game.

In the Cambrian era, 500 million years ago, something broke. In the space of fewer than five million years—a geologic fraction of a moment—there was an explosion of multi-celled organisms. Weird new life forms appeared, such as the world's first predators with teeth and claws. These species were so varied and numerous that their basic makeup underlies nearly all of life today. According to Jeff Bezos, CEO of Amazon.com, "Evolution tried every conceivable path—really fast."

This explosion of new life, which was both amazing and dangerous, is precisely what's happening in business today. Out of this technological primordial pool (called the Internet) are emerging new companies, business models, and corporate structures. It's a period of such chaos and confusion that no one can agree on what's happening now, much less on what's coming next. In the five years since the World Wide Web made the Internet usable by ordinary people, we will have seen an amazing proliferation of new business models.

It's curious then that one of the most prevalent myths being circulated among CEOs and leaders today is that the Internet revolution already happened. If you haven't already grabbed some Internet real estate and established a thriving Web business, you have missed the boat. In fact, nothing could be further from the truth. There is a huge horizon of possibilities and opportunities, so don't panic.

In fact, before you develop a strategy or invest heavily in it, you have to recognize how fast today's successful business models are changing. For example, said Kaplan, "In 1999, the dominant marketing strategy was to become a portal like Yahoo!, Excite, Amazon, or eBay. By January 2000, people saw that many of these portals were indistinguishable from one another. As a result, they started running away from the portal strategy and started to specialize."

The point is that we can still expect to see momentous upheavals in what companies in every industry are doing to deal with marketing and customers. Companies that have established an Internet beachhead can't sit back and say, "Lock up this e-business model in the office cabinet."

As soon as you think you have arrived and you can write the formula down, you're in trouble. What would happen to Amazon.com if suddenly books became downloadable directly from the publisher?

At the beginning of the twenty-first century there is an unprecedented window of opportunity to create powerful new enterprises, as every traditional industry restructures itself in light of the Internet. Yet in the span of the next five years or so, that window of opportunity may close forever. To be sure, there will be many nontraditional industries created in the future and new opportunities yet to come. Perhaps the best words of advice then would be to seize an opportunity when it is presented to you and jump into action.

Mindset 2. The Internet is going to impact your business, whether you believe it or not.

"It's amazing how many company leaders assume that their business is 'immune to the Internet,'" Ken Kaplan said. The CEO of Mont Blanc pens, for example, made a strategic decision in 1998 to not sell the company's products over the Internet. The thinking was that Internet sales would dilute the luxury brand and force the company to lower prices. However in 1999, Mont Blanc received a letter from someone who had reserved Montblanc.com as a Web site address. Wresting the dot-com name away from the enterprising soul who had reserved it wound up costing the luxury pen maker almost $12 million.

Whereas some leaders adopt an attitude of "Internet immunity," others adopt a wait-and-see attitude, preferring to let others in their industry break the trail and deal with the scratches and bruises that result. As mentioned earlier, that strategy certainly didn't help Eckhard Pfeiffer, CEO of Compaq Computers. He simply watched Dell reap the first-mover advantage and lost his job.

Tony Tjan, co-founder and EVP of Zefer, cautions, "If you are a CEO (or leader) of a business unit, you have to adopt a mindset that the Internet is going to profoundly impact your business, whether you believe it or not. The question then becomes, how will it do that and how do I respond creatively and powerfully?"[6] This might involve something as profound as transforming your entire business model or something as simple as finding a better way to achieve cost efficiencies.

Tjan emphasizes, "This means you have to stop looking at your e-business activities as some kind of experiment and see it as running through the core of your business." A typical scenario today is a business leader who says, "We have to do something about the Internet." The leader assigns one or two people to the project, and they put up a home page, scan the company brochure onto the Internet, and buy a $25,000 e-business software package. It would be much more effective to call a time-out and examine your whole portfolio of Internet opportunities to see which ones will give you the most leverage and then act decisively in those areas. (See strategy workshop at the end of the chapter.)

Mindset 3. Don't redesign your Web site; redesign your business.

Want to create a super-successful Internet business strategy? Are you already halfway through your second iteration of your Web site? Before you go further, stop and think for a moment about the difference between a successful dot-com company like Amazon.com, eBay, or Landsend.com, and a *dot bomb* that makes a lot of noise with its advertising and then disappears up in smoke.

The real dot-com companies have developed a strategic business model that is designed to leverage the distinct features of the Internet: (1) creating a one-to-one relationship with customers— *Amazon.com*; (2) leveraging the network effects of the Internet—*eBay*; (3) providing a revolutionary new service that was difficult, impossible, or even unthinkable before the Internet—*E*Trade*; or (4) leveraging the Internet across the value-chain to increase speed and decrease cost and waste—*FedEx*. Figure 2.2. describes these four Internet adoption strategies.

> **Put the customer in charge of your business.**

Most business leaders, in their haste to put something up on the Web or to redesign their site, fail to consider these factors. In most cases, they simply take their existing business strategy model and use the Internet to automate direct marketing or sales. However, such a path doesn't fundamentally change the company's strategic business model and doesn't give the advantage over its competitors that the Internet can give. As David Siegel, who has consulted on hundreds of Web sites in large and small companies, puts it, "Don't redesign your Web site; redesign your company."[7] Begin this by putting your customers in charge by designing your business around them rather than designing your business around your products and services.

Most businesses tend to follow the "product category.com" model. There are companies called furniture.com, pets.com., lightbulbs.com. There is even a com-

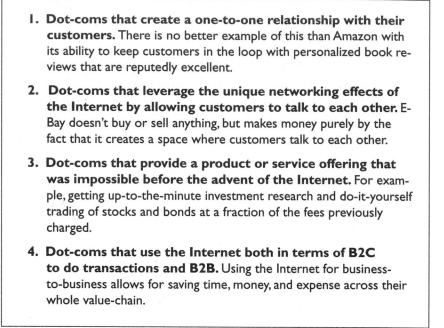

1. **Dot-coms that create a one-to-one relationship with their customers.** There is no better example of this than Amazon with its ability to keep customers in the loop with personalized book reviews that are reputedly excellent.

2. **Dot-coms that leverage the unique networking effects of the Internet by allowing customers to talk to each other.** E-Bay doesn't buy or sell anything, but makes money purely by the fact that it creates a space where customers talk to each other.

3. **Dot-coms that provide a product or service offering that was impossible before the advent of the Internet.** For example, getting up-to-the-minute investment research and do-it-yourself trading of stocks and bonds at a fraction of the fees previously charged.

4. **Dot-coms that use the Internet both in terms of B2C to do transactions and B2B.** Using the Internet for business-to-business allows for saving time, money, and expense across their whole value-chain.

FIGURE 2.2 Internet Adoption Strategies

pany that is called Justballs.com that sells bowling balls, tennis balls, golf balls, and so forth. The mistake these companies make is assuming that the customer will be loyal to a Web site that is no more than the customer-facing entity for a supply chain of mass-produced goods.

These businesses are still part of the i-economy, which was based on a *push model*—pushing products and services from the supply chain down to the customer who was happy to get whatever merchandise was on the lot. In the e-economy, that assumption has been turned on its head. We have shifted from a push economy to a *pull model* of the economy where the customer is in charge.

The Web gives customers what they have always wanted—an opportunity to express what they really want, to get honest answers to their questions, and to freely exchange information with other customers. As a result, companies must treat customers fundamentally differently, not as segments, categories, or "Web hits," but as human beings.

In creating a successful e-business, the single most important premise to keep in mind is the shift from a chest-pounding, egocentric organization to a more demure, customer-centric organization. "I always hear phrases like: 'I want to be the market leader' or 'We should be the authoritative source,' or 'We will use the Internet to reinforce our brand,'" says David Siegel. "Where is the customer in all of that?"

If you don't start with the right questions, you wind up with the wrong answers. There are two essential questions to ask in creating a successful e-business model. They have nothing to do with technology and everything to do with customers. First, who are your most important customers? Second, how can you help them solve problems?

The traditional business marketing approach was all about spin. You created an advertising campaign to sell products through a series of transactions and then hid any negative information about what you offered. Today, we are living in a *truth economy* where any attempt to hide information will be revealed almost immediately.

It's not only important to provide honest information about your products (as well as your competitor's), but to also provide the forums for your customers to talk to each other. This allows them to share information about things like "what's the best product for the best price" or to provide each other support in using the services of a given vendor.

Make it possible for customers to solve problems by talking to each other.

A colleague tells a story of going to an e-commerce site and looking for stereo cables, having read that the best cables were XYZ brand and cost $350. While at the Web site, the colleague joined a discussion group where he learned from a stereo aficionado that, while it was true that the best stereo cables sold for $350, to most human beings, the sound was indistinguishable from that of the $35 cables.

It's not only important to create communities where customers can talk about products and services they want to buy, but also about how to use them. For example, while writing this book, I came across an ad by Oracle, the software company, seeking to hire 20,000 consultants to help customers who purchased Oracle software learn how to implement it.

Several days later, I had a conversation with Keith Fox, a marketing VP from Cisco Systems, who said in effect, "We didn't want to be like Oracle and hire an army of consultants, so we set up Web-based customer groups. Today, a very high percentage of customers' implementation issues are handled by customers supporting other customers as they engage in dialogue through our Web site. Our role is to act as facilitators."[8]

A paradigm shift question to ask when designing a successful dot-com (rather than a dot bomb) is: "What can we do today that was difficult, impossible, or even unthinkable before the Internet?" Tens of thousands of companies create Web sites every week, but only a very small fraction of them are able to answer this question.

Jeff Taylor, founder of Monster.com (and profiled in Chapter 7) is a good example of someone who was able to successfully address these questions. When I spoke to Taylor, he told me that before Monster.com (the 484th registered Web site), with the exception of executives, most people could only search for a job in their local newspapers. Employers could only select talent from their region. Monster.com opened the job search process up so that many more job openings could be discovered and the search could take place independent of time and distance. On any given day, there are more than 384,000 jobs advertised and, in most cases, anyone who fills out a resume is likely to get at least one job offer. This would have been impossible without the Internet.

In answering the question posed, "What could we offer customers that was difficult or impossible before the Internet?" don't limit yourself to the Buy It.com mentality. It's not only important to consider the B2C (business-to-consumer segment, often referred to as e-commerce), but also to consider the B2B (business-to-business or e-business) segment, which is in fact much larger. According to Forrester Research, an Internet research firm, in 1999, the B2B segment was $109 billion—about six times larger than the e-tailing sector.

Mindset 4. Make reinventing your business model an ongoing process, not an isolated event.

CEOs face a dilemma. On the one hand, they are under enormous stockholder pressure to come up with a powerful Internet strategy. On the other, the capital investment involved may send their stock in a nosedive. Thus, creating an Internet strategy that is powerful in terms of the marketplace and that will be accepted by the board means company leaders must often do some hard thinking.

Today, every CEO not only has to have an Internet mindset, but the skills that go along with it. The essential one is to be able create or transform business models at Net speed. The first thing you need is a place to start. As Robert Lessin, chairman of WIT Capital, suggests, "It may be a good idea to alert your board (or senior leaders) that you will need to spend 50 percent of your time thinking about your Internet strategy, which will create some breathing room." If you are an entrepreneur, plan to spend the same amount of time doing the same. Once you have done that, you will be able to take a reflective stance rather than just reacting, as many managers are doing today, out of desperation or panic. To get there faster, you need to slow your thinking process down. You need to spend time thinking hard about your business strategy or model.

Provide a revolutionary product or service that was impossible before the Internet.

A business model is basically a *theory of business* that holds up under public scrutiny and, most importantly, in actual practice. In constructing a business model for today's e-economy, it is important to keep in mind three points: The purpose of any business is to *create a customer* by providing value; the goal of a business is to deliver on economic performance; and the Internet can be leveraged to help you do both.

Here are three generic business models that you may wish to draw on in developing your own.

The Niche Specialist Model—click with variety and choice. The company CD-NOW.com was created because its founders, two brothers, Jason and Matt Olim, were jazz fans who couldn't find much jazz music at local music stores. They started the company after going into one music shop and asking the manager what recordings he had of Miles Davis. The manager had never heard of Miles Davis. The Olims set up shop in their parents' basement, financed their start-up on their credit cards and within a short time the company was offering 3,000 jazz recordings over the Internet. They then went on to build the same in other categories.

The Auctions Model—click with dynamic pricing. Adauction.com offers a highly perishable item—unpurchased advertising. When a magazine is about to go to press and has empty ad space, it goes to Adauction.com, and puts the space up for bid. The ads are sold at a fair price 97 percent of the time, and Adauction, which does not make or sell products of its own, takes a small slice.

The Infomediary Model. An infomediary is a Web business that focuses on one customer segment. It provides specialized information while also giving people price and choice. The first mover definitely has the advantage with this model. Once an infomediary establishes itself on the Web in a particular segment, in come the buyers, which in turn attracts more sellers, which in turn attracts more buyers. This is becoming the model of choice of the business-to-business e-business area. This could include offering goods through a catalog model such as Grainger.com, which stocks over two million hard-to-find items though a network of over 500 alliances.

Creating a Super-Successful Internet Business Model

Use the following four steps to begin to build a super-successful business Internet model.

1. Start with some customer reconnaissance and intelligence gathering.

The first thing to consider in creating an e-business is to ask yourself in broadbrush terms Peter Drucker's classic question: *"What is our business and what should it be?"* This forces you to look beyond whatever your business is now and to consider new possibilities and opportunities.

It also forces you to ask yourself the all-important question: *Who is your most important customer?* There are too many companies that think they can build a business model by trying to serve five or six customer segments. That may have been possible in the world of mass production, but today, customers have become very demanding and require very personalized products and services.

Though it may sound counterintuitive, the best way to grow a business may in fact be to say that, "We will do everything to say 'yes' in the service of . . . , which in turn may force us to say 'no' to some others." The best e-businesses have been designed like this. For example, Priceline.com doesn't serve business customers. Rather, it services budget travelers. The Hewlett-Packard Village Web site doesn't service the budget shopper; rather it serves the customer who would rather buy a sturdier, better designed LaserJet printer, even though it means paying $399 instead of $299.

> The difference between a dot-com and a dot bomb is doing something that was impossible before the Internet.

Once you have decided who your customers are, the next step is to spend some time with them finding out not only their desires and needs, but most importantly their big dissatisfiers or chief frustration points.

For example, after this chapter you will read about Kevin McCallum, former product manager of Procter and Gamble (P&G) and now vice president of 1 800 CONTACTS, which provides contact lenses. While still at P&G, McCallum and his team invented a product called Dryel, which may one day replace your local dry cleaner.

McCallum didn't come up with the idea out of thin air; rather he interviewed four hundred women to find out what their cleaning problems were. He wasn't even thinking dry cleaning when he started. Today, he is doing the same thing, interviewing customers to find out their problems, at 1 800 CONTACTS, except at Internet speed.

The point is that success in business, whether on the Internet or elsewhere, has little to do with being a creative genius, it has to do with customers. Once you establish customer intimacy, it is much easier to come up with a preemptive business strategy based on a highly innovative product or service than it is by sitting in your room throwing darts at the wall.

2. Create a Strategy of Preeminence— assume the mantle of leadership.

Being a worthy competitor is not enough in today's fast-paced, highly innovative e-economy. If you think about Amazon.com, AOL, and Priceline.com, it's clear to see that the e-economy favors those who come up with a business model that allows them to become the preeminent, predominant, defining force in their field.

To create what Jay Abraham, chief strategy officer for a number of highly prominent Internet firms, calls "a strategy of preeminence" involves three simple steps.

Gather your findings from your customer reconnaissance and highlight customers' desires, needs, frustrations, and dissatisfiers with the way business is carried out by your industry, by your competitors, or by your own company. For example, before Monster.com, job seekers *desired* to be able to find jobs where they didn't have to settle for less and they were *frustrated* with the Sunday newspaper and *dissatisfied* with employment agencies.

Start developing your strategy of preeminence by seeing and thinking in terms of breakthroughs. Start by asking yourself the paradigm shift question: Given your customers' desires, needs, frustrations, what can you provide that was difficult, impossible, or even unthinkable before the Internet? Or ask: How could your company leverage the unique properties of the Internet? What, new, innovative, competitively advantageous product or service could you offer? In thinking about this, let go of your attachment to the standard practices of your own industry. Look at what other industries have done to leverage the Internet. You will be amazed at how easily you can adapt these practices to your own industry or situation.

Innovations in strategy must be supported by innovations in infrastructure.

Seize the first-mover advantage. There is no great idea today that is so original that you can be assured that you are the only one who has thought of it. If you don't act right now, immediately, you may be too late. Speed is a tremendous advantage. So rather than perfect your strategy, plan so that it's directionally right, then iterate.

One of the most important things in any business is location, location, location and the same thing is true on the Internet. As soon as you have a broad-brush idea of what e-business you want to be in, register your domain name. This has the effect of declaring your e-business into existence, as well as reserving the Internet real estate you want.

Figure 2.3, which shows the Internet Adoption Curve from *The Clickable Corporation*[9], will give you different ideas about how you might want to build a strategy of preeminence. Over time, you may want to include more of these aspects in your e-business.

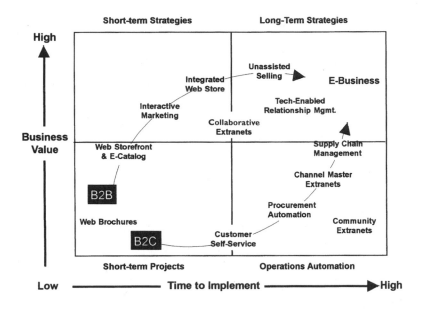

FIGURE 2.3   Internet Adoption Curve

3. Choose partners wisely so as to leverage your strategy.

Many e-commerce businesses are subject to the Wizard of Oz syndrome. They make a great deal of noise about the great Oz—their Web site, brand, offerings. Yet, when you pull the curtain back, there is nothing there except a little old man from Kansas.

Your business model not only has to be based on a marketing strategy for creating customers, but also on your organization's infrastructure. It's one thing to establish your Web site and have great merchandising skills; it's another to capture information about your customers so you can personalize your offerings or make sure that orders are processed and shipped swiftly with a minimum of expense.

Think in terms of creating a blueprint of your e-business. Ask: What is our business strategy? What kinds of processes do we need to set up: brand and demand creation, product design and development, or logistics?

Obviously, it's important to focus on the one or two things you do well and create partners who can give you leverage and whose businesses are interoperable with yours. As Laurie Tucker, senior vice president of e-commerce at FedEx, who is also responsible for customers having a great experience in dealing with the company, says, "The digital world moves too fast for even the biggest companies to do it all on their own."[10]

Finding the right partners then is an essential part of your business model. Who could you align yourself with that could offer you a powerful assist in speeding up time to market, increasing productivity, and reducing costs? At the very least, take the time to figure out the efficiencies to be gained by electronically integrating operations with them. Obviously, in selecting partners, you have to choose wisely. Take into consideration both personal and cultural compatibility.

4. Enable your business design with relationships technology.

Any successful business model today must take into account the reality of "business without borders." This means that you not only have to form process teams and partnerships, but also that your business model must be designed so people can connect and collaborate across boundaries. The power of the Internet is that it makes available relationships technology that allows you to do that at a relatively low cost.

Whenever you invest in technology, take the time to think about the downstream requirements of integrating that technology so that your entire business becomes interoperable. Be prepared to answer how a given technology will not only empower your business, but those of your customers, clients, and partners. Show how you will use the Internet and relationships technology to make this easier.

In the 1990s, many companies made huge investments in ERP software from companies like SAP. However, these had to be abandoned in the year 2000 or so because the proprietary ERP software was not interoperable with their partners' systems. Companies also found that it was easier to connect and collaborate using simple, low-cost Web browsers than the fancy software.

It's not only important to think in terms of how Internet technology can improve the performance of physical processes, but also how it can improve human performance. For example, consider PlanetIntra.com, a very successful software company nominally based in Mountain View, California. The CEO, Alan MacMillan, is a Canadian who has been working in Hong Kong. The company's product has been written by a software team in Croatia. The vice president for technology lives in Russia, while the vice president of international sales is a German living in Tokyo. They use the Internet, in fact their own product, to collaborate with each other and their customers across borders. They also use their software to coordinate the sales and distribution of their product through partners around the world. Leaders in the future will need to be able to "coach" meetings like this over the Internet with skill and dexterity.

The Clickable Corporation

"The high-richness, high-reach, high-speed Internet has forced many to design their entire business strategies around the click of the mouse or around billions of mouse clicks performed by millions of users." In the book, *The Clickable Corporation*, Jonathan Rosenoer, Douglas Armstrong, and J. Russell Gates outline eight value propositions that companies can offer customers through the Web. Figure 2.4 shows these.[11]

A Game-Changer Process for Discovering the Genius in Your Group

In early December 1999 an urgent, confidential memo was sent to seventy managers of J. P. Morgan & Co from Thomas Ketchum, the bank's chief administrative officer. The essence of the memo was, "drop what you are doing right now." The message directed thirty-five managing directors, as well as the seventy employees, to report to an unmarked room in a building in the Wall Street financial district. The message told people to drop all holiday plans because everyone would be tied up for weeks.

When Phil Weisberg, then a manager in the derivatives section at the bank, saw the e-mail, he wondered what could be so important? A huge merger maybe? It wasn't the case, but something considered even more important to the company. It was the launch of a project called "eswat," a six-week brainstorming session in which the big New York bank's most creative brains tried to determine, with military zeal, how to adapt to the Internet age so as not to be left in the dust of history.

"If J. P. Morgan isn't an e-business coming out of this," said J. P. Morgan's chief executive, Douglas J. Warner III, "we're history. There is an e-tech wave coming, and

1. **Click with information:** Make it possible for your customers to gather information about products and services that they could only get before with great cost and difficulty.

2. **Click with Convenience:** Provide customers with convenience in a fundamentally different way by using the Web to disappear barriers of time and space.

3. **Click with Customization:** Learn to customize your products and services on a one-to-one basis through an interactive dialogue with customers that previously would have been impossible without the Web.

4. **Click with Choice:** Act as a super middleman that allows customers to discover who has the best prices, and find hard to find products.

5. **Click with Savings:** Assist B2B customers by seeing where your business is interoperable and where you could provide an on-line service that reduces their costs.

6. **Click with Community:** Invite customers to join communities online, e.g., investors, retirees, new mothers. By focusing on their values and interests, you can efficiently offer products and services to a group that is already pre-niched.

7. **Click with Entertainment:** Make buying what has been a boring product or run of the mill service an experience that is fun.

8. **Click with Trust:** Resolve the trust issue by ensuring privacy for your customers and educating them about the Internet's ease and efficiency.

FIGURE 2.4 Eight Successful Strategies to Create Successful Customer Relationships

we aim to be at the top of that wave riding it." Warner showed up at the meeting first thing Monday morning doing everything possible to make it happen. He said, "I wanted to do this in a collaborative way with the bank's best brains, no hierarchy, no offices, no structure." He told the group, "Nothing is too sacred to question." He later added, "We want the most creative, radical thinking possible." Then he set a deadline. "You have six weeks to do this and I want no more than ten ideas."

The session produced the ten big ideas and a new section of the bank with 200 employees called Lab Morgan.[12]

Sponsor a Collaborative Strategy Design Workshop

The story illustrates that today in every company there needs to be at least one person, the CEO or someone close by, who takes responsibility for creating a game-changing business strategy in light of the Internet. Furthermore, every enterprise should have a game-changer process whereby this happens on a regular basis. This process must be distinct and stand out from all other run-of-the-mill organization activities.

The fact is that most companies do not have a forum for strategic-brainstorming conversations to take place. The annual process of planning and budgeting doesn't provide a forum for people to fundamentally question the business strategy model. At the same time, when strategic discussions do occur, they are usually comprised of people from on high who were the authors of the present business model and who usually have more invested in the status quo than they do in change.

The intent here is to support you as a leader in facilitating a strategic business model renewal process through a collaborative strategy design workshop. The suggestions offered below are based on a process I use in working with companies that is called the *CollabLab-accelerated solutions environment.*

The CollabLab is not a meeting, a training session, or an exercise. The idea is to provide an *accelerated solutions environment* that will allow people to deal with complex issues in days, rather than weeks or months. It is, therefore, highly effective in creating or transforming business models at Net speed. Figure 2.5 shows some of the accelerators in a CollabLab.

The Strategy Session in Three Phases

The idea of the strategy session is to have a purposeful conversation that leads to a game-changing business model. To ensure a rich quality of dialogue, draw people out and invite them to give their honest opinion when asked, as well as to ques-

Collaborative Session *Accelerator Principles*

Juxtaposition: Innovation comes from differences. Who you invite to the collaborative session is as important as anything you put on the agenda. One of the key leadership roles for the next millennium will be to be a *convener* whose job it is to *get all the stakeholders in one room* with a shared understood goal—CEO's, middle managers, partners, and even customers. Remember, it's juxtaposing multiple talents and perspectives in dialogue that lights creative sparks which often lead to strategic insights. Include people you usually wouldn't think of. Need someone who is e-savvy? Invite that 29-year-old new hire in marketing. Need someone who is an expert on potentially disruptive technology, or virtual supply chains? Use the Web to find an expert and invite that person to the session.

Socialization: Treat each other as colleagues. Spend the first 30 to 60 minutes or so of the session with people getting to know each other and building a basis of authentic communication and trust. The time spent in socializing interimly slows things down, but ultimately speeds things up. Two of my favorite ice breakers are: 1) Offer a welcome drink so that people can mill about, meet each other and talk; 2) Ask people to sit down in pairs to interview each other on who they are, their background, and interests. Then ask the interviewer to introduce that person to the group. Also, ask people at the beginning of the session to agree to treat each other as colleagues.

Imagination: Play "What If?" It's my experience that what makes a CollabLab strategy session powerful is making each aspect fast-paced and fun. For example, ask the group to do the following exercise. *Fortune* magazine runs a cover story on how your company achieved a dominant position in eCommerce in your industry. How did you do it? Or ask your group to write a *Wall Street Journal* headline that describes your own company's death scenario. "XYZ Associates' stock drops from 85 to 14 as a result of failure to respond to the Internet." Then ask people to say why this happened.

Diversion: Use colorful language. People tend think down the same logical track leading to "better sameness." Encourage metaphors, analogies, and colorful language to divert people from the same old track and to spark creative thinking. For example, the Internet makes it possible to have "richness" and "reach." Richness comes from enhancing the value of products, services, and information through customer interaction. Reach comes from doing transactions independent of time and distance. How could we use the Internet to improve on both? Or you might ask: Are eMay's "auctions" a better metaphor for our EBusiness than zNET's "online catalogue"?

Interaction: Plan so it's directionally right, then iterate. Individual geniuses don't sit down, ponder a topic for an hour or two, and then say "Eureka, I've got it!" Instead they stuff their head full of information, mull on it for a day or two, and come up with an insight that is directionally right. Then usually the next day they iterate. In most cases, each iteration takes half as long and doubles the output of the previous one. A key to discovering group genius is to design iteration into your conversational process (it usually gets left out) so that the team gets another crack at things like the business mission, infrastructure design, or enabling technology. Today, it is possible to reconvene groups to iterate independently of time and distance through groupware and virtual teamrooms. Use it!

FIGURE 2.5 Accelerator Principles for a Collaborative Session

tion what they have taken for granted. To make sure the conversation stays focused, I recommend a conversational recipe. One that we often use in the CollabLab is a three-step process called *Scan, Focus, Act.*[13] In Scan, you develop a wide variety of e-business alternatives. In Focus, you select which alternatives to focus on. In Act, you begin to prototype different aspects of your business model. Let's look at each phase of the strategy session.

Phase One: SCAN for Successful Business Models

The purpose of the Scan phase is to enable you to step back from your "legacy" mindset or particular perspective and see things you didn't see before. If you don't take time to scan to learn, you will probably wind up recreating a more, better, or different version of your current business model. Scanning also makes it possible for you to develop a vibrant and varied portfolio of business possibilities.

1. Begin by scanning the environment to find out which e-business models are succeeding and what you can learn from them.   Scan companies both in your industry and beyond it that you can role model in some way.

Look for companies that have few assets or atoms. A good principle to follow in creating your successful e-business model is to look for products that are information-rich, high price, and low weight. It's no wonder that one of the first successful e-business companies was Amazon.com, which sells books, a product that can be placed in a FedEx envelope in seconds and shipped anywhere in the world. Think about the difficulties in running a successful e-business on a global basis if your product were cement. Other e-business products that are high price and low weight are financial instruments, silk ties, and cigars.

Look for companies that provide a powerful and distinct service that was not possible before the Internet. For example, Autobytel.com makes it possible for its customers to connect to 2,700 dealers across the country to get the best price for the car they want. It also provides car-buying information and consumer reports.

Look for companies that leverage the powerful networking effects of the Internet. EBay doesn't buy or sell any products whatsoever. Instead it creates a space where almost anyone who wants to sell a certain item can find a buyer through an online auction. It does this not by direct marketing but by inviting its members to invite other friends to participate as buyers or sellers and thus feed the network. The more people who participate, the more the company grows.

Look for companies that establish brand recognition. The Internet gives the guy a chance to make it big by selling a powerful and unique product and service. As businesses in every conceivable category proliferate, the power of brands becomes not only important, but also essential. In designing your business model, think about where it is that you already have some brand power and, furthermore, what you can do to leverage it. If you are a new company and have no brand recognition, see if you can create a partnership with a company that already has a brand established.

Look for companies that are "bricks" as well as "clicks." The Internet makes it possible for a company to promise anything, but it can leave questions in people's minds as to what they will deliver. Most purchasers would like to have the convenience of shopping over the Internet, but like to know that there is a bricks-and-mortar outlet somewhere where they can see a face, pick up a product, or get reliable service. Would you rather buy a computer on-line from Gateway, knowing that there are retail outlets where you can first see the computer and also service it, when and if you have a problem, or would you rather buy one on-line from "computersomethingorother.com"?

2. Now scan your more immediate environment by doing a "constituent or competitor analysis." Some questions to ask are:

- What trends do you see in your industry, as result of e-commerce, that are likely to reshape your industry?
- What are your nearest competitors doing with respect to e-commerce?
- What will happen to you if you don't?

3. Take the point of view of the customer.

- What are your identified customers dissatisfied with today? What is frustrating them?
- What alternatives are your customers interested in? What kind of benefit would erase their dissatisfaction?

- What do your customers aspire to be or achieve? How can you help them do that?

4. Develop your e-business portfolio of options.   Once you have gone through the exercises above, begin to look at all of your business assets—brand recognition, innovative product development, supply chain management, customer service, and human performance—and start to brainstorm what your e-business options are, especially those things you could do much better through Internet adoption. What could you do that would allow you to be the definitive, preeminent, predominant force in your industry or field? I have discovered in working with companies that only by brainstorming your whole portfolio of options will you be able to select the best ones.

Phase Two: FOCUS on Your Best Alternatives for Business Models

The purpose of the Focus phase is to allow you to select from your list of options those items or combination of items that are of the highest leverage.

1. Choose which options to focus on.   Some questions to ask are:

- What are your best business advantages today?
- Which one of these advantages could you leverage on the Internet? (For example, how could you extend products, improve service, streamline processes?)
- Which potential advantages could you develop further in light of your current business relationships?

2. Write a mission statement.   This should take the form of a long sentence or, at most, a short paragraph. The following questions will help to frame your statement:

- What is our highest goal and aspiration as a business? What are our best business opportunities? Where can we assume the mantle of leadership

or what will we do that separates us from all the other *me, too* competitors?

- What can we do to create new value that was impossible to do before the
  Internet? What can we do to create customers, innovate new offerings,
  streamline processes, and improve service?
- Which strategies of the clickable corporation can we apply? Click with:
  Previously hard-to-get information, mind-blowing convenience, a
  much higher range of choice, one-to-one customization, surprising
  cost/time savings, community, or entertainment. (See Figure 2.4.)

3. Set up solution-specific criteria that are focused on what is core.   Ask
yourself: Are the options that we have come up with: *High impact and easy to do,
low impact and easy to do, low impact and difficult to do, or high impact and difficult
to do?* Rate each option. (See Figure 2.6.)

4. Design your organizational infrastructure.   Once you decide what
your mission is, think about the specific people you will need to champion your
business. It may be better to "hive off" a new business unit with people from the
outside rather than to drag people out of your existing culture. Ask the group to
identify the organizational processes that will allow you to succeed (for example,
e-business development, production, service). Identify potential business partners, especially those whose processes are interoperable with yours.

5. Enable your business with technology.   Ask people to think of what
disruptive technologies are occurring in other industries that could impact your
business. Then ask the group to determine what they have to do to respond to it.
Also look at what leading-edge technologies could make a difference.
   Some questions to ask are:

- What are your customers' connectivity needs?
- What issues can they solve on-line?
- How can you use technology to streamline processes or internally im-
  prove customer services?

Rate Criteria Using the Following Scale

Low Impact Easy to Do	High Impact Easy to Do
Low Impact Hard to Do	High Impact Hard to Do

FIGURE 2.6 A Template for Rating Your Options

(If you are not sure of the answers, go back and do another iteration on scanning your environment for examples of how companies have used technology to solve problems similar to yours.)

Phase Three: ACT by Creating a Prototype Together

Once a clear picture of the business model begins to emerge, the next step is to begin to take some action while in the same room rather than talk about what you will do later separately.

1. Create a series of blueprints regarding the different parts.   This could be a Web site design, process map, or talent-acquisition method. The idea is for the different stakeholders to create some rapid prototypes together. Thinking and working together on the prototypes of the various components of the design can spark creativity and save a huge amount of time.

Leadership is a way of being, not just a set of functions.

2. Use the breakthrough technique to initiate powerful action. Another strategy for gaining speed involves looking at your e-business model and then focusing on what's core to getting it up and running. Once you discover what is core (as opposed to the bells and whistles), go for some quick wins. Use the Breakthrough Technique as shown in Figure 2.7. Groups can continue projects in collaborative workspaces on-line after the group disbands.

To Reinvent Your Organization, You Must Reinvent Yourself First

Take a moment to reflect on how you personally have to change to be a leader who is taking responsibility for transforming or creating new business models, and especially doing so in an ongoing way. Again, I suggest using the triple-loop learning approach. As outlined in Chapter 1, the process starts with looking at your goals and aspirations, and then learning to alter who you are, as well as your thinking and behavior, until you are able to reach the goals, especially in light of unintended results. Let's say that your goal is to create a strategy of preeminence

---

Breakthrough Technique Basic Guidelines

1. Identify a high-leverage business opportunity

2. Decide on a team leader and team

3. Create a razor-sharp goal to be completed in weeks, not months

4. Spend one day creating a written work plan

5. Get going and produce some results, right now, immediately!

FIGURE 2.7 The Breakthrough Technique

in your company and that in order to do so, you realize that something needs to change for you, your team, and your organization—you need to become game-changers rather than playing the game as it has always been done in the past. Let's go through the steps of triple-loop learning.

Triple-Loop Learning

How do you need to be different?

In terms of making the shift from leader who is a game-player to a game-changer, think about who you have been as a leader in the past. Begin to recognize the patterns that have shaped who you are and start to expand your horizon of possibility as a person. Instead of seeing who you are and your way of being as "fixed" or immutable, start to see yourself as a possibility again. You will also begin to have some choice around your actual behavior.

"Thinking drives behavior."
Michael Gerber

Write a sentence that states the belief or beliefs that have fundamentally shaped, limited, and defined who you have been in regards to being a game-player. This statement should get at underlying beliefs and assumptions. For example: "Don't rock the boat, play it safe, stick to the knitting and do what has made us successful in the past."

Now think about how you need to be different to be a game-changer and to create a strategy of preeminence. For example: "I have to be willing to take a risk, there is no safety, I need to be willing to shake other people up as well and confront them with the uncomfortable questions about our company's future (and the future of each of us)."

Write one sentence that represents a new leadership declaration with respect to making the shift from a game-player to a game-changer. For example: "I can no longer play it safe and ride on the success of the past, but must question what I have taken for granted in order to be a preeminent force in my field."

Double-Loop Learning

How do you need to think differently?

Your leadership declaration is a self-expressive, self-defining, existential act. It represents a sincere and honest commitment to intervene in the historical background that has shaped who you are. Double-loop learning represents a sincere attempt to intervene both in the corresponding mental models that have come from that, as well as the standard practices of your particular field of play.

When people see things differently, they can act differently.

Write one sentence that describes the mental model that has shaped your leadership style based on your immediate environment. For example: "Find out what the rules are and do what you do well." The next thing to consider is whether or not this mental model works for you now, and if you might want to revise it.

Write one sentence that describes what your new mental model might be that could be the basis of a new leadership style that would support you in being a game-changer. For example: "The rules have changed. I need to consider how the Internet has and will impact our business and rethink how we do everything in light of it."

Single-Loop Learning

How do you need to act differently?

I have found in coaching hundreds of executives that, if people try to seek prescriptions before they have reframed their thinking and actions, they usually revert to form. However, once people have the "right" mindset, a prescription or tip can be very useful.

Think about the prescriptions you have acted on in the past: "Follow the rules," "Don't rock the boat," and so forth.

Write down some prescriptions which might go with your new leadership declaration or mindset. For example: "Question how things are done and get others doing so too," or "Learn from what others are doing that is working in the Internet world."

Transformational Learning—
Guidelines for Reflection-in-Action

Figure 2.8 provides some guidelines that may help in making a shift in your way of being, thinking, and acting. The idea is to put some of these notions into practice and then to reflect on what happens. This is called reflection-in-action. The intention is to keep adjusting your way of being, thinking, and acting according to the feedback you are getting.

How do you need to *be* different?

- From CEO as "conformist to corporate tradition" to the CEO as "revolutionary who creates a new tradition"

- From being a "doer who reacts to people and circumstances" to being a "chief strategist with a reflective stance"

- From being a "game-player, who does things by the rules" to "game-changer, who invents new rules"

- From being a "crowd pleaser and predictable" to being "joyously creative, contrarian, and an iconoclast"

- From being a "tentative Web person who experiments with the Internet" to being a "full-fledged Web fanatic who drives the Internet into every aspect of your business"

How do you need to *think* differently?

- From bricks-and-mortar thinking to Internet thinking

- From thinking in terms of running a business to thinking in terms of continually reinventing business models

- From asking yourself, "What is possible to do with our current business design?" to asking, "What can we do that was impossible to do before the Internet?"

- From thinking B2C (Amazon) or B2B (FDX) to C2C (eBay) or C2B (Monster.com)

- From thinking in terms of following standard rules and practices to thinking in terms of creating new practices

- From thinking in terms of making decisions at bureaucratic speed to thinking in terms of making decisions in Internet time

How do you need to *act* differently?

- Create forums for strategic conversations to take place

- Pose powerful questions and draw people out to tap the group genius

- Continually scan the environment in order to learn and gain new perspectives

- Continually question what you take for granted

- Focus on what's core

- Get going and produce some results right now, immediately!

FIGURE 2.8 A Template for Becoming a Leader Who is a Game-Changer

Interlude

Kevin McCallum,
Franchise Manager
at Procter & Gamble

Create a Strategy of Preeminence

"Jason? Can you stop at the dry cleaner's on the way home today?"

At some point during his four-year marriage to Marcie, this question—or one of its variations, "Can you pick Billy up from day care?". . . "Can you pick up some milk?". . . "Can you stop at the bank?". . . "Can you come home at a decent hour?" —had replaced the long embraces and whispers of "I love you" that once occurred regularly on the front porch of their home at 7:30 in the morning. Now, Jason is propelled into his workday with a travel mug of coffee and a directive that he will have to remember nine hours later.

"The game has changed," he thinks, as he peers over the mountain of clothes in his back seat and pulls out of his driveway. He knows it is normal for couples to evolve from a stage of honeymoon infatuation to one marked by necessary routines and requests. He and Marcie are a team—an efficient union—each with their list of errands that allow them to function effectively as a family. He is happy to help out. If he only remembers . . . .

•   •   •

"Jason?" He hears his name at the same time he sees the shadow of his boss spread like ink across his desk. The hairs on the back of his neck stand on end. "Free for lunch today?"

"Sure," Jason replies, clenching his teeth in a smile that he hopes appears genuine.

"Great. A couple of new clients are coming in today, and I thought we could take them to that Italian place in Santa Monica. We need to make a really good impression on these guys."

"Sure," says Jason again, wondering why he is always the one targeted for these meetings.

"Oh, one more thing." His boss sticks his head back into Jason's cubicle. "Can you drive? My car's in the shop."

"Sure," replies Jason one final time. He smiles and thinks, "At least if I'm driving, I won't have to be such an active participant in what will be an excruciating conversation on the way to the restaurant."

●   ●   ●

It is 12:30 p.m., and Jason has already forgotten about the dry-cleaning errand after work. He's also forgotten about the pile of clothes in his back seat. As he approaches his car with his boss and the two Italian venture capitalists who warrant such a good impression, he remembers. He can't help but remember, for in front of him he sees the chaos of shirt collars and pants rising like a volcano through his rear window. To make matters worse, the sleeve of one his wife's blouses hangs out of the car, pinched in the door and crumpled sadly on the asphalt.

So much for good impressions.

Jason is like many of us. He faces typical demands. From his marriage. From his job. From the constant struggle of balancing the two. Even from his dry cleaner, who closes promptly at 6 p.m.

There's a theory in psychology known as *learned helplessness*, which was first observed in laboratory rats but later witnessed in human beings. The premise is simple: Over time, if you are consistently punished (or not rewarded) for your behaviors, you *learn* to expect nothing else. You learn to be helpless, unable to see alternatives. You are resigned to your fate of mistreatment. I bring up this lesson from Psychology 101 because it reminds me of what happens when consumers go to the dry cleaner's. Like the maître d' of the finest restaurant in town or, to be more dramatic, like the IRS threatening you with an audit, the dry cleaner has all the power and sets his own rules. He has something you want and need—the ability to clean dry-clean-only clothing—and there's no competition. He can charge whatever he wants. And if you want to wear silk or rayon or cashmere, you will drive around like Jason, with piles of laundry in your car, until you're able to fit the dry cleaner's schedule. You will play by your dry-cleaner's rules. But do you really have to?

"Not at all," according to Kevin McCallum, former franchise manager at Procter & Gamble.[1] He should know. As mastermind behind P&G's at-home dry cleaning alternative, Dryel, McCallum was one of the first to change the game of an industry that had flourished, unchanged, for twenty-five years. Now, he's doing the same thing with another product/service line at 1800CONTACTS.com, where he is in charge of marketing contact lenses to consumers on-line.

I first met McCallum when the Dryel brand was being launched nationally. His strategy and approach to product development was, I thought, unique yet simple. When I heard he moved to 1800CONTACTS, I wondered if the same principles that worked so well for product development would apply to on-line service development. He assures me that the principles are the same. But the rules have changed. Kevin McCallum is blending tried-and-true marketing strategies with new rules of on-line conduct. As a result, he's definitely changing the consumer game of buying contact lenses.

McCallum's approach to changing the game—be it dry cleaning or contact-lens shopping—involves what some refer to as an "optimist/maximist strategy." That is, in order to change the game in any industry, you don't necessarily have to start from scratch (although it may not be a bad idea). You might be able to salvage existing structures or processes that work well—or will work well with a bit of tweaking. Be optimistic about what already works. For McCallum at P&G,

what worked was the company's ability to develop new products, as well as its supportive structure that encouraged "out-of-the-box" thinking. At 1800CON-TACTS, he is also using what works—in this case, an appreciation of the customers' role in creating a business and successful marketing strategies—to be more than a worthy competitor. That is, he is using the power of customer insights and his own experience to change the game.

What's the Game?

Remember what life was like before you had a VCR? Or a CD player? Chances are, you don't. These electronic components have become ubiquitous over the past twenty-five years and have changed the game of home entertainment for each of us. In many instances, technologies and new products are driving these movements toward convenience, but that's not always the case.

Consider, for example, that there was a time when it was unthinkable to call a restaurant and request a meal to be delivered to your home within the hour. It was also not so long ago that mailing packages involved a trip to the post office. Now, a host of delivery services will come right to your door. Banking used to require long waits in front of a teller's window. Today, ATMs are located on every street corner. A more recent example is seen in the emerging trend of automobile maintenance centers establishing satellite offices in parking lots of major corporations—changing oil and rotating tires while the owners are busy at work. The Internet is the latest service channel finding its way into consumers' homes. You can now buy almost anything you want on-line—from groceries to stamps to airline tickets to retail products—and have your purchase delivered to your door.

Whether it is with a new product or new service, game-changing in the marketplace typically evolves from a pronounced need to make our lives more convenient. According to McCallum, the challenge lies in identifying this market need, scanning the existing playing field for solutions, and then developing something new and valuable for the consumer. To succeed in changing an existing seller-driven game, you need to put the customer first. When you do that, you will invariably reach an insight, which you must be able to build upon with creativity to make something happen.

Taking the Customer to the Cleaners

Cotton is out. Silk, rayon, acetate, linen, and nylon are in. And dry cleaners around the world are grinning ear to ear. These are not the types of fabrics that consumers can easily toss into the washing machine with their jeans and T-shirts. To get them cleaned, millions of consumers each day travel to the local dry cleaners, spending up to five dollars per item. In Europe, the cost is easily three times as much. That's billions of dollars each year going to the dry-cleaning industry. Surely, there's an opportunity to change the game.

Kevin McCallum and his team at Procter & Gamble were given the formidable (and vague) task of growing the P&G laundry products business by creating something new. "It was pretty daunting," said McCallum, "to be faced with the challenge of growing a business by 20 percent in one year. But we knew that we could do it. It just depended on an attitude of discovery, a plan, and a process." When the team members set out to offer a new product to consumers, they weren't thinking about dry cleaning. In fact, they weren't thinking about much of anything. Instead, they were counting on the consumers to guide them to the opportunity.

"The process always begins by defining your target and identifying your customer," said McCallum matter-of-factly. Once you've done that, you have the source of all your insights in front of you. He refers to the next phase of the game-changing process as "casting the net." Another way to think of this is personalized market research, which involves physically moving into the marketplace, homes, and lives of your identified customers. Specifically, you're looking for three things:

1. The dissatisfiers—what are your identified customers dissatisfied with today? What is frustrating them?
2. The benefits—what alternatives are your consumers interested in? What kind of benefit would erase their dissatisfaction?
3. The aspirations—what do your customers aspire to be or achieve?

These are the questions that McCallum and his seven team members set out to answer. To do so, they spent time with their consumers. Lots of time. McCallum estimated that each team member invested about fifty days observing approximately 800 consumers on "laundry day" in their homes. "We watched them. We talked to them. We followed them around. Our goal was to understand how they managed the task of laundering clothes." From that understanding, the insight that eventually led to Dryel was revealed.

"It was this simple," began McCallum. "We were noticing that piles of clothes existed in consumers' closets across the country. When we would ask about the pile, people invariably responded with, 'Oh. That's just the pile going to the dry cleaners on Thursday.' When we would then meet again as a team and compare notes, it became clear that everyone was witnessing this pile of clothing. A trend had emerged. And that's what this phase is all about—identifying trends."

McCallum's approach enabled this trend and the resulting insight to emerge. It is doubtful that a survey would have captured the need for a dry-cleaning alternative. "You can't just ask people on the street, 'What do you want out of your laundry experience?' Rather, you need to observe them experiencing their frustrations. That's the only way they will be able to really articulate their needs."

Once the P&G team members agreed that the pile of dry-clean-only clothes might be a source of insight, they returned to the consumers and tried to better understand the relevance and frustrations of dry cleaning in their lives. "We heard things like, 'I have to take those clothes in on Wednesday. It's such a drag,' or 'I can't believe how much they charge,' or 'They broke a button last week.'" What became clear during these conversations was the fact that consumers were, on the whole, dissatisfied with their dry cleaning experiences. To get a well-rounded view of the situation, the team also visited dry cleaners. This was necessary to better understand the value that dry cleaning was providing and shed new light on the sources of dissatisfaction.

"At this point, our 'casting the net' phase was over. We had learned that the $8 billion dry-cleaning industry was not satisfying its customers. We knew there was a tremendous opportunity here." The opportunity had been identified by going into the field—not from sitting behind a corporate desk, trying to answer the daunting question of "How will I grow this business by 20 percent?" Consumers revealed the insight. They also provided important additional information. "We learned that people don't get dirty while wearing dry-clean-only clothes. They wear these clothes in three basic venues—to work, to social functions, and to places like church or synagogue. People aren't mowing their lawns in silk." While such an observation may seem apparent, it was important to include it in the initial analysis. If people weren't getting dirty while wearing their clothes, why were they having them cleaned at all? What were the benefits consumers were seeking from dry cleaning—or from a dry-cleaning alternative? The reasons were to remove odors and specific stains and to make the garment "fresh" again. Knowing this helped focus the development of a dry-cleaning alternative.

Once the consumer has helped identify the general area of opportunity, the creative process begins. With the Dryel team, this took the form of brainstorming. "We started thinking of all possible solutions to dry cleaning at home—liquid products, buckets, sponges, sprays, things in the dryer. All ideas were tossed on the table, and together we put the puzzle pieces of possible prototypes together."

The challenge at this point was creating a product that consumers would purchase and use. It might seem obvious that, when given a more convenient, more economical alternative, consumers would flock to the new dry-cleaning alternative. Not necessarily. To go back to the *learned helplessness* scenario mentioned above, numerous studies have demonstrated that once the punishment is withdrawn, rats and people continue to act as if they will be punished. Rats won't eat, even though the electric shocking mechanism has been turned off for days. This example is, of course, extreme. But the basic premise remains the same. Would dry-cleaning consumers be able to appreciate the alternative that P&G was preparing for them?

From the dozens of ideas that emerged, several P&G prototypes were developed and tested with consumers. "The customers who had given us the original insight into this dry-cleaning need now provided valuable information that helped us make the product better. They would try out the prototypes and report back to us with suggestions and comments. We'd listen and go back to the drawing board. We learned from them. And we had to think about it all over again. Learn . . . . Think. Learn . . . . Think. That's the only way you can create a successful product."

The result of this iterative development process was Dryel, the at-home cleaning system for dry-clean-only garments that is available across the country today. The concept is straightforward. The Dryel kit cares for up to sixteen garments and contains a bottle of stain remover, absorbent pads, dryer-activated cloths, and one reusable Dryel bag. Once the stain remover is applied to stains, garments are placed in the bag with the absorbent pad and cloth, and then placed in the dryer for thirty minutes. Dryel removes small spots and stains and cleans away odors such as smoke and perspiration, leaving clothes smelling fresh.

According to McCallum, Dryel was developed to complement—not replace—professional dry cleaning. It shouldn't be used on heavily soiled items, or for garments made of leather, suede or fur. What Dryel can do is provide an economical and convenient way to freshen clothes and extend the length of time between trips to the dry cleaner.

As for pricing and distribution, McCallum turned once again to the consumer. "We looked at how much they were paying for professional dry cleaning, and then we asked them how much they would pay for the product. We let them assess the value and determine the price." As for distribution, test-market consumers indicated they would expect to find Dryel in grocery stores, mass merchandisers, and local drug stores. Wisely, that's where P&G placed the product.

Dryel was tested in Columbus, Ohio, for one year before its national launch. The results were convincing. In fact, if the test market results were accurate, it would prove to become one of the largest, most successful product launches of the decade. Indeed, they were accurate. During its first year on national shelves, Dryel was a $450 million business. It was projected that within three years, sales would reach $2 billion. In 1999, Dryel was ranked a *Good Housekeeping* product of the year, and *Advertising Age* ranked it one of the top twenty-five brands of the new millennium.

Would this consumer-driven approach work as well in the service industry, where there was no one product to develop? Kevin McCallum was about to find out.

Creating a New Vision for the Eye Care Industry

In March 2000, Kevin McCallum left Procter & Gamble after eight years as manager of many of the company's leading brand franchises. He had honed his skills in product development and felt the same principles that had led to successful product launches (such as Bounce and Downy, which he grew from a $1.2 million business to a $2 billion business in five years) could be applied in the service sector. So when 1800CONTACTS, a direct provider of contact lenses, asked him to be the company's first Internet marketing director, he jumped at the chance.

The company has already achieved remarkable success. In the last five years of the 1990s, sales jumped from $3.6 million to more than $100 million. In fact, in 2000, 1800CONTACTS delivered over 100,000 contact lenses to customers every day, making it the largest direct marketer of contact lenses in the world—by far. With $15 million in inventory on-hand in the company's Draper, Utah, facility, 1800CONTACTS is able to meet any consumer's need. And the company can do so quickly (because it has everything in stock) and more economically (because it has the volume to drive down price).

The company's Internet presence (www.1800CONTACTS.com) is fast becoming a focus for the business. More than 1,000 on-line orders were processed each day. That has translated into $31 million in Net sales during the first quarter of 2000. More than half of the company's on-line customers are repeat buyers. It's easy to see why. The average customer saves twenty-five dollars to fifty dollars per year, receives free shipping right to his or her door, and does not have to waste time traveling back to the optometrist's office to pick up the lenses.

But back to McCallum. Could he successfully move from developing a dry-cleaning alternative to marketing contact lenses? To some, that might seem like a gargantuan leap. He was, after all, moving from the product sector to the service sector, from manufacturing to selling. He was moving from one of the largest, most well established brick-and-mortar operations in the world to a small, though rapidly growing, Internet company. These differences, however, were outweighed by the positions' similarities. Both dry cleaning and contact lenses represent an $8 billion market. Both industries target consumers who make a choice to satisfy more "refined" needs—wanting to wear dry-cleanable clothing instead of machine washables and wanting to wear contact lenses instead of eyeglasses. Both industries enjoy a stranglehold on the consumer. Consumers wanting to have their clothing dry-cleaned have no choice but to go to the dry cleaners. Consumers who want contact lenses have to purchase these through their optometrists. Not anymore. In industries with little choice and virtually no competition, there is tremendous opportunity to create a new space for consumers. This was the greatest similarity of all—the opportunity to carve a customer-driven niche in multi-billion dollar industries. The opportunity to give consumers control and value.

In the contact lens industry, consumers go to an optometrist for an eye exam. Once that is completed, they are given a prescription for lenses and offered a choice—often limited—from their doctors' list of preferred vendors. Optometrists typically do not stock large quantities of these lenses, so they must be ordered from the manufacturer. These orders usually take time because optometrists want to order from manufacturers only once they have a large enough shipment to make it worthwhile. And, because they are the only game in town, optometrists are often able to make a handsome profit on these sales. To make matters worse for consumers, they must often wait two weeks for the lenses to arrive, and then they must go back to the optometrist to pick them up. It's a process that is expensive and inconvenient. Certainly this game can be changed.

Indeed it can, if McCallum has anything to say about it (which he does). The same guiding principles that changed the game in dry cleaning can be applied to contact lenses. The foundation of these principles lies in the golden rule: *The source of all insights comes from your consumer.*

"Customer contact is key," said McCallum. "At P&G, I went to consumers' homes to better understand their laundry needs. I'll do the same thing here, going with consumers to their eye appointments. By doing that, I'm going to understand their experience and gain insights into how we might improve it." Put another way, 1800CONTACTS.com is going to ask consumers to change their contact lens-buying behavior. To get them to do that, 1800CONTACTS.com needs to be able to talk to them about their experience in a meaningful way.

Once again, McCallum will cast the net to explore his consumers' dissatisfactions with their current method of purchasing contacts, as well as the benefits they would be most interested in. The net to be cast at 1800CONTACTS, however, will be much smaller than the one used at P&G. Whereas McCallum devoted fifty days to gathering consumer insights that led to the three-year development of Dryel, he won't have that luxury of time with the Internet start-up. "Instead of talking to hundreds of consumers, I'll talk to, say, fifteen initially. We'll see what insights we glean and go from there."

McCallum recognizes that iteration will play a larger role in the Internet space than in the brick-and-mortar world. Consumer contact will be an ongoing process, one that improves the service delivery at 1800CONTACTS.com on a continuous basis. "We will have to move forward, even if we're not 100 percent sure that we're going in the right direction. And we'll have to be agile enough to change direction, or modify our direction, if that is what is needed." McCallum is confident that this is the right thing to do.

This is a very different mindset in the Internet economy. Most e-organizations are focused on speed—getting their Web site up and running ahead of the pack is the most important thing. They pay much less attention to consumer needs. This "build it and they will (hopefully) come" approach differs from McCallum's method, which is "build what they need and they will come."

Is McCallum nervous about the fifty competitors already on-line in the contact lens market space? "No. None of those guys have talked to the consumers. That's how I'm going to be able to distinguish 1800CONTACTS.com—by gathering the information that will lead to the greatest value for the customer." McCallum acknowledged that speed is vitally important in the electronic economy. But he was quick to add, "If you don't hit the mark, you're dead." To make sure he hits the mark, he is slowing down—just a bit—in order to gain the consumer insights that will make a difference.

While the Internet presents a challenge in terms of speed, it also presents a great opportunity. That is, the Internet provides the vehicle by which an on-line retailer or distributor can build a solid, ongoing relationship with the consumer. Brick-and-mortar operations tend to create a mass media relationship with consumers, dependent primarily on blanket advertising. It's a one-way channel: I sell, you buy. You're never sure who your customers are. The Internet, on the other hand, provides a two-way channel, one in which the seller and buyer are able to establish a relationship and, ultimately, loyalty to one another. This means that e-commerce organizations are more likely to secure customers for life. After all, if you know your customers and have managed the relationship well, you will understand how their needs change as they grow.

Recruiting the Team to Change the Game

According to McCallum, team members who work together to create a product or product-delivery channel must all possess one primary characteristic—an appreciation for the customers' insights. Other than that, he hopes that there are marked differences in the skills team members bring to the table. "I want to surround myself with people who think differently from me," he said. "I need people who have different opinions and a willingness to explore different hypotheses."For McCallum, this means assembling a team of people from different backgrounds. The P&G team, for example, comprised members from various functional areas of the firm—marketing, sales, research, finance, information systems.

It is also important for leaders in e-commerce to take the time to fully understand customers' needs. This may seem like an oxymoron in an industry that offers everything *but* time, but—as McCallum has illustrated before—you have to have the determination and the capacity to devote a certain block of time to consumer interaction. That's what will ultimately set you apart in the marketplace.

Spending time with consumers yields another benefit. "Leadership of your organization is much more likely to buy in to your ideas if you can back them up with specific information that relates to the consumer's desires. Saying 'we talked to 200 consumers and they have this problem' will catch the attention of decision-makers. And you don't need tons of quantitative data. Anecdotal evidence that shows you're developing something that the consumer wants is all you need to get the green light."

The Internet has the potential to change the game of every industry. Never before has it been so convenient for consumers to purchase and receive products or services in the comfort of their own homes. Never before have consumers had so much purchasing control. The games will continue to change as consumers refine their needs and help on-line vendors better serve them.

The bottom line from game-changer Kevin McCallum: "Consumers will tell you what they want. You just have to ask them."

From Top-Down to Lateral Leadership

*The so-called Information Revolution is, in reality,
a Relationships Revolution.*

In Chapter 1, we looked at the shift from CEO as steward to the CEO as entrepreneur. In Chapter 2, we looked at developing your own strategy of preeminence by coming up with a game-changing business model that has the power to revolutionize your industry. The question we will be addressing in this chapter is what kind of leader you need to be to marshal the strategic and organizational capabilities to move from where you are to where you want to be.

In doing so, we have to take into account that there will be more confusion in the business world in the next decade than there has been in any previous decade, perhaps in all history. I can't think of any other era that brought the kind of topsy-turvy change that we are experiencing now, the pace of which is only going to accelerate.

As such, most of our old beliefs and assumptions about the era in which we live, the nature of leadership, and organization are up for grabs. For example, as Michael Schrage, author of *No More Teams*, has pointed out, one of the most enduring clichés of the postwar era is the "shift from the industrial to information age." Yet the irony is that this metaphor may be more myth than reality. "We are neither in the beginning, middle, or end of the information age," says Schrage.

A simple observation of the impact of today's dazzling digital technologies on our daily lives, pop culture, management, organizations, markets, transportation, and healthcare reveals the following, according to Schrage: "The impact of the digital technology is not in the easily manipulatable bits and bytes of information they store, but in the relationships they create." I am speaking of relationships between employees, relationships between customers, relationships between organizations, relationships between networks. The so-called information revolution is in reality more a relationships revolution.[1]

Reorient Your Worldview of Power and Control and Adopt a Relationships Orientation

In the past, wealth came from focusing on productivity and efficiency. Today, wealth will come from focusing on increasing the quality and quantity of economic relationships. It's relationships between talented people and groups with different views and perspectives that lead to opportunities and innovation. Business leaders would be wise to stop thinking in terms of the deft management of information to achieve higher efficiencies and instead focus on the deft management of relationships to produce higher innovation.

Stop focusing on the deft management of information, and focus on the deft management of relationships.

The genius of the leaders of such companies as Dell Computer, Federal Express, and eBay is their ability to connect physical networks, digital networks, and human networks in ways that result in the creation of new value. They create new value not just by connecting people outside of their firms but also by fostering creative collaboration internally on customer desires, needs, and frustrations. They also know that the Internet expands our ability to create relationships exponentially and they leverage that in every way possible.

Perhaps the most essential leadership skill or capability that you and I as leaders must have will be the ability to distinguish and create those relationships that are the greatest source of economic value. It may well be true that you are a strategic thinker of the highest order with a brilliant business model and venture capitalists banging at your door, with cash in hand, but it is only through sculpting new patterns of relationships and interaction that you will be able to translate your business model into a thriving enterprise.

The same applies if you are the leader of a big established business. The emerging model seems to be to focus on your circle of competence and increase relationships with other firms.

The image of the *top-down* hierarchical leader who manages the corporation with a vertical value chain, giving orders to the same five direct reports, is becoming increasingly irrelevant. It is being replaced by the lateral leader who leads across a shifting enterprise-web composed of collaborative teams and a virtual value chain made up of insiders and outsiders he hardly controls. The role of such a leader is to orchestrate new patterns of relationship and interaction that result in a customer-centric organization and a high level of speed and innovation.

> *"No one is in charge any more. Control is an illusion."*
> **Avram Miller**

As Avram Miller (see Interlude after Chapter 3) has pointed out, in a network economy, no one is in charge any more and control is an illusion. Company leaders cannot boss their talented knowledge workers any more than they can give orders to their strategic partners or dictate to their customers what they will buy.

To create the desired future, leaders today will have to let go of the power and control orientation that was acceptable in the past and adopt a relationships orientation. The leadership paradigm has been altered in this way in the past decade as a result of the advent of talented knowledge workers who could pack up and leave tomorrow, as well as the rapid increase of mergers and acquisitions. Yet the introduction of the Internet has greatly accelerated it. Here's why.

In the past, information was the glue that held a company's hierarchy, its value chain, and its supply chain together. Information was the link between its brand marketing, its design and development department, its manufacturing capability, and its customers. Today, as companies increasingly leverage the Internet to build enterprise-webs, information melts so that it is no longer possessed by one enterprise, but by every node in the network.

In the process, leadership authority becomes decentralized and traditional organizational structures just blow apart. Boundaries within and between companies and their suppliers, and even their employees, are disappearing. Keeping an organization on track now is no longer about managing one person or group; it's about managing the relationship between all of the different parts, especially the way people think and interact together.

What are the implications of all of this in terms of leadership? Evolutionarily, it's the equivalent of the first fish flopping up on the beach one dark and stormy night in the Cambrian era fifty million years ago and needing to transform into a frog by the next morning. What's required here is a real alteration of substance, not a change in form.

The Paradigm-Shift Question: How Do I Lead When I am Not in Charge?

Think about what it would feel like if you were a CEO or leader who had been born and brought up in the leadership paradigm of the twentieth century—command leadership and vertical value chains—to be suddenly thrust into this brave new world of collaborative leadership and virtual value chains. Suddenly you are no longer the boss and have to share power. Suddenly you no longer have your hands on the levers and controls of a centralized company. Suddenly amidst all the pressures of your job, you feel your stomach dropping and you ask yourself, "Do I have what it takes?"

Perhaps it happens when you are trying to put together a merger that looks good on paper, but you are unable to establish the kind of relationship you need with the CEO on the other side of the fence. Or perhaps it happens when you do your first IPO and discover that your VC wants to take an active hand in managing your marketing campaign. Or perhaps it happens when you lose your best "employee" to a firm that regards people as "talent."

The fact is that many CEOs and leaders today are holding their leadership skills in question. *The Economist* magazine, in a survey of 3,000 board-level leaders, found that only 4 percent believed they possessed the necessary mindset or skills to lead the virtual corporations of the twenty-first century. The key questions these leaders were concerned with were: How do I lead when I am not in charge? How do I communicate more collaboratively? How do I learn to be a good partner? How do I learn to negotiate and manage conflicts more effectively? In essence, these CEOs and leaders are asking to learn about lateral leadership.

> **Leaders will need to articulate shared goals that inspire collaboration, while creating as much opportunity as they possibly can.**

Let's create a snapshot of what lateral leadership looks like. First the CEO's (and manager's) number-one job will be to articulate throughout an entire enterprise-web goals and challenges that inspire commitment and collaboration. A key in this is to be able to show people and groups the opportunity for them. As John Chambers of Cisco Systems says, "I constantly pay attention to creating as much opportunity for our employees, partners, and customers as I possibly can."[2]

Leaders will need to be much more open and curious to both ideas and people, less closed and circumspect, to accommodate the shift from the *closed* to *open corporation*. The old managerial frame of reference—*strategy, structure, and systems*—will be replaced by a new one—*purpose, processes, and people*. The corporation will look less like an organization and more like a busy swarm of bees moving at a high rate of speed.

At the same time that company leaders discover the rush of being able to build a scalable business fast by constructing an extended enterprise-web, they will also discover the pain that goes along with the loss of control. This means that leaders must not only learn to let go at the top, but become ambassadors who can move their agenda forward in a world where partners may have different priorities at any given moment. In the same sense, employees, such as project managers and tech reps, must become diplomats in the process of negotiating and managing conflicts.

Orders coming from above will be increasingly replaced by ideas coming from anywhere and everywhere about new ways to create and add value for customers. And it will be the leader's job to help connect the best people and ideas in a way that leads to something powerful and new. Company leaders must learn not only to manage teams as they did in the twentieth century but to piece together collaborations that contain extraordinary combinations of people from around the block or around the world.

Leaders will have to act much more like ambassadors, employees, and diplomats— negotiating and resolving conflicts.

Our managerial frames of reference must shift in order to be able to operate at Internet speed. The leader will have to act less as the decisionmaker and more as a convener bringing people and groups together in face-to-face and virtual meetings to sort through complex issues and make rapid-fire decisions. The notion of making elaborate plans and preparations will be replaced by the notion of making a plan that is directionally right, then iterating.

Figure 3.1 shows some shifts in thinking and attitude that every CEO and manager would be wise to behoove themselves of in order to lead in the twenty-first century. The idea is not to create a blueprint of the leader's new work, but rather to map the territory.

The Men Who Would Be King— From Grandiosity to Humility

Today we seem to have entered into an age of the celebrity CEO whom people revere as gods. Leaders like Jack Welch, CEO of GE, or Bill Gates, chairman of Microsoft, Lou Gerstner of IBM, or Andy Grove of Intel are asked to comment on diverse issues like education, healthcare, social security. At the same time, CEOs throughout the world hang on their every word on how to lead a top-performing business organization. Yet every front has a back.

Harvard's Ron Heifetz has written that many of our leaders fall prey to what he calls "grandiosity." This often starts with a desire to be king of the hill and ends with the disappointments brought on by delusions of grandeur. It was only six months after Bill Gates told AOL's Case "We will buy or bury you" that Gates wound up in federal court charged with predatory and monopolistic practices.

■ **From thinking vertically down the same old ruts to thinking laterally and creatively**

This usually involves connecting the ideas, skills, and capabilities of different people in different fields and/or different industries in a way that results in new value. For example, Jeff Bezos of Amazon. com connected the idea of retailing content to computers and telecommunication.

■ **From the old power of authority to the new power of collaboration**

We live in a network economy in which the traditional corporation has been replaced by the "enterprise," traditional functions have been replaced by processes, and employees have been replaced by talented free agents. The old power of authority no longer makes sense, as people in a network do not report to each other the way they do in a hierarchy. Power will increasingly come from decentralized control and the ability to collaborate.

■ **From the stand-alone corporations to the enterprise web**

The traditional "corporation" as we have known it may disappear in the next ten years except as a legal contrivance in the office of lawyers. The "collaborative" corporation is replacing it. Whether you work for GM or for one of the 10,000 parts suppliers that GM relies on to produce cars, may be more a matter of your point of view than reality.

■ **From IQ to EQ or from managing your organization to managing relationships**

Daniel Goleman, author of *Emotional Intelligence,* has pointed out that most executives have an IQ of 120 or so. However, IQ is a washout. The distinguishing factor in terms of who succeeds and who doesn't is EQ or emotional intelligence. It may take IQ to be able to come up with business strategies and analyze who the right set of partners might be, but it takes EQ to be able to manage yourself and those relationships under the inevitable stress and pressures that will arise. Most managers who derail do so because of a lack of this kind of intelligence.

FIGURE 3.1 The New Leadership Paradigm: A Shift in Mindset and Skills

Heifetz says that most leaders start out with an attitude of "How can I help you?" They become CEOs when they prove they can help the organization solve its problems. Then their "How can I help you?" attitude often transforms into grandiosity, a condition that causes them to adopt a superior attitude, to have difficulties creating successful relationships, and to overestimate their omnipotence in the face of outside threats.[3] It's no wonder that seven out of ten mergers end in failure.

Plan so that it's directionally right, then iterate.

Perhaps one of the most important shifts that the leaders of our corporations need to make in the transition to the new economy is the shift from grandiosity to humility.

The Men and Women Who Would Lead from the Side

I predict that in the future we will still have a handful of grandiose, top-down CEOs who manage to grab a huge amount of our attention by virtue of their charismatic personalities or accomplishments. Yet I also predict that we will see a dramatic increase in the number of lateral leaders who embody the opposite set of virtues. In some ways, their strength will not be their ability to stand out in a crowd, but to articulate a purpose that inspires commitment and collaboration without their egos getting in the way.

As Joan Holmes, executive director of the Hunger Project, an organization committed to ending world hunger, once told me, to be a leader in the future, you will not only need to have a strong vision and bring people together around it, but also have the ability to orchestrate relationships from behind the scenes, which requires getting your ego out of the way.

Drawing an analogy, Holmes said, "In the U.S. Senate, all eyes are on the senators. But the people who really make things happen are the staffers who frame the issues so as to spark dialogue, make the connections between key stakeholders from different sides of the political spectrum, and then make sure the meetings happen."[4] Tomorrow's leaders will have to develop the ability to not just lead from the top, but also lead from the side.

The same thing applies in the business world. When I spoke to Roger Ackerman, former CEO of Corning Incorporated, the leader of the fiber optic telecommunications revolution, he told me, "Corning invented fiber optics in the '60s. It was a narrowly used industrial product until someone in our company made a connection to the telecommunications industry and came up with the idea of fiber optic cable. However, at that time, we knew a lot about fiber, but we didn't know anything about cable. I saw my role not as leading a revolution, but as trying to find an alliance partner who had the capabilities that were needed to make this thing happen before the window of opportunity closed. So I went to AT&T and talked to CEO Paul Allen, but he was basically not interested due to AT&T's investment in telephone lines. So I then went to Siemens and we made a great deal."

Ackerman's experience with AT&T led him to initiate a cultural revolution at Corning based on what he calls quirky leadership practices like "openness" and "relatedness." Today, Corning's fiber optic telecommunications business is growing at 100 percent a year, and, said Ackerman, "Half the people in the world have still not received their first phone call."[5]

How Would You Recognize a Lateral Leader?

In my view, the e-leaders of today and tomorrow will balance the traditional leadership virtues of the past with the new leadership virtues of the future. At the same time, in another sense they will represent a new genetic code for leadership and exhibit the traits of a new leadership species. One question audiences often ask me is how could they recognize a true e-leader or lateral leader if they saw one.

I tell people to look for four distinct things: co-CEOs who thrive amid change and complexity; executives who think laterally and act like artists; leaders who manage by "six degrees of separation"; and leaders who are like "Jack be nimble, Jack be quick."

Look for Co-CEOs Who
Thrive Amid Change, Complexity

When Steve Ballmer became CEO of Microsoft, leaving Bill Gates in the role of chairman, Ballmer commented both on the changing leadership roles and Microsoft's new grand strategy to shift from stand-alone products like Windows NT into one seamless Internet-based offering, requiring extraordinary levels of collaboration.

"Bill has an amazing personal capacity to keep a lot of complex issues in his head, and be the point of integration for collaboration. But I don't think either Bill or I is up to what this company has to do at this level, and at this scale." It can't be all kept in one person's head.[6]

The game plan is for Gates to lead less from the top and more from the side as a master strategist who shapes the company with lateral thinking by connecting different emerging trends in technology, while Ballmer leads the charge and orchestrates the necessary levels of creative collaboration.

The cerebral Bill Gates and the passionate Steve Ballmer may not be the perfect example of lateral leaders but perhaps their thinking has changed and they are moving down the right track.

Look for Executives Who
Think Laterally and Act Like Artists

In Paris, I took a group of executives to the Louvre as part of a leadership development program. On the side of the building was a huge cloth banner on which was printed a picture of Picasso with a rose in his mouth. On the bottom right, a Macintosh logo, replete with the tag line, "Think different." Picasso not only had the ability to think different, he was constantly creating, and abandoning what he had created to art dealers.

I predict that in the coming years the most successful CEOs will be like Picasso and other artists whose greatest satisfaction is the sheer joy of creating something that jars our normal perspective. For example, Steve Jobs was personally and directly involved in the creation of the Apple Lisa, the Next Computer, Pixar, a new method of graphic film animation, and the tangerine-colored iMac.

Another dimension of the CEO as artist is demonstrated by Jim Clark, who searches for the new thing and at a certain point moves on to the next thing in a continuous process of creation and generation. His success at becoming a billionaire in three separate businesses—Silicon Valley Graphics, Netscape, and Healtheon—shows that, to be a leader today, you no longer have to have a plan for what a company will look like when it reaches maturity.

Arthur Clarke, historian and science fiction writer, noted in his book *The Act of Creation* that creative people exercised lateral thinking or what he called "thinking aside," long before Edward DeBono coined the phrase. Clarke said that the act of creation has to do with being able to connect ideas from different frames of reference in a way that resulted in something startlingly different and new.

The creation of the World Wide Web by Tim Berners Lee was basically the result of connecting the idea of isolated computer terminals, with isolated telephones, and the ability to find whatever information content you needed through a search engine.

Look for Leaders Who Manage by Six Degrees of Separation

Dee Hock is the founder and CEO emeritus of Visa International, a company that clears over $1.4 trillion a year, has 15,000 owner members, operates in 200 countries, and has a quarter of a billion customers.

A simple quotation distinguishes Hock from the narcissistic leaders mentioned earlier. "Today, before any audience in the world, I can hold a Visa card overhead and ask, 'How many of you recognize this?'" Hock says. "When I ask how many can tell me who the CEO of the company is, where its headquarters are, or how to buy shares, a dead silence will come over the room." The audience members recognize at that moment that something extraordinary has occurred in American business and that they haven't a clue as to how it has happened.

The results of this organization are apparent, but the leader, structure, and whereabouts are completely invisible. At that point, Hock tells his audience about Visa's history, eschewing the grandiose and demonstrating profound humility about both his successes and failures. He started the company by managing through the metaphor expressed in the play and movie titled *Six Degrees of Sepa-*

ration, which involves a young man's knowing who he has to talk to in order to wrangle an introduction to the right person.

In many ways, Visa is a perfect example of a virtual company; it has only 500 employees and very little bricks and mortar. Its main product/service is processing Visa's credit card information and transactions for its 200,000 banks and financial institutions around the globe. Hock saw his role as inventing a forum where members of Visa could develop a shared purpose and principles of governance that would shape their behavior. He also saw his role as framing issues that were ripe for discussion, and ripening others.

Visa is a company that embodies the essence of decentralized control, or is what Hock calls a "chaordic organization," a combination of chaos and order. When the company's fifteen interlocking boards discuss a proposal, none can individually pass it and each can veto it. Yet somehow Hock's concept of the chaordic organization seemed to work. "No part knew the whole. And the whole did not know all the parts, and none had any need to."[7]

This seems like an organic, self-regulating model for other chaordic organizations such as the brain, the biosphere, a forest, or an e-business like eBay or Amazon that leverages the networking effects of the Internet. Interestingly enough, Visa creates new industries and new businesses in the tens of thousands, first by creating the conditions by which member organizations could connect and create without limitation, and by making unsecured credit available to millions.

Look for Leaders Who are Like "Jack Be Nimble, Jack Be Quick"

Today, ever-increasing customer expectations, hyper-competition, disruptive technologies like the Internet, and talent wars that are as hotly contested as the National Basketball Association draft have put the ability to react swiftly and nimbly at a premium. To be able to act agilely and quickly requires people who are not rule-bound, even if they themselves are the ones who created the rules. It requires leaders who are rule-breakers and rule-makers.

For example, what good does it do you if you are Fred Smith, CEO of FedEx, and are able to deliver documents *absolutely positively overnight*, if suddenly everybody has e-mail and they can send the same documents in less than a minute? It doesn't do you any good, unless you can figure out something else fast, like delivering packages for Internet firms or selling your logistics services to other Internet firms.

What good does it do if you are Steve Case of the competitive AOL and able to offer the best on-line service for a healthy fee, if all of a sudden giving away Internet access becomes the competitive standard of the industry? If you want to stay in the game, you start thinking fast in terms of selling advertising on your site or home financing or acquiring a cable wire company so that you can sell faster broadband service, movies, and what not.

What good does it do if you talk about the importance of hiring the best talent in your company, if the two weeks it usually takes your HR group to read resumes, conduct interviews, and make a deal results in the new hire being snapped up in two days by someone else? If you have some hot talent at bay, you cross over the levels of the often-bureaucratic HR department and pick up the phone and make a sweet offer.

Lateral Leaders Create Collaborative Corporations

One of the first signs of the emergence of the collaborative corporation was the merger mania that took place in the mid-1990s. Daimler Benz bought Chrysler, Travelers bought Citibank, and Ciba Geigy bought Sandoz. In the first half of 1998 alone there were over 10,500 mergers worldwide.

The words of CEO Daniel Vasella of the new Novartis, a combination of Ciba and Sandoz, were echoed by many, "Our intent is to not only make a company that is bigger but to make a company that is better."[8] Yet in fact, very few of these mergers seemed to pan out that way.

> *"Every time the word 'threat' comes out of your mouth, think alliance."*
> Laurie Tucker, FedEx

Around the same time, another movement toward the collaborative corporation was taking place that had to do with moving from a physical to virtual supply chain through outsourcing. This allowed companies to focus their activities on the circle of competence, whether marketing or product innovation, and farm out the rest. In many cases, this has actually resulted in companies that are smaller and better.

For example, if you visit the Misummi Corporation in Japan, you won't be greeted by a secretary. A life-sized silhouette cutout of Marilyn Monroe that stands beside a desk with a telephone and a directory will greet you instead. The company, which used to produce parts for the auto industry, only has about a hundred employees but does almost a billion dollars a year in business.

It has over 500 outsourcing relationships, including finance, design, development, manufacturing, purchasing, administration, and human resources. The staff on hand is comprised of two teams which focus on two key areas, coming up with new business ideas and coordinating Misummi's various outsourcing relationships.

Create Collaborative Networks Among Business Units to Capture Synergies

It's important to point out that when most people think of the collaborative corporation they often think in terms of the collaboration happening between partners. An issue of equally great importance is how to create synergies between the multi-business units of a company, as well as between individual groups.

In traditional corporations, the collaboration between multi-business units tends to freeze into fixed patterns. Business units share intangibles like brand name, tangibles like manufacturing facilities, or organization capabilities like design and development. Once the patterns are established, they tend not to be revisited.

Kathleen Eisenhardt of Stanford University has observed a different model practiced by the leaders of collaborative companies that she calls "co-evolution." It involves senior leaders setting the stage for individual business units to co-evolve by collaborating in response to market opportunities or operational issues. Instead of thinking in terms of fixed collaborations, these leaders think in terms of "Velcro organizations." This usually involves creating shifting collaborative webs or patching together different skillsets from different organizations to meet customer demands.[9]

Gary Wendt, former CEO of GE Capital, is an example of a company leader who believes in co-evolution. GE Capital was created as a collaborative link between GE's consumer businesses, such as dishwashers and dryers, helping to set up financing for consumers. As time went on, GE Capital's financial expertise evolved and it began offering its services to GE's industrial businesses, like jet engines.

Today, GE's jet engines division, with the help of GE Capital, has been able to get a jump on Rolls Royce for Boeing contracts by designing a more sophisticated high-tech product, with faster product cycles. The key to success has been to defray costs not by selling the engines, but by leasing them the same way Gateway computer leases PCs. Every three years the airlines can trade in the engines for an upgraded model. The introduction of leasing the engines not only creates a demand for the product but also the turn-around of products helps to speed up the product-development cycle.

> **Teams are used for problems of higher complexity. Collaborations are used for problems of the highest complexity.**

Companies like Disney are also intensely involved in co-evolution, creating shifting collaborative webs. For example, Disney World and its Big Boat Cruise Division collaborate on joint vacation plans to boost revenues. ESPN managers work with Disney's Internet business to share sports content, and with theme parks to open ESPN restaurants. The webs aren't static but shift according to changes in the marketplace. It is particularly in the bailiwick of senior leaders to make sure such collaborations happen.

As a lateral leader focused on opportunities to co-evolve, you can act as a pollinator of ideas as you travel among the different business units or teams. You may also have the opportunity to stage collaborative gatherings where you bring business leaders together to socialize, to converse, and to find collaborative opportunities. You can play another role in an approach Eisenhardt calls "patching," which is based on the idea of seeing the lineup of different business units against different market opportunities in the same way that a sports coach sets up the optimal lineup against different teams.

Five Steps to Jump-Start New Collaborative Networks Among Units

1. Begin by establishing at least monthly must-show meetings between different business chiefs that allow them to socialize and see collaborative opportunities.
2. Make sure the conversation stays focused on core strategies and real operating basics that build an understanding of the businesses' different roles and intuition about where links might be found.
3. Recognize and dispel the myth that "good people collaborate, bad people don't." Business leaders will probably always be rewarded by the performance of their individual units, no matter how much this is criticized. Show them that by collaborating, they can meet those self-interested goals and get an edge up on the competition.
4. When opportunities to collaborate arise, keep in mind that many managers get trapped in the "brilliance" of their first idea. Ask them to brainstorm to come up with other ideas—from shared strategy to shared assets and from collaborating at different points on the value chain to simply sharing information.
5. Fine-tune as you move along. Look at the benefits and costs of the most promising collaborations. Do experiments. Making plans up front will never substitute for real-time learning. Finally, know when to pull the plug on collaborations that are unproductive.[10]

All collaborations involve teamwork, but not all teams are collaborative.

Creative Collaboration versus Teamwork

Finally, we should mention the power of putting together collaborative teams within a single organization to produce innovations, reach breakthrough goals, and solve complex problems. It is important to note that while all collaborations involve teamwork, not all teams are collaborative.

The difference is that collaborations are usually focused on creating something that never existed before and usually involve extraordinary combinations of people, whereas teams tend to be focused on incremental improvements and usually involve people from within a single function—the marketing team or the engineering team.

The leader has a special role to play in collaborative teams. For example, according to John Seely Brown, chief scientist at Xerox's Palo Alto Research Center (PARC), the organization that invented the PC windows, the mouse, the Ethernet, precursor of the Internet, and many other breakthroughs, "My job as a leader is to foster innovative solutions to complex business problems. Where does innovation come from? It comes from differences. From juxtaposing people with different perspectives, talents, and gifts in focused dialogue.

"At PARC we start with a customer problem. Then we bring together extraordinary combinations of people: physicists, MBAs, computer engineers, artists, software programmers, and anthropologists to brainstorm around it. In conversations, we take the problem, explore it from every perspective that we can imagine. This allows us to constantly reframe the problem until we get to the root of it and crack it wide open."[11]

Create Virtual Team Networks

Creating a network of strategic alliances or shifting collaborative webs and teams is proving to be a highly effective way of making one plus one equal three. But how do you do this when people in groups are spread out all over the world? The leaders of the new economy are finding innovative ways to use virtual team technologies to bring talented knowledge workers together from far-flung regions to share knowledge and accomplish what would otherwise be difficult or impossible.

One CEO who believes very strongly in the virtual team-room approach is John Browne, CEO of BP Amoco, a company that is 80,000 people strong and spread out around the globe. In many ways, it resembles a Silicon Valley start-up more than a stalwart of the oil and gas industry. Browne's personal leadership mission is to create a company where they "use knowledge more effectively than their competitors do."

All employees at BP Amoco have the authority to create their own home pages, in which they portray not just their picture, but also their passions, talents, gifts, and value-added expertise. They are also asked to share what kind of projects they're involved in and which kind they would find fascinating or intriguing in the future. If you need to find someone who has an interest in working on a breakthrough oil exploration project in the North Sea or an expert on sustainability, you can find him or her with the search engine.

> *"Everything that can be done face-to-face can be done virtually."*
> **John Browne**

Browne also believes that everything that can be done in a face-to-face meeting can be done virtually. Where most companies' people are still at the stage of trying to nurture collaboration through face-to-face meetings, conferences calls, or e-mail, which all have limitations, Browne has introduced something called the Virtual Team Network, a special computer system that not only boasts video conferencing, but a *team room* capability based on groupware, replete with electronic blackboards and scanners, to allow people in remote locations to formulate strategies, work on projects, or share knowledge.

During a special project that involved the development of the Andrew Oil Field in the North Sea, BP Amoco used the Virtual Team Network to discover oil through a new drilling method and to pass on lessons from the revolutionary project in real time. People who were directly involved in the critical decisions that occurred daily were not on the rig at all but were in remote places around the world. This included oil rig contractors from the UK, the experts who invented the new technology from Alaska, and pipe technicians from Columbia.

John Browne initiated a cultural revolution to make this kind of effort a success. This not only required that he and other leaders set a new collaborative context, but that they get directly involved in training and coaching so as to shift attitudes and behavior. "We realized that virtual teamwork required a new set of behaviors, such as people collaborating and being cooperative about what they know rather than possessive."[12]

To Reinvent Your Organization, You Must Reinvent Yourself First

The question you may be asking yourself at this point is: How do I transform myself from a hierarchical boss to a lateral leader? Or, how do I transform a traditional, stovepipe company into a truly collaborative corporation? Let's say that your goal is to create the relationships you need to make your game-changing business model a success. Let's use the triple-loop learning approach introduced in Chapter 1 to get insight into who you need to be as a lateral leader and how your thinking and actions need to change to make your business model a success.

Begin by thinking about your new business model and your circle of competence. Then write down the other capabilities you will need to realize it. For example, Web site design, product development, supply-chain skills and talent acquisition. Now think about the specific relationships you need to create with other talented people, partners to actually bring those capabilities on board. Jot down a few points about what you would do to create a world-class collaborative organization.

> Transformational learning shifts our way of being and the thinking that drives our behavior. Transactional learning shifts only the information in people's heads.

Triple-Loop Learning

How do you need to be different?

To make the shift from top-down to lateral leadership, think about who you have been as a leader in the past based on your history or background. Begin to recognize the patterns that have shaped who you are.

Write a sentence that states the belief or beliefs that have fundamentally shaped, limited, and defined who you have been in regards to lateral leadership. This statement should get at underlying beliefs and assumptions. For example, "In one word, my belief in 'bosship,'" or "I must have unilateral control."

Now think about how you need to be different to create the relationships you will need to reach your goals. For example, "I must let go of the need to be the boss and be more of a partner," or "I need to let go of the need to *be* so task-oriented and *be* more available for relationships." It is important to keep in mind that it is our way of being that shapes our thinking and influences our actions.

Write one sentence that represents a new leadership declaration with respect to making the shift from top-down to lateral leadership. For example, "I will be less task-oriented, more relationship-oriented."

Double-Loop Learning

How do you need to think differently?

Double-loop learning, as we said earlier, represents a sincere attempt to intervene in the corresponding mental models that come from your fundamental statement about who you are as a leader and to intervene in the standard practices of your particular field of play. For example, a participant in one of my leadership workshops told me, "My parents were very stern Mormons and John Wayne rode through my entire childhood teaching me everything I knew about power and authority. This predisposed me to adopt the prevailing mental model of organizations—command and control."

Write one sentence that describes the mental model that has shaped your leadership style based on your immediate environment. For example, "My leadership style is one of command and control," or "A good manager is a good delegator." Then look at whether this mental model works for you or not.

Write one sentence that describes what your new mental model might be that could be the basis of a new leadership style that would support you in collaborating. For example, "My leadership style is collaborative," or " A good manager works in partnership with others to reach difficult goals."

Single-Loop Learning

How do you need to act differently?

Think about the prescriptions you have acted on in the past. "Show that you're the boss," "Delegate," or "Check up on people."

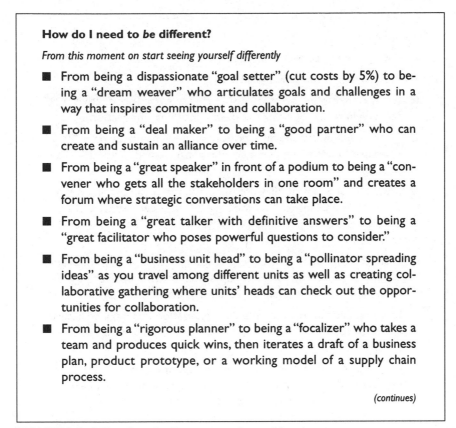

How do I need to *be* different?

From this moment on start seeing yourself differently

- From being a dispassionate "goal setter" (cut costs by 5%) to being a "dream weaver" who articulates goals and challenges in a way that inspires commitment and collaboration.

- From being a "deal maker" to being a "good partner" who can create and sustain an alliance over time.

- From being a "great speaker" in front of a podium to being a "convener who gets all the stakeholders in one room" and creates a forum where strategic conversations can take place.

- From being a "great talker with definitive answers" to being a "great facilitator who poses powerful questions to consider."

- From being a "business unit head" to being a "pollinator spreading ideas" as you travel among different units as well as creating collaborative gathering where units' heads can check out the opportunities for collaboration.

- From being a "rigorous planner" to being a "focalizer" who takes a team and produces quick wins, then iterates a draft of a business plan, product prototype, or a working model of a supply chain process.

(continues)

FIGURE 3.2 A Template for Becoming a Lateral Leader

Now write down some prescriptions that might go with your new leadership declaration or mindset. For example, "Treat everyone as a colleague," "Instead of delegating, create a collaborative team," "Be a thinking partner rather than checker." Figure 3.2 may assist you in making these shifts as well as give you some guidelines for reflection-in-action, which will help you adjust your way of being, thinking, and acting according to the feedback you are getting.

Letting Go at the Top

I would like to tell a story to remind you that transforming who we are, shifting mental models, and altering our old patterns is not an intellectual exercise; it's al-

(continued)

How do you need to *think* differently?

From this moment on start thinking differently

- From thinking in terms of doing things right (productivity) to thinking in terms of doing the next right thing (innovation).

- From thinking that being a good manager means being a "good delegator" to thinking that a good manager equals a good "collaborator."

- From thinking, "What different people in the organization do I delegate this problem to?" to thinking, "What new patterns of relationship and interaction do I need to create around this problem to solve it?"

- From thinking that "control" of the value chain is what's important to thinking in terms of giving up some control in exchange for speed (i.e., instead of thinking to do it yourself, think alliances).

- From thinking in terms of a fixed organization (strategy, structure, systems) to thinking in terms of an open organization (purpose, processes, partners).

- From thinking that who is on the team are the people in the building to thinking who is on the team are the people who have the most value to contribute independent of time and distance.

(continues)

ways an emotional process. It requires letting go of ways of being, mental models, and behavior patterns that have long been a part of us. And as I said before, this is not so easy to do.

Clergia Sturdy, a trainer for the Stucki Group in Switzerland, runs the Challenge Program for Alusuisse (Algroup), an outdoor program designed to help leaders let go at the top. She is standing on the edge of a cliff overlooking a gorge, talking softly to a vice president of manufacturing who is literally shaking in his boots. In one hand he has a bungee cord, which is attached to a tree above him and belayed to his belt. In the other hand, he has a nice fresh egg. That's right, an egg!

(continued)

How do you need to *act* differently?

From this moment on start acting differently

- In answering the question, "How do I lead when I am not in charge?" ask, propose, and collaborate instead of yelling, telling, or selling.

- Based on your business model, create a mind map of the a) capabilities, b) specific individuals, c) groups you need to partner with.

- Make a habit of the idea "Never waste a lunch." Use lunches to manage by six degrees of separation—to wrangle the introductions you need to build your enterprise web.

- Ask questions like, "What are you doing that's cool?" to find out what people are doing in a given business unit, then pollinate those ideas in other groups.

- Sponsor a collaborative gathering of different units' heads to socialize, talk, and explore collaborative opportunities.

- Shift from passionately advocating your views at meeting in order to win, to balancing advocacy and inquiry to build shared understanding.

Sturdy has explained to him and others in the group that the objective of the challenge is not only to jump, but also to have the experience of letting go. One of the ways to tell whether they did this or not is if they clench their fists and break the egg when they jump. If they crush the egg when they fall, they have not really let go.

"So do it now," she murmurs in a tone so supportive that participants often feel she is an angel of mercy. "Breathe in and jump when you exhale." A moment later, the executive jumps and discovers to no one's surprise that he has egg over his hands and face. "Letting go is the real challenge" he shouts, "not the jumping," and he asks to do it again.

To use the story as a metaphor, today there are many leaders who are jumping from Fortune 500s to Netcos and from bricks-and-mortar organizations to virtual ones without ever letting go of the thinking and attitudes of the past. They have transformed their businesses without necessarily transforming themselves, and they will probably wind up with egg on their face.

What does letting go at the top mean? First, it means to accept that, even if you are the CEO, you are probably not in charge. There is no CEO who would say they were in command of a big Fortune 500 organization that is so complex. Second, it means accepting that control today is an illusion. Do you really control your people, customers, and partners? Finally, letting go at the top means accepting that talented people don't need someone to command them, they need to be inspired. The egg-in-hand story also indicates that letting go is not just an intellectual exercise; it's an emotional process.

In conclusion, the old power of authority is giving way to the new power of collaboration as we move from stand-alone corporations to extended enterprise-webs and from functional teams to creative collaborations. This will require you and me as individuals to make profound transformations in our thinking and behavior, which will require letting go, reflection and action, coaching and mentoring. The ability to make these transformations will have a huge impact on our being able to take our business model and build the necessary strategic and organizational capabilities to succeed.

Interlude

Avram Miller, EVP of Business Development at Intel

Connect and Collaborate Across Boundaries

Nathan Green is waiting.

Nathan is always waiting, it seems. . . . for his Venti Skim Latte. . . . for the graphics department to complete adding the "bells and whistles" to his latest industry presentation. . . . for his son, Josh, to get tired of the Barney video and fall asleep in his arms. . . . for the competition's latest Web site to download.

"I'm waiting," he says quietly one evening to his wife, Jane, as she stoops to pick up the macaroni Josh has tossed from his high-chair tray, "for my life to start."

Jane looks up, the paper towel in her hand still moving in circular motions across the linoleum. She blows a stray hair from her face. "What are you talking about? Your life has definitely started. Right, Josh?" she asks as another noodle lands nearby.

"Started!" exclaims Josh, clapping his buttery hands together for added effect.

Nathan grabs a washcloth and heads toward his son for the post-dinner wipe-down. "You're right. Of course my life with you and Josh has started. That's not what I mean."

"What do you mean then?"

"Work. I keep waiting for some sort of epiphany that I'm doing what I should be doing."

"But you like your job."

"Yeah, I know. It's just . . . I mean, it's so . . . ." Nathan has never known how to put it into words.

"It's just what?" Jane sinks into the kitchen chair, absently twirling Josh's Tigger by the tail.

"I want to make a difference."

"But, honey, you do make a difference! You wouldn't have been promoted four times in the last three years if you didn't."

"I want to have control."

"I don't understand. You lead 100 people everyday. I'd say that's 'control.'"

Nathan pauses. Then it comes to him "No, Janie. That's not control. That's just the illusion of control. There's a big difference."

•   •   •

Avram Miller understands the difference that Nathan alludes to. As vice president of Intel Corporation, he came to the same conclusion in 1999. At that time, Miller was director of corporate business development for the microprocessing powerhouse. He played a leading role in establishing Intel as the leading corporate high-tech venture organization and managed a billion-dollar portfolio. He was at the top of his game. Or so everyone would have thought.

Was Avram Miller making a difference at Intel in spring 1999? Of course he was. Was he considered one of the first leaders to recognize the potential of the Internet to become a powerful new medium? Unquestionably. Was he a voice to be reckoned with in new media circles? Undoubtedly. Had I ever heard of him? Never.

Now, my ignorance of Miller's accomplishments in no way diminishes them. In fact, perhaps I exaggerate. I probably came across his name in any number of newspapers, read about his vision for Intel in a variety of trade publications, or even saw him speak on panels describing the future of the Internet. But when I did, I didn't remember Avram Miller's words. I remembered the words from "that guy at Intel." As Nathan acknowledged, "There's a big difference." I don't think Avram Miller would take umbrage at my mistake, if you can call it that. In fact, it is that lack of distinction between an executive and his or her corporate "persona" that led Miller to make a drastic change.[1]

According to Miller, he spent a good portion of the 1970s applying computer technology to the medical care industry. Later, in addition to leadership positions in a number of computer companies, Miller served as president of Franklin Computer Corporation and as group manager of Digital Equipment Corporation. Confronting change, then, was nothing new to him. In May 1999, he left Intel— and the corporate world that he had known and, in fact, developed for fifteen years. I bet you're thinking he was lured away by some sexy Internet start-up that dangled a large carrot of options in front of him. Or maybe you're thinking he left to found an Intel competitor, which many folks in similar positions seem to be keen on doing. You'd be wrong on both counts. As Miller explains, "I left to become the CEO of my own life."

It was through this message that I first took notice of Avram Miller—Miller the man, not Miller the corporate spokesperson. His radical departure from corporate life was profiled in the *Wall Street Journal* (Interactive edition, July 8, 1999) and *Fast Company* magazine's "Who's Fast 2000" article (December 1999). The *Fast Company* editors had chosen Miller as one of sixteen "unsung heroes and rising stars . . . who use their energy, their brain, their passion, and their commitment to make a difference."[2] Some may consider it ironic that he was selected for inclusion in this prestigious group, credited with creating and holding the future, *after* he left Intel.

Now that I've met Miller, I don't find it ironic at all. In fact, it makes perfect sense. Now that Miller has shed the corporate coil of Intel, he's finally able to truly create the future—his own and that of the world of work. He is the new kind of leader emerging in, and empowered by, the new electronic economy. He is a leader with no one reporting to him. A leader with no one to whom he reports. A leader with no corporate philosophy with which he must align. Yet he leads. He leads other leaders to each other. He leads a good idea from one industry to a complementary vision in another. He does so with his influence, his creativity and—as *Fast Company* rightly concluded—with his energy, passion, brains, and commitment to making a difference. And he's doing it on his own terms. Avram Miller is a true example of what we call a lateral leader.

The Tugboat Turned Speedboat

Ever since the industrial revolution, most people have found themselves working within a corporate structure of some sort. Jobs are carried out for the service of a company. In fact, it's common to hear someone ask, "Whom do you work *for*?" as if the company has a human persona. It's equally likely to hear, in response, "I work *for* Company X." Imagine how strange it would be to hear someone say, "I am employed *by* Company Y, but I work *for* myself, *for* my own agenda, and *for* my sense of identity." You're not likely to hear a statement like this because it would be, simply, untrue. With corporate structures as they are today, you cannot work *for* yourself while employed *by* another. A corporation shapes you and, at least during office hours, expects you to "tow the company line." If you don't, you'll find yourself out on your ear. It's not surprising, then, that your loyalty aligns with the company's agenda. Sure, you may try to impact or modify that agenda. And if you're the CEO, you may have some success. But if you're a middle manager, you won't have much influence on changing the broad corporate culture that dictates your every move.

Even as vice president at Intel, Avram Miller knew his influence was limited. "I was a corporate troublemaker. I would work in the 'discomfort' zone, and really try to move and shape the company's culture. I felt like a tugboat, trying to steer a massive, lumbering ship." His transformation from "tugboat" to "speedboat" was completed in spring 1999 when he realized that he would be much more content shaping his own agenda and steering his own course. That was when the fifty-five-year-old Miller decided to step down from Intel and launch Avram Miller Co. in San Francisco.

The Avram Miller Co. describes itself as a strategy and business development corporation. Miller serves as CEO of the one-man operation in its San Francisco "world headquarters" office. In this role, Miller serves as an important link between the computer, communications, and media industries. He sits on the board of several major global Internet players, including Alta Vista, CMGI, World Online International, and Pacific Century Cyberworks. From this vantage point, Miller is able to "stitch together a worldwide platform by developing relationships between those companies."[3]

In his new role as CEO of his own life, Miller claims that his interests haven't changed. "What's changed is my ability to act on those interests. Whereas some of the things I wanted to pursue in the past—like my interest in consumer electronics—didn't necessarily fit with the prevailing corporate agenda, now everything 'fits.' Anything I want to do fits my agenda."

Today, his agenda is simple: to apply his knowledge and know-how in computer systems and Internet technology to the consumer electronics industry. To carry out this agenda, Miller often wears many hats—business strategist, venture capitalist, deal-maker, and integrator of business opportunities for just a few. In order for leaders to take full advantage of the intersecting space between the communications, computer, and media industries, Miller believes they will have to do more than create one top-down company. "We've already seen the shift from top-down to horizontal organizations in corporate America. Companies are figuring out their areas of expertise, focusing on those, and then working with other companies to develop a complete system. That's becoming even more and more common in the Internet space."

The Role of Activist Strategist

It's also becoming more and more common in Miller's day-to-day activities, which involve integrating a network of companies from around the world to provide dramatic and cutting-edge products and services to consumers. Miller acknowledges that it is important to distinguish between his role as board member/adviser—which takes a lot of time and is generally *reactive* in nature—and his role as an "activist strategist" in which he *proactively* pursues areas of greatest interest to him. The latter role is the one Miller is most excited about. "If I just developed a strategy for these companies, they more than likely wouldn't do anything with it. I typically have to do the work, as well." It is by serving as an activist strategist that Miller sees his greatest opportunities. "It has to do with impact, not money. I identify or invent those opportunities that will deliver the greatest potential impact. And that's thrilling to me."

"The beauty of the arrangements are that I have a very real relationship with the companies, but I don't work *for* any one company. I'm not subordinate to anyone, which gives me a level of freedom to explore options and pursue opportunities." The downside, Miller says, is that he must always be wary of potential conflicts of interest. Interestingly, the issue of "loyalty" that shapes the thinking of so many executives in traditional corporate settings is also an issue at the Avram Miller Company. How does Miller handle the issue of loyalty? "In discussing deals, I always try to put myself into the shoes of the other person. I won't pursue an opportunity if it's not beneficial to all parties."

A New Set of Abilities for the Internet Age

This, it turns out, is one of Miller's strengths as a lateral leader—his ability to be a good partner. This leadership trait comprises several components. First, a good partner must be able to recognize the other parties that might be appropriate for a partnership and asks "how are these organizations or individuals going to add value to each other?" Once this is accomplished, the parties must establish relationships and trust. "In the past," says Miller, "you might have been successful if you knew how to build a company from top to bottom. Today, you need a completely different set of abilities, the most important of which are networking and communication skills." Miller has these skills and many others. He can communicate effectively with anyone—from twenty-something-year-old whiz kids to corporate CEOs. "The most important thing is to get rid of all your prejudices. You have to open your mind. It doesn't matter if the people you're talking to are twenty-two years old or fifty-seven years old. It doesn't matter what their color is, what their gender is, what language they speak, how big their company is, or even if they were a success before." According to Miller, "The playing field in the e-world is much more level than it has been in the past. Everyone can potentially contribute." By leveling the playing field, the Internet is diminishing the power of the hierarchical organization.

Like many others, Miller believes the Internet has already become *the* medium of distribution for information, products, and services. Our current uses of the Internet for e-mail, Web sites, and e-commerce are, however, just the tip of a new economic iceberg. As the most powerful laboratory for business reinvention that's ever existed, the Internet is poised to create innovative economic models and re-define industries. As a laboratory, the Internet encourages experimentation. And experimentation requires a stomach for iteration. This is Miller's second charac-teristic of lateral leadership.

If, for example, a product wasn't selling in the old business paradigm, a leader might call upon his or her marketing team to come up with a strategy that would convince consumers to buy it—whether they wanted it or not. Today, consumers are too savvy for these sorts of shenanigans. They will let you know immediately, with one click of the finger, whether they are interested in what you are selling. In the Internet world, the question is no longer "how can we get customers to buy our product?" It is "what product do they want to buy?" Leaders need to be able to change course quickly in order to respond to the consumers' demands. Changing course quickly requires a willingness to try a new thing, and then another, and then another. "Iteration," according to Miller, "is necessarily related to speed, which is all-important in the e-economy. But it is also—and perhaps more im-portantly—related to opportunity. We can now try our hand at new opportuni-ties very quickly. This is, of course, much more feasible when the cost of iteration is low."

Related to the ability to change direction on a dime is the important character-istic of being able to give up control. To Miller, this is not difficult, since "most folks have very little control anyway. They have the *illusion* of control." The Inter-net has made this crystal clear. The success of an e-business is determined by cus-tomers, not by the company structures that provide goods and services.

Consider how the typical company has changed over the past twenty years. In the heyday of self-contained structures and vertical management, a company did everything—research and design, manufacturing, distribution, marketing and sales. In this scenario, a company did have control over its operations, its employ-ees, and, if there was little competition, its customers. With the advent of net-worked technology, however, this all-in-one model fell to the wayside. The hori-zontal company emerged, focusing on the one or two core areas that it did extremely well. It depended on other companies to carry out pieces of its strategy. Control was relinquished and replaced by dependence on others. Then came the Internet, which threw the concept of corporate control completely out the window. In the new Internet economy, companies are working together (more and more often with the help of someone like Miller) to "make something happen" in the marketplace. And nothing is going to happen in the marketplace without improving the end-value for the consumer—who is the only one with any real control these days.

What's replacing the control, or illusion of control, that existed in companies and in leadership for so long? Miller points to the rebirth of intuition. "In our society, we often don't want to admit that we know something if we don't know *why* we know it. At Intel, I used to have a horrible problem. I'd go into a meeting and I'd be very convinced about something, and people would say, 'What evidence do you have for that?' And I'd say, 'I don't have any evidence.'"[4] For his colleagues at Intel, and presumably in corporations around the world, evidence, or a rationalization for a hunch, was required. No longer.

The speed with which the Internet changes business models requires that leaders develop their sense of intuition. The days of pondering an idea with a group of colleagues are over. Decisions must be made quickly, often overnight. You won't have evidence. You won't have research to back up your claims. What you will have is a gut feeling. An instinct. An intuitive feeling that you are headed in the right direction.

In the Internet economy, the old paradigm of "ready, aim, fire" has been replaced with "get ready as best you can, fire, aim." Leaders have to be more than quick in making decisions. They must also be willing to take risks. And they must be willing to go in a direction that will not produce value in the near future. Miller gives the following example, "Let's say you give a CEO two choices. You say, 'Here's your business. It's growing at 4 percent a year, and if you keep going in that direction, then it will eventually flatten out. In five years, it will probably start declining.' Or you say, 'Here's another business, whose revenues will decline 3 percent a year for the next three years. But in five years, it will be worth twice as much as it is now.' I don't believe there's a CEO in the world who would take the second business option. He or she would take the first option and say, 'I'll figure out a way. I'm not going to make a decision today that's going to hurt me in the short-term.'"[5] Miller believes that CEOs will soon come to realize that they must take risky positions to create long-term value and success. As an example of a business sector that must change its thinking, he points to the music industry, which is facing a technologically enabled music distribution system that must be reckoned with.

Another characteristic vital for lateral leaders is self-confidence. Miller's journey to lateral leadership was charted through several corporate cultures, within each of which he gained experience and strengthened his reputation. Is this type of corporate apprenticeship required for anyone wishing to become CEO of his own life? Absolutely not, Miller says. "There's certainly not just one way to do things. This background helped me, but would not have been helpful to someone else. What's most important in moving to a role of self-CEO is how you think about yourself. This is the greatest limitation for all of us—not how others think of us, but how we think of ourselves." We are all born with our greatest potential, and then our parents, schools, and ultimately, corporate institutions beat that potential right out of us. And with the potential goes the self-confidence needed to be your own CEO. Miller knew as a young child that he was destined to change the rules of leadership. "I always knew that organizations like schools were inhibitors. As a kid, people kept telling me to be like everyone else around me. Well, to be honest, there didn't seem to be a very compelling reason to do that."

Just as the luxuries of corporate control and analytical decision-making have become less important, so too has the notion of experience. According to Miller, "The important skills in the workforce today are the 'raw materials' of intelligence and attitude. With things changing as quickly as they are in the Internet age, experience becomes much less relevant." This does not bode well for middle-aged corporate CEOs thinking of jumping ship to Internet start-ups. "If experience is less valuable, then age becomes less valuable. Being fifty-five and having worked for thirty years may actually become a disadvantage." Miller's point makes sense. Many people might question the value you bring to an Internet company when you've been mired for years in a corporate bureaucracy that shaped your thinking and values in a way that are inconsistent with the new business landscape.

Breaking the Binds of the Corporation

We are seeing, however, that people—even brittle, rigid, brick-and-mortar executives—have a tremendous capacity to change. Just look at Avram Miller. "When I was working at Intel, I was constrained by thinking about the world from Intel's point of view. The conventional wisdom is that corporations are the leaders that make things happen. But I'm suggesting something fundamentally new: Can we imagine a world in which leaders can leave their corporations and continue to lead? Do I have to be part of a corporation to use the power of a corporation?"

Another way to ask this question is: "Can a tugboat captain become a speedboat racer?" The answer is a resounding yes. Miller successfully made the transition by not relying on another corporate structure to buoy him. Instead, he stepped outside the typical corporate structure and now *uses* the corporate structures around him to make deals and break new ground. "I don't think of myself as a free agent," concludes Miller. "If I want to accomplish something, maybe I can better accomplish it without being part of any one company—by being part of multiple companies. I'm hoping that other people will follow this model. Then we could have some great minds working on problems—minds that are unconstrained by their companies' agendas."[6] Above all else, Miller is interested in human potential and looking at how people succeed and thrive in an environment that is stacked against them from the start. "I look at everything out there as a constraint to true human potential. Doing away with all the constraints will allow you to rediscover that human potential that was with you at birth."

Avram Miller is a great example of a lateral leader—one who works as a partner with other leaders to set a bold new direction. To become this type of leader, he had to set out on his own. Now he is able to drive his own agenda, follow his own course, and make a difference—on his terms. What's stopping you?

4

From Production-Builder-in-Chief to Brand-Builder-in-Chief

To be sure, being entrepreneurial and creating a game-changing business model is critical to success in the new economy, but you won't get very far if nobody knows about you. This chapter is devoted to building a powerbrand that will make your company stand out from all the other "me, too" competitors. It will show you how building a brand is the key to being able to grow your business exponentially and multiply your profits.

• • •

"Buon giorno . . . Sono Fulvio Bussandri," says a charming, disarming, and deeply melodious voice that reminds me of the late great actor, Marcello Mastrianni, on a wireless voice mail, first in Italian, then in French, and then in English. "It is my pleasure to receive your call. I would be delighted to return you message. Please leave a number where you can be reached. And I promise to make it my utmost priority to get back to you as soon as possible. Arrivederci!" Beep.

Have you reached someone in the Vatican in Rome, or the Armani fashion empire in Milan, or someone in Boston's "little Italy" famed North End? Truly, not a chance. You have reached one of the most prodigious and successful brand builders in North America, Fulvio Bussandri, CEO of Microcell Solutions, the fastest growing wireless communication company in the world—almost 10 percent a day. The man is a natural brand builder—right down to the distinctive voice mail message. Of the thousands of voice mail messages you have received in your life, this one truly stands out.

So does Fulvio Bussandri himself, in his impeccably tailored *business cazj*, blue sport shirt and white silk and wool pants. "In the last eight quartiles, we have gained more Net subscribers than any other player out there," he says. "We're growing at 8 percent a day. And bonissimo, it feels good to win," he adds, with the huge smile of someone who not only has a zest for winning, but a zest for living.

It was only a short while ago that Bussandri, whose family immigrated to Canada from Italia when he was a child, was tooling around Rome in a Mazarrati, his favorite sports car. He was chief brand builder for Coca Cola in Italy, a job he took over after leaving Pepsi. It was with Coke and Pepsi that he learned about mass branding ideas and techniques.

If you haven't already heard about Microcell, you no doubt soon will. In just two short years, after being granted a license for mobile phones, Bussandri and his colleagues have built an impressive company from scratch. With heavy competition like AT&T and Bell Canada, the only way to survive and win was to build a powerbrand fast. That's just what they did. "We have built the Microcell brand at the lightning speed of the Internet," Bussandri says.

Today, Microcell Fido is the number one recognized brand in Canada in something ad agencies call unaided awareness, and the third most recognized brand in aided awareness behind Coca-Cola and McDonald's. However, Bussandri is faced with a new challenge: As the Internet converges with the wireless, the phone in your pocket is about to become a portal offering an infinite variety of Web-based services such as "m-commerce," location-based services such as how to find the nearest Italian restaurant within three blocks, and entertainment services from games to theater tickets. It is being hailed as the wireless revolution, a tsunami event that will bring about cataclysmic changes in the business landscape.

Seize the Mantle of Leadership— Get There First With the Most

As the battle lines are drawn between the competition worldwide, Bussandri and his team are sitting around a fashionable cigar bar in Montreal engaged in a heated dialogue about how to reinvent the Microcell brand for the new world of "wireless in cyberspace." "Did you know that 71 percent of Internet users are also wireless phone users?" Bussandri asks his team, gesticulating with his hands. "If we can grasp the first-mover advantage like many of the Internet firms did a few years back, we have here the possibility of unheralded growth and profits."

In the next few weeks, Bussandri and company work with my company, MasterfulCoaching.com, to create a strategy of preeminence based on the ambitious aspiration: "Leading the Wireless Revolution by transforming the way people live, work, and communicate." The tag line, referring to the brand name of their phone/portal, is: *Fido simplifies life.* "You have to seize the mantle of leadership," Bussandri says, "but in today's copycat economy, there are no killer apps. Establishing your brand is a matter of getting there first, with the most."

He passionately holds forth on how his company got where it is by "democratizing the mobile phone" and getting there first with the most. "We were first with the most with $40/400 minutes, first with the most with marketing prepaid cards through ATMs, first with the most with a GSM world phone, and we intend to be first with the most with wireless in cyberspace." Get ready for m-commerce, location-based restaurant recommendations, downloadable video and music, and e-customer relationships management.

Today Every Leader Must Realize That Brands Are More Important Than Ever

It all depends on how fast Bussandri and his team can create more brand equity in this new arena. "Today," he says, "brands are everything, and without a brand you are nothing." That's why almost every company—from running shoes to pizza and from cars to coffee—is trying to figure out how they can transcend the confines of their category and create a Fubu-, Abercrombie-, or Tommy Hilfiger-type buzz. A brand not only makes you stand out, but also cuts through the clutter and makes you the only choice in the customer's mind.

If you are a business leader trying to establish an e-business, branding is all the more important. "Have you noticed?" asks Bussandri. "There are no number two and three brands in the e-economy? And there is lots of money to be made, but only if you get there first." Home Depot versus Home Supplies, Starbucks versus Dunkin' Donuts. Amazon.com versus Barnes & Noble, eBay auctions versus whomever . . . No contest!

> **How do you decide which Web sites to visit, which to bookmark, and which to return to a second time? The answer lies in the power of the brand.**

From the customer's point of view, almost anybody can build a Web site and promise anything. And because anyone can, everyone will. How do you know which sites are worth visiting, which sites are worth shopping in, and which to bookmark or return to a second time? The answer lies in the power of their brand.

Brand names and their URL addresses will be the source of almost everything that is of value in business. Business leaders and their organizations will succeed or fail on the basis of a powerful name, a few consonants and vowels, a circle with a W, a swoosh, or an apple.

Today Every Business Leader Must Become a Brand-Builder-in-Chief

In January 2000, Jacques Nasser, CEO of Ford, picked up the newspaper and was shocked to discover that Yahoo's market capitalization had exceeded that of the Big Three Detroit auto firms. What he wanted to know was what was behind this dramatic redistribution of wealth to Yahoo! and other Internet companies? The answer lay in the power of Yahoo's brand—not in the power of its assembly plants, or inventories, or distribution network.

With a powerful brand, you have the magnet to draw people to your site and to offer them almost an infinite array of products and services without being weighed down by the cost of capital or physical assets. With that, Jack Nasser drew his executives together in the silver headquarters tower in Dearborn, Michigan, and announced that Ford was going to become an e-business and its number one priority was to build brands.

Nasser told everyone in the room, guys who had grown up in the auto industry assembly plants, that starting right then they were going to need to see themselves differently—as *brand-builder-in-chief*, instead of seeing themselves as production-builder-in-chief. Fundamental shifts in thinking and attitude would be required.

He then explained why in the past few years he had made acquisitions of companies with strong brands, like Jaguar, Land Rover, and Volvo—companies with few manufacturing assets. He wanted to make a bold move to announce to the world Ford's intention to become an e-business. He had decided to return over $10 billion dollars over-slated for manufacturing to investors. Ford would immediately begin spinning off its parts plants to a new venture called Vesteon, itself an e-enabled company.

While Nasser was taking the lead in transforming his company, he was in a sense only following in the footsteps of other e-leaders. People like Michael Dell of Dell Computers, John Chambers of Cisco Systems, and Carly Fiorina of Hewlett-Packard had recognized years earlier that the re-distribution of wealth, capital, and competitive advantage taking place was occurring as a result of a shift from the *production-owning model* of business to the *brand-owning model* of business.

Every Business Must Shift From the Production-Owning Model to Brand-Owning Model

The shift from *production-owning* to *brand-owning* model has been driven by two corresponding other shifts. The first is a shift from a *push economy* to a *pull economy*, and the second, a shift from a *management-led* company to a *customer-led* company.

In the *push model* (supply-driven model), company leaders focus their attention on production. They invest a great deal of working capital in physical plants, equipment, and inventories, and direct most of the human capital toward improving processes and getting productivities and efficiencies. Marketing is done through mass advertising and selling through a dealer network, not to the actual customer.

In the *pull model*, a company leader devotes the bulk of his or her attention to being a brand builder and creating a customer-led company. Most of the human capital of the company is directed toward market relationships and toward building a flexible supply chain that allows the company to react quickly to market changes or customer demands. The company is organized around key customers, not product divisions. Marketing is done on a one-to-one basis—where the customer pulls for the products and services they want.

Are you a management-led company, organized around product divisions, or a customer-led company organized around customers?

Michael Dell seized upon the brand-owning model from the start—*Dell Direct*—selling computers directly to customers out of his college dorm. The company is a *pull*-driven company, organizing itself around customer groups—big business, small business, and so forth, and with a virtual supply chain. Dell usually has no more than three days' worth of inventory in its supply chain. And it gets paid for the computer you buy before it's even built. The point is that Dell, and others, like Apple, are not in the business of selling PCs, they're in the business of selling their brands.

John Chambers of Cisco Systems also decided to adopt the brand-owning model when he became CEO, and he has worked hard to position Cisco as the train that the Internet runs on. Cisco is a *pull*-driven, customer-led company in which customers talk to each other over the Cisco Web site about what products they want, as well as how to install and use them once they get them. Cisco doesn't make most of the stuff it sells. If a customer orders something from Cisco, the order will go to someone in its supply chain 50 percent of the time. The supplier will also ship the order. Cisco will charge a premium for its brand capital and pocket the difference.

Other company leaders such as Jack Nasser of Ford, Carly Fiorina at Hewlett-Packard, and Chris Galvin of Motorola are following suit with the brand-owning model. In the future, essentially every other successful company will, too.

Becoming a Brand-Builder-in-Chief

At first glance, for a business leader to become a *brand-builder-in-chief* may not seem that daunting. But if you have spent your entire career as a traditional manager or technician, it's a radical transformation. You have a lot of history to overcome and until now your winning strategy told you that the answer lay in getting those productivities and efficiencies, not in building a powerbrand.

If it's difficult to think of yourself as brand-builder-in-chief for your company, start thinking about building what Tom Peters has described as "the brand called you." That's right, you are your own brand as a leader. The more power the brand "you" has, the more power you will have to get and use power intelligently. What do you think your brand equity is as a leader today? Is the power of your brand equal to or greater than your dreams and aspirations? Is it enough to get you the job you want? Is it sufficient to give you the clout you need to make the difference you want to make in the company?

> *"We're launching companies that are 100 percent funded by the power of the brand."*
> **Richard Branson**

Think about it. The top CEOs in the world today are those who have built a brand "you" that is in some ways stronger than the companies that they work for. When you think of GE, who or what do you think of? You think of Jack Welch and his management style, not jet engines, light bulbs, or financial services. When you think of Cisco Systems, who do you think of? You think of the big smile on John Chamber's face, not Internet routers and switches. And when you think of Intel, who do you think of? That's right, Andy Grove, then maybe "Intel inside," a Grove initiative.

Take a Stand for Marketing Your Game-Changing Idea

When you take a stand for marketing your game-changing idea, it will make you and your brand stand out. Leaders project a brand power that other people are attracted to—a halo effect that others want to rub off on them. The power of the brand has little to do with the positional power, being the CEO of XYZ, and little to do with having a big corner office. It has lots to do with reputational power and lots to do with credibility.

It comes from taking a stand, as a leader for a big idea. It comes from accomplishing something in that particular area, and it comes from putting yourself out there. Just think of how many times you have seen the faces of a Welch, Chambers, or Grove on the cover of *Business Week*, *Fortune*, *Forbes*, and so forth. However, don't be distracted by celebrity and glitterati. Each of these leaders knows that it is the message, not the medium, that matters.

The key to being a brand builder in today's economy isn't deciding what advertising agency you should use and whether you should run your ads on TV, on radio, or in the newspaper. The key is for you as a leader to stand for an idea. Ideas, not stuff, are the currency of the new economy. You win with marketing of your ideas—which are the new basis of competition. You don't win with better shipping, better production scheduling, or better bill collecting.

In Welch's case, the idea that he stands for is that with a true entrepreneurial spirit and an anti-bureaucratic attitude, you can transform a big company. In Chambers's case, the idea is that "every business is an e-business." In the case of Scott McNealy, CEO of Sun, it's "the network is the computer," not the PC on your desk. Lofty and high-sounding though these ideas may be, they wind up establishing brands and selling tons of light bulbs, switches and routers, and pentium chips.

> *"If you can get people to accept, embrace, adore, and cherish your ideas, you win! You win financially, you gain power, and you change the world."*
> Seth Godin, *Permission Marketing*

Let me share an example of how a leader's speaking and listening can build a brand, especially when it shifts the prevailing paradigm. In my own work with Masterful Coaching with executives, I consciously and intentionally speak and listen so as to shift people's paradigm around coaching. I say that coaching is about creating a powerful future, not filling gaps; that it's about accomplishment, not therapy; that it's a day-in, day-out process, not an isolated event. As people grasp these distinctions, my brand is established and a level of permission is created that leads to engagements.

The More People Talk About Your Game-Changing Idea, the Greater the Power of Your Brand

One of the things you will discover is that the power you bring to developing the brand "you" can be directly brought to bear on building a powerful brand for your company. As Jeff Taylor, CEO of Monster.com, told me, "In the new economy, there is a very short distance between whatever the CEO personifies and the company." It's what you stand for as a CEO that inevitably shapes who you are as a leader and in turn inevitably shapes your company's brand.

"Markets are conversations."
Christopher Locke,
The Cluetrain Manifesto

This gets to the very heart of leadership, which I assert arises in discovering ourselves as the stand that we take (not our position in the company). Think about it. We change the world with ideas that we passionately believe in and draw our identity from, personally and collectively. The products and services we offer follow in the footsteps of these ideas. It was a leader taking a stand for an idea whose time had come that resulted in the automobile era, the affordable ranch house in the suburbs, the personal computer, and the Internet.

It's a leader taking a stand for an idea that is the single most powerful way to build a brand. Not by talking at people through conventional advertising, but by talking with people or better yet getting people to talk to each other about the product, service, or customer experience you offer. The bigger the number of people that you can get talking about you and the big idea that you and your company stand for, the bigger your brand will be. This is a very powerful brand-building strategy in the e-economy where everyone is connected.

Richard Branson of Virgin Brands is an excellent example of a leader who personifies his brand by taking a stand for an idea. He has always thought of himself as a David standing up to Goliath, pitting Virgin against companies like British Airways and Coke and Pepsi Cola. "We look to compete with companies that fit our David to their Goliath image, big bad wolves that dramatically overcharge and under-deliver," says Branson.

> **What does it take to win in business? Ask yourself: What do I need to do to change the conversation and to change the world?**

The old conversation in the marketplace was "you had no choice." Branson has changed the conversation to, "yes, you do have a choice." For example, most airlines offer an economy-class ticket (with a cramped seat) at $1,200 on international flights and a business class with a roomier seat at an exorbitant $5,500. Branson changed the conversation about what was possible by offering a super-economy seat that was much roomier at around $2,200.

Branson is onto another secret: The way you get people talking about you and your company is not by blowing a lot of money on subway or bus ads. You do it through word of mouth. Word of mouth is as old as the oldest profession. Branson's publicity stunts, like driving a tank down Wall Street to launch Virgin Cola and declaring his intention to win the Cola wars against Coke and Pepsi, get lots of people talking about him, what he stands for, and, of course, the Virgin brand.

Today, word of mouth is much easier to get going due to the fact that everyone is connected, whether through Internet, PDAs, or mobile phones. In fact, "word of mouse" beats word of mouth, as most of us talk to more people through e-mail than we ever did through meetings, telephone, or letters. This means that today, a leader's standing for an idea that makes a difference and passionately communicating it has a greater possibility of establishing that idea than ever before.

> *"Get personally, directly, and emotionally involved in building your brand on a daily basis."*
> **Richard Branson**

Perhaps more than anything else, Branson's skill as a brand builder is a matter of his willingness to get involved in publicizing his company. It was Branson who when Virgin Air first started, served drinks and played songs on his guitar to passengers on New York-to-London flights. It was Branson who decided that, when and if a Virgin plane was significantly late, he would show up at Heathrow airport to apologize to the passengers. And it was Branson who more recently opened the new Virgin brides shop in London by waiting on customers himself, offering to personally deliver flowers and champagne to the wedding.

If Who You Need to Be to Build Your Brand Is an Extrovert, Be One

I know what you're thinking. It's OK if you're someone like Branson who is a natural showman. In fact, in order to become a marketing wizard, Branson had to fundamentally alter his personality. "Before we launched the airline, I was a shy and retiring individual who couldn't make speeches and get out there. I had to transform myself from introvert to extrovert."

Branson tells other CEOs that they can do it, too, although he is pleased that they remain behind the parapets. According to a BBC report, ninety-nine out of one hundred invitations to British chief executives to appear on network television are refused. I have a friend who tells the story of working in a large traditional company in London where the CEO still carved the roast every day for lunch in the executive dining room! As a result of Branson's willingness to put a face on his brand and get personally and directly involved, he has built a portable brand that can be used to sell almost anything.

The Seven Immutable Laws of E-Powerbranding

Whether you are the CEO of a Global 2000 firm or the founder of a new dot-com enterprise the seven principles of e-powerbranding will guide you in building a successful brand in the e-economy. They will inspire and empower you in transforming yourself from a production meister to marketing wizard who worships brand equity and knows exactly how to create it. They will enable you to understand the differences between building a brand on- and off-line, and help you devise strategies and tactics that you can immediately apply to your business.

Before introducing the seven principles, there are some preliminary things that are important to think about. For example, it is much more effective to have a brilliant business strategy and poor advertising and publicity than it is to have a muddy strategy and great advertising and publicity. Here are a few things you can do to set the right context to be able to implement the seven e-powerbranding principles powerfully:

Set unreasonable expectations for the growth of your company.

This forces you to come up with a number of nonconformist brand-building strategies. For example, Fulvio Bussandri and his team at Microcell took a stand to "Dare to own the wireless revolution," then promised to deliver between 50 percent and 100 percent growth a year. A goal of 5 percent or 10 percent would probably only produce mediocre strategies.

Stretch your definition of yourself and your brand.

Ask yourself, "Who are we?" and "What are we capable of?" rather than, "What have we done?" It may be useful to think of reinventing your company so that what you are selling is your brand through a portal rather than selling a particular product or service. To be able to do this, you are going to have to reinvent yourself as a leader—to draw your identity from your brand rather than your present product catalog or production facilities.

Immerse your customers in a total brand experience.

I spoke to Chan Suh, CEO of Agency.com, about the difference between e-branding and the traditional kind. He said that traditional marketing is strongest in making claims at the beginning of the sales cycle, and then starts to weaken as the sales cycle progresses. Why? Most traditional marketing takes place before the sale. It's the effort to get people into the store. Chan Suh says, "On-line branding is radically different. It can be the advertising medium. It can be the information/ demonstration kiosk. It can be the store. It can be the customer service center. On the Web, you can immerse your customers in your complete brand experience—all in one place, all at one time. That can be a great blessing or your worst nightmare, depending on how well you manage it."[1]

> You need to view the brand and the Internet as the business, not just as advertising or a medium.

Now we are ready to look at the seven principles of building an e-powerbrand.

E-Powerbrand Principle #1: The Internet—Decide Whether It's a Business or a Medium

Al Ries, one of the authors of *The 22 Immutable Laws of Branding*, says that the Internet could be seen in two ways—as a business or a means of communication.[2] First it is a new medium of communication in the same sense that newspapers, magazines, radio, and TV were new mediums. The Internet can be used as an effective medium for stores like Sears, Wal-Mart, or JC Penney to let people know its store hours in a particular location, its special sales, and its employment opportunities, all in one place. In this sense, it is an improvement over the newspaper, magazine, or TV ads.

On the other hand, the Internet can be viewed as the basis of a new business itself, one in which you do your brand marketing, product development, distribution, sales, and service completely over the Web. Amazon.com, eBay, and Yahoo! don't use the Internet to inform you about what they are doing; they are businesses that exist purely in virtual space.

Most people don't distinguish between seeing the Internet as a way to communicate their brand and seeing it as a business to build their brand. So ask yourself, does your Web site exist to support your off-line brand, or does it exist to support your on-line business? There is a real danger that in trying to do both, you will do neither. Once you make your decision, based on the *law of either-or*, things will start to fall into place.

If you want to build a new brand based on providing customers a new experience not attainable without the Web, then it's essential to view the Internet as a business, not just as a medium. You have to see the Internet as something that represents an extraordinary opportunity to create whole new categories, to offer distinctively new and different customer experiences. This is just what Jeff Bezos of Amazon and Louis Borders of Webvan, the grocery-delivery service, or Lands' End are doing with Internet retailing.

One note of caution. Because many people get confused as to whether the Internet is a brochure or a business, they often make the mistake of insufficiently resourcing their Web site. A brochure, whether it's on or off the Web, doesn't need an organization, processes, support staff, and so forth. A business on or off the Web does.

E-Powerbrand Principle #2:
The Name is the Game

If you are attempting to build a bricks-and-mortar business, the name is important. If you are attempting to build a point-and-click business, the name you choose can be the one thing that makes a difference. Think about the physical world versus the Internet. If you're looking for a computer repair shop that's at the corner of Main and Olsen, you don't have to know the name, or how to spell it because you have physical clues. In the virtual world, coming up with a name that is memorable becomes absolutely crucial.

The same applies to being able to spell the name. Do I need to know how to spell Abercrombie and Fitch to go into it on the mall and find this hot brand? No; again, I have physical clues. Yet on the Internet, if I can't spell "Abercrombie and Fitch," I am never going to be able to find the Web site, put things in my shopping basket, or make any purchases there. It is important on the Internet to find a name that is easy to spell.

A third factor in choosing an e-brand name is that it conveys a sense of personality along with being creative and unique. For example, Jeff Taylor got the idea for Monster.com when he woke up from a dream at four o'clock in the morning. He saw a monster board full of jobs for people, rather than a board with a puny few. He purposely chose the name, even amid heckling, because it suggested something more creative than a name like jobsearch.com or careers.com. Monster.com was not only the first into the field, but also the first to offer talent auctions and site career management. (More on this in the interlude after Chapter 7.)

A lot of companies make a mistake in picking a name. They pick a generic name that will be easy to find on the Internet, like drugs.com, pets.com, or furniture.com. While these strategies may give companies a temporary advantage, in the long run, it's a disadvantage because it makes it hard to distinguish their business in the eyes of the customer.

Instead of thinking of a generic name, think of something creative. When Fulvio Bussandri and his company Microcell were looking for a name for a new mobile communications company, they didn't pick a name like "Cell City," or "Mobile One." Instead they decided to pick a name that had some personality and that stood for proximity and reliability. The name they came up with was Fido—yep, the phone company's brand is based on the name of a dog and almost every ad has a picture of a loyal dog in it. The brand became hugely successful within two years. For the wireless in cyberspace the company adopted the name IFido.

In most cases, instead of trying to leverage your parent company's venerable name, it makes more sense to launch your on-line brand with a new, different, even quirky, name and then find a way not to compete with the parent company but to partner together. For example, Outpost.com allows you to buy DVDs online and pick them up at West Coast Video.

Compare the list of successful Web names below for both personality and uniqueness with those of the established brand.

- Monster.com versus Jobfind.com
- Yahoo! versus Library of Congress
- Tax Momma versus H&R Block

- Outpost.com versus JC Penney
- Razorfish (consulting) versus Mckinsey or Andersen
- Oxygen Inc. (advertising) versus Ogilvy and Mather
- Vertical Net (trade association) versus The Chamber of Commerce

E-Powerbrand Principle #3: The More You Focus, the More Powerful Your Brand

Leaders have to make tough decisions about focusing their brand. The key is to find an area where you can assume the mantle of leadership and focus on it. If your business is not in an area where you can be a leader now, narrow your focus until you find one. A brand becomes stronger when you narrow its focus, weaker when you expand it.

One way to focus your brand is to make it your personal leadership mission to own one word or image in the mind of the customer. For example, what word comes to mind when you hear the word Starbucks? "Great coffee." How did Starbucks get ownership of that word? Focus! In every town and city in America there are a number of small coffee shops that serve sandwiches, pies, and a mediocre cup of coffee. Starbucks became a great brand by focusing on providing a variety of quality coffees, making pastries or sandwiches secondary. As a result, Starbucks has been able to add two dollars and eighty cents to the price of a fifty-cent cup of coffee.

Let's take an example of brand expansion. What comes to mind when you hear the word "Volvo?" Most likely it's the word safety. Yet, while Volvo has established its brand in the mind of the customer with the word safety, it has tried to build its business by designing convertibles and high performance cars. For a company like Volvo, the correct strategy would be to try to build its brand by selling safe cars. One market would be every soccer mom in America. Here would be a creative, provocative Volvo ad to soccer moms and dads: "Do you own a Volvo? No. Shame on you!"

The same could be said of Amazon.com, which used to mean books. Today it means being the biggest e-tailer in the marketplace, which has diluted the power of the brand at least to some extent. Amazon sells lots of books but only 5 percent of the books in the United States. A more powerful strategy might have been to go after the other 95 percent, and then go global.

How do you find the one word to focus on that will differentiate your brand? It's my observation that the best place to start is to gain some customer insight with your most important customers. I did a brand-positioning project for Hans Peter Frei of Zurich Financial Services for a proposed Web site, riskengineering.com. (The group inspects your plant and tells you where you have a potential for a fire, blow up, or shutdown, and then recommends what to do about it.)

I interviewed a dozen risk managers in big companies like ABB, Alcatel, and Shell who were in some cases responsible for hundreds of plants. I asked them: What are your desires, needs, frustrations, and dissatisfiers? They told me that they were afraid that too many of the risk management reports hibernated and didn't get acted upon. There were too many written paper reports for any human being to read and stay on top of. The unspoken concern was that hidden in their files was a disaster waiting to happen.

The customer insight I was seeking to position the brand came to me in a brilliant flash of the obvious. The risk managers wanted the experience of being in control and they felt somewhat out of control.

We then held a group meeting in one of our *CollabLabs—accelerated solutions environments* about what the brand positioning should be based on this insight. I suggested that the group choose a metaphor for a situation that would give the risk managers the experience of control. The one that was chosen had to do with putting the risk managers in the cockpit of an airplane. With a click of a mouse, one of the group members, Marcella Ruppli, shifted the screen on her laptop from my Power Point presentation to a Web registration site and laid claim to a new website: "myriskcockpit.com."

The Web site was designed around this metaphor. There was a "flight navigator" where inspection reports could be accessed virtually from around the world. There was a "radar screen" that would light up with code red risk alerts and draw the risk manager's attention to unexpected risks that might be coming at him. And of course there would also be a "two-way radio" where risk managers from different companies could engage in dialogue with each other about industry-specific risk topics.

> ■ Keep focusing your brand until you find a category you can be a leader in
>
> ■ Find a large, easily targetable market and sell to it
>
> ■ Go after a small little market no one cares about and turn it into a bonanza

FIGURE 4.1 Branding Focus Principles

This Web site was received with great enthusiasm by Zurich's Global 2000 customers. What made it particularly powerful was that it represented a convergence of style and substance. It virtually eliminated the need for paper reports and put risk engineering at the fingertips of the risk managers, giving them the experience of control that they needed and wanted.

E-Powerbrand Principle #4: Create a New Category Based on an Idea That Gives Customers a New Experience

When CEOs say, "We need to grow the business by building our brand," what are they really saying? For the most part, they are saying they want to capture a larger share of a market that already exists. The fact is, however, the most powerful way to build a brand has nothing to do with increasing a company's market share in a given category. The most powerful way to do that has to do with creating a new category in an area where no market exists.

Again, this requires that the CEO take the attitude of being an entrepreneur and create a new business model, as opposed to a steward who just relies on what was created in the past. It also sometimes takes playing David to the other guy's Goliath. To build a new powerbrand starts with recognizing that customers don't care about new brands, they care about new ideas, and new categories that provide new experiences. Once an idea catches on, everyone swarms to it. Just look what happened with the fax machine, gourmet coffee, e-mail and, more recently, the rebirth of the scooter.

Have you noticed? Ideas are driving the new economy. Ideas are resulting in people who never expected it becoming wealthy. Ideas are changing the way people live, think, and work. If you can get people to listen to, embrace, cherish, and act on your ideas, not only can you get rich and gain power, you can change the world. This was summed up well when I came across an advert with a picture of a young Asian man sitting on the floor of an empty room staring into his laptop portal. *Before the IPO, before the billions, before the Learjet, just you and an idea— IBM e business.*

What's the connection to branding and marketing? If ideas are the gold standard of today's economy, then the objective of branding and marketing is to create an "idea virus."[3] An idea that just sits there unrecognized is worth little. Yet an idea that magnifies, spreads, and infects everyone it touches can be worth lots. Such an idea has the possibility of becoming an "idea virus."

> **If you can get people to accept, embrace, adore, and cherish your ideas, you win! You win financially, you gain power, and you change the world.**

An example of an idea virus is "Hotmail." The company didn't start by investing $2 million or $3 million in advertising. It started with the idea of a "free Web-based e-mail system that could be accessed from any PC," and in a short time, the idea went viral in the B2C segment. Amazon created a new category of idea virus called "e-tailing" by selling books and later other things on-line. Today, there is an idea virus in the B2C category called "collaborative commerce," which involves competing companies banding together to purchase and move goods at lower prices.

One of the best ways to create a new powerbrand is to come up with an idea that will give customers a new experience. Nokia started marketing the idea of "connecting people." They weren't only marketing the idea, but the experience of being connected. Remember when you first saw people walking around with mobile phones and you said to yourself, "I'll never buy one of those things." Then your friends, family, and colleagues got them. All of a sudden, you had to have one too—you were bitten by the idea virus. Soon you were reveling in the experience of being connected without being tied down to your home or office. "This is great!"

Fortunately there are proven techniques for caring and feeding an idea until it goes viral, just as there are proven techniques for providing customers new experiences, ones that lead to unheralded profits and growth. Some questions to ask yourself are:

- What kind of on-line experiences can we create for customers that will offer them something completely new, an experience they can't have off-line? Or what kind of on-line experience can we offer customers that duplicates an experience customers have off-line, but does it better, faster, and cheaper?
- What can we do to communicate the idea with such power and velocity that it goes viral, bringing us access to a large group of customers we are targeting without having to spend a lot of money on publicity or advertising?
- How will we be able to fill the vacuum for this idea so completely that we not only build a brand, but also create a brand fortress that competitors can't penetrate?
- How can we get permission from customers to keep up an ongoing dialogue with them so that we can build the relationships, and the product or service, and gain a larger share of wallet?

E-Powerbrand Principle #5: Launch Your Brand by Generating a Conversation That Makes Your Idea Go Viral

As the Internet revolution dawned, our TVs, radios, and news periodicals became crammed with Internet ads. GoTo.com, Pets.com, Somebodyorother.com, or Anybody.com—all spraying money like water on expensive ads in the *Wall Street Journal* or a barrage of local radio spots. In many cases, these companies made some kind of impression, but unfortunately, one that was forgotten moments later.

As Seth Godin has pointed out, traditional advertising methods based on "interruption" leave customers cold. *Interrupting* your customer's favorite TV show or radio program, or even their Sunday newspaper, leaves them irritated, agitated, and turned off. Furthermore, it takes a huge number of repetitions to get just one customer to put up their hand and say "I'm ready to buy."

In the new economy, consumers have built up antibodies that resist traditional brand-building and marketing techniques. Instead of looking at your ads, they will go to powerful search engines on the Internet to find a product that meets their needs and that they can buy faster and cheaper. In the same sense, it's very difficult to establish a brand based on the merits of any individual product or service, as there are so many *me, too* products and services out there.

So if you don't launch a brand with traditional advertising and publicity, how do you do it? The first step is having an idea that provides people with a whole new domain of experience—a new concept, a new product, a new service offering. The second step is generating a new conversation about your idea with the intent of making it go viral. This is what Jerry Yang did with Yahoo!, what Jeff Bezos did with Amazon, what Marg Whitman did with eBay, and what George Genkins did with Hotmail.

> *"What's a business plan? It's a passionate person telling their story about how they are going to make their business idea come to pass."*
> Gary Hamel

As Victor Hugo said, "Nothing is as powerful as an idea whose time has come." The question is how do you make an idea's time come? The answer is that you and I have the power to make an idea's time come through our speaking and listening, and, by the way, writing on- and off-line. Here are three ideas you can try.

Develop a "teachable vision," write an e-business manifesto.

Remember Steven Jobs and the first Apple computers? Jobs had a teachable vision that he shared with the developers of the first Macintosh. It was to develop a computer that was as simple and easy to use as a bicycle laying against the wall of a garage. This led to a whole new conversation in the world in which people started talking about personal computers that were "user friendly." The idea quickly went viral, and a huge market for personal computers was born. What's your teachable vision? A good way to propagate it on the Internet is to write an e-business manifesto. A manifesto is an idea striving to go viral. Once you write it, put it on your Web site and circulate it to community groups. And of course, ask for "talk back."

Create a cause, not just a business with publicity.

Keith Fox, head of Cisco Systems's marketing, said that Cisco does little or nothing to directly market or advertise its products and services. Instead, it looks for opportunities to publicize how the Internet can help people transform their world. As the idea of the Internet went viral due to all the conversation generated about it, so did Cisco, surpassing Microsoft in market cap. Cisco was, in fact, creating a cause, not just a business, and demonstrating it through community service. The company offers free public forums on subjects like e-leadership, e-branding, e-finance, and even e-education. In 2000, Cisco entered into a partnership with the World Bank's Business Partners for Development program to develop and expand career opportunities for underserved students around the world through education and the Internet.[4]

Create a customer-led listening environment.

As David Siegel, author of *Futurize Your Enterprise,* points out, "If you are an executive, instead of thinking of your job as seeing the future, see it as creating a listening environment to support employees in their conversations with customers." Siegel says, "The best way is to roll up your sleeves, grab your mouse, and participate." Just by spending twenty minutes a day answering e-mail, you can generate conversation about the ideas you stand for and the products and services you have created to put them out in the world. There are a number of other vehicles that you can use as well—personal home pages for all employees that customers can access, chat rooms where customers can talk to each other, newsletters, extranets, community groups, and so forth.

E-Powerbrand Principle #6.
Use a One-to-One Marketing Approach
to Turn Strangers Into Friends
and Friends into Screaming Fans

My son Morgan, who lives in Los Angeles, is crazy about the Kozmo.com Web site. You can go to Kozmo and order your groceries for dinner and then, at the same time, order a video you would like to watch that evening. The order is processed, shipped, and delivered to you within thirty minutes. If you try to tip the delivery person, he or she refuses to take it. Kozmo then leverages the permission it has earned with you by using a database-backed Web site to alert you about special offers on the kind of food or movies you like the most.

In the old economy, you distinguished your brand by your products. As the Kozmo.com example shows, in the new economy, you distinguish yourself by your service and the customer experience you provide in doing so. The reason is that the new era is all about personalization. You achieve this by creating a one-to-one marketing relationship with customers based on an interactive dialogue and customer interface technologies. One of the keys to success with personalization is finding the right balance between people and technologies, high tech and high touch.

The notions of one-to-one marketing (Don Peppers and Martha Rogers) and permission marketing (Seth Godin) are becoming powerful foundations for the new economy.[5] In case you're confused about the difference, one-to-one marketing people strive to shift their orientation from finding as many new customers as possible to getting a greater share of wallet from individual customers. The question is, how do you create the customer in the first place?

The permission marketers, on the other hand, strive to shift their orientation from finding as many prospects as possible to *converting as many prospects as possible into customers for the first time through an interactive dialogue.* The dialogue is aimed at providing value until a level of permission is created that results in an economic relationship. That permission is then leveraged on an ongoing basis.

For example, let's say you are running a consulting company. Someone from a Fortune 500 company in Manhattan hits your Web site and asks a question about a particular topic. You respond by saying that, if they give you their e-mail address, you will send them a free report on that topic. A week or so later they indicate more interest in the topic by asking another question about an upcoming conference. You respond by saying that, if they register for the conference with a minimal fifty dollar deposit you will send them a free set of guidebooks and audiotapes in advance worth $500. A week after they attend the conference, you send them an e-mail and ask them if they would like a free consultation.

As you can see, the purpose of the special report was to increase the level of permission necessary to sell them on the audiotapes. The purpose of the audiotapes was to increase the permission level necessary to sell them on the conference. The purpose of the conference was to increase the permission level necessary to sell them on the free consultation. By this point, you know that the chances are very high that they are interested in engaging your company's services in a significant way.

> Every established brand with a storefront, a plant, and physical assets will eventually create an electronic doppelgänger—a Web site or way of doing business on the Internet. Be prepared!

Of course, you could have offered a free consultation from the outset, but, since most company leaders are somewhat weary of consultants "who just happen to be in the neighborhood and want to meet," this approach would have had a strong possibility of backfiring. Think about how you can apply the principles here in building your own brand and business.

E-Powerbrand Principle #7:
Seek Good Fellowship and Endorsements

Any person or company can make all kinds of promises and claims to its customers, but the question often in the customer's mind is what is the credibility of those claims? In general, traditional brands like Coca-Cola, Heinz, IBM, or Hertz have enough credibility that they don't need to add to it. Yet, if you are a new company, how do potential buyers who have never heard about you or done business with you before know whether or not they can trust you?

Endorsements are a very critical part of any branding strategy of a virtual company because credibility issues are likely to emerge any time people can't go into a physical store and see a person behind the counter they can hold accountable for the company's promises. Priceline.com has done an excellent job using the power of endorsement to launch its brand with William Shatner, Captain Kirk of *Star Trek*, as its spokesman. What would your reaction have been to hearing a radio spot about a company you had never heard of—Priceline.com—that asked you to put your credit card down and name the price of your next airline ticket?

So in building your brand, ask yourself: Who are the authorities in our field that I could ask to endorse our product? Or, what key customers could we get endorsements from to lend credibility to our product? It's important for any leader who is considering this to learn to develop the courage to make powerful requests. What makes any request powerful is knowing that people have the power to say no.

Another approach to building your brand, market reach, and credibility is to practice good fellowship and align yourself with a company that already has built up a great deal of brand equity either on- or off-line. Though we are living on the electronic frontier, most new companies need to associate with a physical entity somewhere. People still trust the physical world. They believe in bricks and mortar and assets. And most of all, they believe in companies with a recognizable brand.

Though it's fine to talk about the new economy, we should still believe deeply in the old economy, because that's where the brand recognition and equity are unassailable. A corporation with a huge marketing budget has the option of simply printing a URL at the bottom of its existing ads and potentially wiping out an Internet start-up competitor. Rather than compete head-on, it would be better for any e-startup to practice good fellowship and align with these companies.

Another strategy for practicing good fellowship is using *affiliates* from other e-business firms to heighten the *richness* of your offer and widen your marketing *reach*. The best place to look for affiliates is up and down the value chain you are on. Ask yourself which companies can become more successful by making your company successful. And vice versa. Barter is often better than buying. So make requests to do things like trade e-zine article space, trade banner headlines, trade killer content.

Sponsor a Collaborative Design
Workshop on Building a PowerBrand

The best way for CEOs or leaders to deal with the power principles above is not to sit in their offices and try to come up with the packaged solutions and ultimate answers all by themselves. One person, however brilliant and strategically positioned, tends to operate from a singular perspective and is likely to be blindsided by that perspective in changing, complex situations.

"I will never compete against an established brand. I will partner with it."
Robert Lessin, WIT Capital

I have seen through experience that a collaborative branding session with a team of people drawn from different quarters of a company, as well as from different industries, and a variety of subject-matter experts can come up with creative and innovative marketing and advertising solutions that can outperform any consulting firm or advertising agency.

Whom you invite is a critical part of the design.

As mentioned in Chapter 2, innovation comes from differences, from juxtaposing multiple talents and perspectives in focused dialogue. For example, I orchestrated a session like this for the National Hockey League. We invited the commissioner of the league, a number of different team owners and players, and all the licensees of the National Hockey League's sport logo products. We then invited outside subject-matter experts from Procter & Gamble, Gatorade, and Hallmark cards.

Come up with some conversational recipes that will guide the process.

There are five conversations you need to have to create an e-powerbrand. These can be put in the form of five areas of questioning.

- *What's your customer insight?* Ask your most important customers about their desires, needs, frustrations, and dissatisfiers. Keep asking questions until you come to a moment of true customer insight you can use to build your brand. Think first in terms of the experience the customer wants, not products and services.
- *What's your differentiator?* How can you leverage your brand heritage you have built up in the past? How can you use the insights you gained to differentiate yourself from all the other "me, too" competitors in your industry today? Write down your positioning by describing three core values—Starbucks, for example: (1) great coffee, (2) warm ambiance, (3) socializing.
- *What is the core offer based on that?* After you have your positioning, what is your *core offer* to customers to deliver on it? It is important to focus on "what's core" offers rather than a laundry list of everything you can do. Write a short list of three to five items that represent what's core.
- *What is your Web site concept?* Ask your group to design three different Web sites based on a key design metaphor that represents your positioning. At Zurich, the customer wanted to have the experience of control, so we named the Web site myriskcockpit.com and then built the positioning, core offers, USPs, and look and feel around that.
- *Do you have the credentials?* If you are going to make a core offer, you have to make sure you can deliver on it or you will pollute your brand. It is enormously useful to get testimonials from leading experts or customers to establish your credibility. And of course, be able to deliver on your promise (see Chapter 6).

To Reinvent Your Organization, You Must Reinvent Yourself First

Again, we start with the goal. Let's say your goal is to become a marketing wizard and build a powerbrand. Now let's use triple-loop learning to discover who you need to be, how you need to think differently, and how your actions need to change.

Triple-Loop Learning

How do you need to be different?

Write one sentence that describes how you have been in the past as a leader around the issues of brand-building. How has this limited you? Write one sentence that describes how you need to see yourself differently—your leadership declaration. Engage in dialogue with a friend or colleague about the implications of this.

Double-Loop Learning

How do you need to think differently?

Write one sentence that describes your previous mindset around branding. Write a sentence that describes your new mindset or how you need to think differently.

Single-Loop Learning

How do you need to act differently?

Write one sentence that describes attitudes or actions around branding that have not worked in the past. Write one sentence that describes new behaviors you would like to add or old ones you would like to abandon. Figure 4.2 provides a template for answering these questions.

How do you need to *be* different?

From this moment on, start seeing yourself differently

■ From being a widget maker (low-cost producer) to being a marketing wizard and innovator

■ From branding as a Marketing or Advertising job to branding as the job of the CEO and top management team

■ From being laid back in building your brand to being purposely impatient

■ From being an introvert who avoids publicity to an extrovert who looks for opportunities to present your company in a positive light

■ From being expansive in your view of how to grow your business to developing a ruthless focus and making tough decisions

How do you need to *think* differently?

From this moment on, start thinking differently

■ From reengineering and rightsizing processes to branding and buzz

■ From growing your marketing share to creating a new category

■ From brand dilution to brand focus (owning one word like Volvo=safety)

■ From the Internet as a medium for advertising your brand to the Internet as a business to build a brand (vice versa)

■ From wanting your Web-page to do many different things for you to asking what's the one thing you want it to do

■ From stating your brand by making promises in your advertising to living your brand by behaving them

How do you need to *act* differently?

From this moment on, start acting differently

■ Decide whether to use the Web to build your new Web brand business or advertise an existing one

■ Write a new name for your e-company or Web-division that is clear and compelling

■ Take a half-day with your team and narrow your present focus until you find a category where you can be a leader

■ Write a long sentence or short paragraph that defines your unique value proposition

■ Write a short list of places where you are not living your brand and what you will do about it

FIGURE 4.2 A Template for Becoming a Leader Who is a Marketing Wizard

Interlude

Di-Ann Eisnor, CEO of Eisnor Interactive Advertising

Build PowerBrands with Work-the-Street Appeal

Nicole Gibson pushes her way through the crowds of Manhattan's Midtown on her way to work. Her head is down, as it always is on Monday mornings when New Yorkers can be particularly gruff and abrasive. She's not shy. You don't become senior buyer at Macy's by being shy. She's just determined to get to her office and avoid any confrontations along the way.

It's when she's in front of the dry cleaners at Fifty-fourth and Lexington that she sees it. It's in the curb, inches away from a drain opening. A brown leather trifold wallet. Good thing her head was down.

She stops abruptly. A man bumps into her from behind, obviously startled by her sudden stop. "Sorry," Nicole mumbles as she steps a bit to the side. She looks up, surveying the hundreds of people passing her by. She feels nervous. Mischievous. Like she's about to do something wrong.

She knows she will pick it up. She knows she can't NOT pick it up. But can she be so brazen as to actually just scoop it up? No, of course not. She squats to the curb next to the parking meter, out of others' paths. She absently re-ties the laces on her left boot. And then she gingerly, but quickly, picks up the wallet and drops it into her coat pocket.

Once at the office, she closes her door and tells herself, "It's just curiosity. Of course I'll return the wallet to its rightful owner, assuming there's identifying information inside. Of course I won't keep any cash that's in it. Of course . . . ." Before she's completed the moral discussion in her mind, her fingers—as if they were working on their own—are prying open the soft skins of leather. Onto her desk tumbles a ten dollar bill and a small white card. She picks up the card, noticing that it has the same look and feel of Monopoly cards she played with as a child. She turns it over and reads, "Get out of hell free." The fine print points her to a Web site, CharityCounts.com, which serves as an information resource for national not-for-profits.

Nicole smiles. Not only is she ten dollars richer, but she's amused by the clever tactic used to exploit her feelings of guilt at having picked up the wallet in the first place. "CharityCounts.com," she mumbles to herself as she boots up her PC.

●   ●   ●

Howard Kravitz has a lot riding on the game. Fifty bucks to be exact. If the Tennessee Titans can hold out for one more quarter, Howard will be able to take Maureen out to dinner at the new Italian restaurant around the corner. "She'd like that," he thinks.

It's second and eight, third quarter, St. Louis has possession. Twenty seconds left on the clock. McNab runs left and spirals the ball down to the 10-yard line, just beyond the outstretched fingers of Eddy George. "Yes!!!" screams Howard, jubilant over St. Louis's incomplete pass. He rises from his La-Z-Boy as the commercials begin and saunters off toward the kitchen to tell Maureen about their upcoming dinner plans.

Meanwhile, on the television screen, a man sits behind a desk trying to make sense of his financial records. As the mountain of paperwork before him morphs into a monster, he turns on his computer and clicks to OnMoney.com. The site provides him the tools he needs to tame the monster and organize his finances. In the glow of testosterone-induced bravado, the tag line reads "Get your money connected at OnMoney.com."

The thirty-second commercial might have appealed to Howard who, truth be told, does have difficulty managing his and Maureen's finances.

The only problem is that Howard is in the bathroom when the $2 million spot airs.

●   ●   ●

What do Nicole and Howard have in common? For one thing, both are consumers. As such, each of them is deluged with marketing messages and advertising on an hourly basis (although Nicole misses much of it by keeping her head down, her eyes off the billboards). The other thing they have in common is that neither of them saw the OnMoney.com Super Bowl ad.

Their differences, though, outweigh their similarities. They would rarely appear in the same demographic sampling. Nicole is young, single, urban, and wealthy. Howard is middle-aged, married, rural, and solidly middle class. Nicole rarely watches television, but reads *The Economist* and *Harper's Bazaar*. Howard watches five hours of television per night and reads the local paper. From a target marketing perspective, what would be the best way to reach Nicole and Howard? Or would it make sense to even try to reach both of them?

A similar comparison is helpful in looking at CharityCounts.com and OnMoney.com. What they have in common is a need to attract as many visitors as possible. They are both start-ups in the Internet world and are trying to establish themselves and drive traffic to their Web sites. Both must satisfy their stakeholders and, since they are both new to the Internet landscape, this is accomplished more through numbers of "hits" than generated revenue. Finally, in order to encourage consumers to go to their sites, both CharityCounts.com and OnMoney.com have taken very risky approaches to launching their brands. This is where the similarities end.

CharityCounts.com invested a fraction of what a Super Bowl commercial would have cost to create an interactive, meaningful experience for the potential consumer. I, too, am a consumer. Like Nicole and Howard, I see the dot-com advertisements on television and plastered on subway cars. I click my way through the banner ads that populate my favorite Web sites. I hear the radio spots. I skim over the graphically charged, brightly colored ads in *Internet World, Industry Standard,* and *Red Herring*.

Unfortunately for marketers, I don't remember any of it. Well, that's not really true. I do remember one of the first ads I saw on television for a dot-com. It was for an Internet job search company by the name of Monster.com. In the ad, children stare blankly at the camera, sharing their aspirations with the viewing audience: *"When I grow up I want to file all day. When I grow up I want to be a 'yes man'. When I grow up I want to fight my way to middle management."* I think that ad was effective for a variety of reasons. Its simple black-and-white photography and easy pace don't bombard the senses as so many other ads do. Its message is powerful. We're able to see ourselves in the faces of these children. Did we have these same dreams as a child? Of course not. Yet, look what's happened to us! But I think the advertisement was most successful in capturing my attention (and holding it for two years) simply because it was *first*. And while that may not be completely accurate, it is the first dot-com advertisement I recall seeing during the "must see TV" lineup.

I remember thinking at the time how interesting it was for a dot-com company to be advertising on television, a medium that the Internet hoped to displace. By running the ad, NBC seemed to be helping to drive viewers from a television screen to a PC screen. But the fact remains that Monster.com ran the very first television advertisement I ever saw for a dot-com. And it has stuck with me.

The importance of this becomes more pronounced when I share with you that I am hard-pressed to remember any *other* dot-com television (or banner, billboard, magazine) ad I might have seen since then. That's right. Not one.

What's happened here? Could it be that I don't have the capacity to remember more than one television commercial? While I'm the first to admit that that's a distinct possibility, I think the real reason I am able recall the Monster.com ad is that it appeared before the marketing landscape became so saturated with advertising imitators. In the last two years, dot-com companies have cluttered the market space with images vying for our attentions. These companies are pulling out all the stops to build their brands through traditional channels like TV. They're hiring the best directors, actors, and technicians to create the most memorable viewing experience. As a result, ads are getting bolder, sexier, and riskier. But it's a losing proposition. The field is so crowded now that it is virtually impossible to rise above the clutter that bombards us every day. As consumers, we are becoming immune to the powers of traditional marketing and advertising.

We've heard over and over that building a brand is the most important thing a new company can do. Of course, the brand is directly related to things like product/service price, quality, delivery, and customer service. But the brand captures all of these things and packages them neatly into a memorable (that's the key) experience. For the crowded Internet start-up field, building a brand–and doing so quickly—is critical. I have found it ironic that Internet start-ups—which are touting new and exciting ways of conducting business—are relying on the older, more traditional marketing strategies to build their brands. Shouldn't their brand-building activities more accurately reflect the cutting-edge, out-of-the-box thinking that is transforming their businesses? According to many experts in the field, the answer is no. Several leaders told me, "Robert, regardless of whether you're building a brand on-line or off-line, you're going to use the same principles."

I was about to begin believing them when I was fortunate enough to meet Di-Ann Eisnor, who approaches brand-building from a different perspective. She recognizes that consumers are faced with marketing-message overload and that, in order to reach them, you have to go to where the consumers are. Eisnor is a brand-building entrepreneur who doesn't create ad campaigns from a lofty Madison Avenue tower. She and her team create memorable experiences for consumers right in their own backyards or, as Eisnor claims, "in the street."[1]

Marketing as Performance Art

I saw the ad for Eisnor Interactive in *Fast Company* after I had set up a meeting with the company's CEO. The ad presents a strong message and an even stronger image. In it, a young woman is jumping off a subway car. She is full of energy and eager to get somewhere. Most important, she is leaving the clutter and mayhem of the subway behind. She is free. The woman in the ad is Di-Ann Eisnor, CEO of Eisnor Interactive (EI), which develops on-line brands in the off-line marketplace.

She agreed to meet me in EI's new Boston office. I knew she was young (twenty-seven). I knew she was hip. I knew she was unconventional. I also knew that her business was soaring. Given my preconceived notions, I expected the offices of EI to be similar to those of other new Internet (or Internet-supporting) companies that are springing up all over—cutting-edge, gritty, open. I was surprised, then, to find a small but sophisticated office. Here, it seemed, as much attention had been paid to the physical surroundings as to the virtual branding that took place under its roof. And it all makes sense to me after meeting with Eisnor. EI is an agency that exploits the physical world—the consumer's reality—in order to build an on-line brand. It is only natural that this attention to physical settings would permeate the workplace as well.

While the offices of EI initially surprised me, Di-Ann Eisnor didn't. She appeared just as I imagined her to be. Although there wasn't a subway car to be seen, she entered the room with the air of a young leader—free, excited by the potentials around her, and impatient with the chaos of all things traditional. She exuded the same energy as the woman in the ad. She is the EI brand.

Eisnor reminded me of a younger, female version of Jack Welch of GE or Richard Branson of Virgin—someone who embodies the brand of their company by their very nature. Branson is renowned for inserting himself directly into the customer experience—he connects with his public. I knew immediately that Eisnor would serve a similar role for Eisnor Interactive. What you see is what you get. And what you get is a personality and an energy that shouts "We're not your grandparents' branding agency. We're here to give you an unforgettable experience."

Eisnor Interactive is the country's first off-line promotions agency for on-line brands. Eisnor refers to the group as the "Navy SEALs of Marketing." By that she means the forty-plus employees of EI do what it takes to show results. More often than not, what it takes are real-world experiences for individual consumers that drive Internet traffic for her clients in the short-term and customer relationships in the long-term. The New York-based agency (with offices in Boston and San Francisco) has received notoriety and extensive press coverage for its stunts that impact people on the street and get them talking about a digital brand. Clients include Polaroid, Compaq, eGift.com, Reebok, and Staples.com. Billings are expected to exceed $40 million in 2000.

According to Eisnor, the challenge in marketing on-line brands is teaching a new behavior. She asks provocatively, "How do you interact with something that's not physical? How can consumers have a relationship with a digital brand?" The answer lies in creating real-world experiences for people in their daily lives. This is very different from the traditional marketing principles that direct passive campaigns.

A Whole New Ball Game

As Eisnor points out, bricks-and-mortar corporations of the past had thirty years to build their brand. In the new economy, companies have six months. During this period, they must show results for their investors—either in terms of revenue or sales or site traffic. They must also satisfy their other markets—trade folks and consumers being just two. How do you build a brand quickly that satisfies all of these stakeholders?

"Traditional brands," begins Eisnor, "really think about this concept called branding. It's a vague, big, fuzzy notion that means 'spend a minimum of $50 million talking as loudly as you can to as many people as you can.' That approach—that sort of clamoring for attention—is no longer relevant." Rather, Eisnor and her colleagues know they must create an experience that cuts through the clutter of marketing messages, targets their clients' consumers, and generates results. Traditional advertising can't do that. "It no longer has meaning for anyone. It's irrelevant in the Internet era." What then, to Eisnor, is relevant?

Out-of-the-box thinking is what generates the public buzz that is so important in capturing consumer attention. And, as Eisnor points out, this buzz can be created at very little cost. As an example, rather than buying television spots for clients, EI will place provocative advertisements on the sides of trucks and send them around a city for a day. This is much more effective than passive billboards, which people are more likely to ignore. When an advertisement rolls in front of you as you're waiting to cross the street or as you're staring out a cab window, you're more likely to take notice.

EI has also hired actors to pose as chauffeurs in airports, holding up signs that read "Client X for Bill Gates." Passengers—particularly business passengers—disembarking from an airplane are pleased to think they shared a flight with the leader of the computer industry. They hang around, waiting to see Gates. And they remember the client that was supposedly important enough to pick him up. When About.com was launching its brand, EI used the opportunity to address the common concern that many consumers have about the Internet being a cold and human-less space. The agency covered New York with signs, they "branded" bike messengers, and they created dozens of sandwich boards that simply asked, "Is anybody out there?" The answer revealed that yes, there was someone "out there"—the experts behind the topic areas of About.com.

EI was also the force behind Nicole's experience outlined at the beginning of this chapter. Nicole picked up one of 10,000 wallets that were dropped throughout New York City that day. That she picked it up indicates an interaction on Nicole's part. She wasn't a passive observer to a traditional marketing campaign. Rather, she was involved in the campaign and experienced something unique and exhilarating. She, and the 9,999 others who found a wallet that day, are much more likely to remember the brand CharityCounts.com than if they had seen a billboard on the side of the road.

According to Eisnor, what distinguishes successful brand-building efforts from less successful ones is the creation of meaning and value for people on the level at which they exist—on the street. EI creates this meaning and value through unique promotions and real-life experiences. Some refer to these efforts as stunts. Critics call them gimmicks. Whatever they are called, they work. And they work by leveraging two ironies of the Internet economy.

The first is the realization that the most effective way to connect to an increasingly global marketplace is at the "hyper-local" level. "We can create tangible, 3-D experiences for individual consumers only when we know who the consumer is, where he is, and what's on his mind." That means EI spends a lot of time in shopping malls, on Wall Street, and in grocery stores to better understand the needs of the individual customer. Once the EI team understands the consumer's needs and recognizes what the consumer will respond to, it creates the most visceral experience possible.

This is the second irony of the Internet world that EI uses to its advantage: The more physical the interaction between a brand and a consumer, the greater the impact will be in the virtual world. Eisnor is not naïve to the fact that a lot of the branding of an Internet company takes place on-line. "We know the branding will be successful through the development of a relationship with a Web site. But we try to do things that reinforce that *burn personality* in the real world."

Whenever possible, EI will create real-world experiences that deliver value to the consumer. These generate word-of-mouth publicity and establish a sense of customer loyalty—even before the customer has visited a Web site. These are the things that break through the clutter and capture peoples' attention.

For example, EI launched a branding initiative for dealtime.com, a shopping comparison site, that provided something of real value to consumers. Specifically, the agency rented buses, branded them with the dealtime logo and offered free shuttle services for shoppers between all the shopping areas within Manhattan and San Francisco. "It may not sound like much," says Eisnor, "but dealtime received dozens of thank-you notes with messages like, 'no company has ever done this kind of thing for me before.' We added value to people's day, and it meant something to them. That's the kind of interactive dialogue that builds brands."

"We asked the same question with CarOrder.com," continues Eisnor. "How could we provide value to the potential CarOrder consumer that was directly related to the brand of the Internet company?" The answer? For one day, EI arranged for CarOrder.com to pay the tolls for everyone coming into Manhattan during a morning rush hour. For subway users, 50,000 branded metro cards were handed out. This value to consumers generated a lot of positive response. CarOrder.com received numerous messages from thankful commuters (and even sold a few cars that day) and also received significant press coverage for its generosity. These results, coupled with the positive word-of-mouth generated by commuters, made the one-morning branding push more effective than a television spot could have ever been.

These efforts to provide value to individual consumers have led EI to embark on its most ambitious branding exercise yet. With Half.com, an organized on-line marketplace that allows visitors to sell high quality, previously owned goods for at least half off list price, EI has launched a campaign that will bring value not to individual consumers, but to an entire community. Halfway, Oregon, is a picturesque town of 360 inhabitants located forty miles southwest of Hells Canyon near the Idaho border. For the year 2000, it has agreed to change its 200-year-old name to Half.com. Seen as one of the cleverest marketing ploys in recent memory, Half.com has become the world's first dot-com city.

The deal is a good one for both the town and the Internet company. The company has already received extraordinary worldwide media coverage for its innovative brand-building exercise, including coverage from the *New York Times*, the *Wall Street Journal*, CNN, and *Good Morning America* and a live broadcast from Half.com, Oregon, by NBC's *Today Show* in January 2000. In exchange for the name change, Half.com, the town, will also receive significant exposure—something that might help remedy sagging tourism and economic development in the region. Half.com, the company, has built and hosted a Web site for the town and contracts with local developers whenever possible. The company is also donating twenty computers to the local elementary school, providing seed money for local businesses, and discounting the price of Internet access to town residents.

Many outsiders have viewed the Half.com initiative as a mere publicity gimmick. Di-Ann Eisnor disagrees. "In this case, we're looking at social responsibility as media. Yes, our client is getting what they need in terms of publicity and validity, but the town is benefiting, as well. This is a town that has lost its logging industry and several cottage industries. We're wiring the schools and homes and investing in the economic development of the town. That's providing real value to society." Frankly, I think the Half.com critics are probably angry that they didn't think of Eisnor's idea first. What, after all, is gimmicky about channeling money into a community that can really use it? It certainly beats writing an endorsement check to yet another celebrity spokesperson. Sure, EI is getting great publicity from its efforts in Half.com, and I would argue, rightly so. The company is making a difference and adding value in a real and tangible way and deserves to be recognized for its work.

Building on these successes, Eisnor Interactive has developed its own Radical Corporate Responsibilities Initiative (RCRI). This initiative will further explore opportunities to view social responsibility as media opportunities. "The bottom line," says Eisnor, "is that if you provide real news, you'll get media coverage. It's not as easy as buying a radio spot, but it's much more valuable. There's tremendous opportunity here for clients who can, for example, commit to helping the unemployed or homeless. Working with them, we can develop a solution to a specific problem and take a social stance in the process."

As an example, EI is currently working with a client and several employment agencies around the country to train and educate 100 people and bring them back into the workforce. "It's cheaper than running a national TV ad for a month, and costs probably the same amount as running five ads in the *New York Times*. Neither of these traditional marketing techniques do anything to break through the clutter. Our program does. We're planning to help 100 people get back into the workforce. That's important and compelling. The media will be interested."

Eisnor counts on the media's being interested in her socially responsible marketing tactics. She agrees that press hits are important. But what is more important is the opportunity—Eisnor calls it an obligation—for dot-com companies to take a leadership role in solving the country's problems. "If we can be entrepreneurial and start companies and make a ton of money, we should be able to put that back into society. We're approaching an age in which we shouldn't separate work and charity."

The Half.com initiative clearly shows how the right brand-building exercise will generate more publicity than traditional advertising techniques could. What is less obvious are the cost savings for clients. The Half.com deal cost about $110,000, a fraction of what it would cost to create one thirty-second television commercial. Paying tolls for commuters or distributing wallets throughout New York are similarly cost-effective ways of providing value to consumers and an opportunity to build consumer interest and loyalty.

Take for example the 2000 Super Bowl commercials, like the one that Howard missed at the beginning of this chapter. As many people know, the Super Bowl commercials, particularly those airing in the third and fourth quarters of the game, are the most expensive television spots an advertiser can buy. The payoff is that the coverage supposedly reaches 135 million worldwide viewers. As Howard demonstrated by his timely trip to the washroom, that figure is perhaps unrealistic. In any event, seventeen dot-coms paid an average of $2.2 million each to air a Super Bowl commercial in 2000. While many of these (OnMoney.com included) claim that their advertising investment reaped huge pay-offs, industry analysts are not convinced.

One dot-com advertiser claims that traffic increased 550 percent as a result of the Super Bowl ad. That percentage is, indeed, impressive, but becomes less so if it translates into an increase in hits from, say, 200 to 1,300. Another way to look at this sort of advertising investment is to look at the bare statistics. According to the *Industry Standard*, Internet companies spent a total of $75 million on television advertising on Super Bowl Sunday. In addition to the broadcasting fees, we can assume that each commercial cost approximately $500,000 to produce. Media Metrix figures indicate that total traffic to these advertised Internet sites grew by 1.1 million. If we do the math, we can see that it works out to a cost of more than $75 per new visitor.

For many companies, however, the prestige of advertising with "the big boys" makes the investment worthwhile. For certain Internet companies, those with products or services related to sporting goods or beer, this risk may, indeed, be worthwhile. But what about OurBeginning.com, a site catering to life event planning and targeting, particularly, brides-to-be? Obviously, the Super Bowl audience, the most massive of all mass markets, does not comprise large numbers of this target demographic. Perhaps no one told OurBeginning.com that bit of marketing wisdom, given that the Internet company spent more than $4 million to air five spots on game day.

According to Eisnor, taking such a risk on Super Bowl advertising—particularly as a way to *launch* a brand—is irresponsible. "If you're an established brand, fine. Do a spot on the Super Bowl. The whole country is your market, and this sort of advertising makes sense. But it's just ridiculous to launch your company—and spend your entire marketing budget–with one Super Bowl ad." That kind of straight talk is indicative of a young, energetic leader in the emerging Internet market space.

Stunt Woman

Di-Ann Eisnor attributes her success to what she doesn't know. "I start from scratch with all my thinking. I've never learned the things that I would need to unlearn now." In fact, Eisnor knows quite a bit. Armed with a double major in painting and business from New York University, common sense, ambition, and the support of a mother who encouraged her to follow her dreams, she began her marketing career at Dentsu, a large Japanese agency. After college, she moved to Dentsu's European headquarters and rose to the rank of senior account executive. This was in the early '90s, before the advent of on-line marketing. When she returned to New York in 1995, she signed on with SiteSpecific, an early Internet direct marketing company whose clients, a mix of traditional companies and Internet start-ups, were making their first forays onto the Web with brochure-ware. Two years later, SiteSpecific was sold to CKS.

"As soon as the CKS deal was inked," says Eisnor, "I left the company to start Eisnor Interactive. I knew I had a combination of skills in off-line and on-line promotions, and I knew my clients at SiteSpecific were asking, 'what's next?' They realized that they were going to have to do something new and different to break through the usual marketing clutter in order to build relationships and brands with their customers. Based on my skills and what clients were asking for, the creation of Eisnor Interactive was a natural evolution. It's what needed to happen."

She formed Eisnor Interactive to help digital clients develop relationships with consumers. "There was, and is, a real barrier there. As an example, one of our first clients had been successful in using on-line advertising to generate traffic to their Web site. But their market, at the time, was quite small. As the market grew and competitors came onto the scene, it became much more important for the client to be able to ensure potential customers that there was a 'real' company and 'real' people behind the Web site. Their existing promotions didn't engender the same type of feeling a customer enjoys when walking into a shop. We helped them realize that if you make an effort to talk to your customers and, above all, are *relevant* to their needs, you'll have a much better chance of securing their loyalty."

EI created a program whereby the client would talk to people on the streets, create 3-D experiences for consumers to remember, and come away with a solid understanding of consumers' thoughts and concerns about particular products and services. These conversations, carried on by trained actors and accompanied by innovative product giveaways, revealed a lot of useful information for the client. "This is where we differ from traditional branding promotions," explains Eisnor. "We provide a forum for customers to interact and share information with us. And we use that information, something many companies don't do. We recognize that what we do allows two-way communication. Traditional branding can't claim to do that."

Like her mother before her, Eisnor has learned by doing. She's been fortunate not to have worked for companies that stifled her energy. Instead, they allowed her to follow her own intuition. Eisnor still follows that intuition in all of her decisionmaking: "If it feels right, I just have to go in that direction." The company is now two and a half years old and has been profitable since the first quarter. Ironically, EI doesn't have to do much to market itself. "Most of our new clients come to us through word-of-mouth, public relations, and friends we have in the industry." Many others are drawn to EI's reputation as a cutting-edge marketing leader in on-line branding.

In its short history, EI has carved out a space in which it has created a hybrid scenario of marketing that falls "somewhere between traditional branding and direct-response initiatives. Something new is emerging in that space, and it's very exciting." In addition to clients, investors are also taking notice. EI has recently signed a strategic alliance with Omnicom, which will not only allow EI to expand more rapidly, but also supply knowledge and resources to Eisnor's management team. "Venture capitalists give you money," explains Eisnor. "But strategic alliances give you so much more. I'm very excited by what we'll be able to learn from Omnicom."

Stunt Leader

Di-Ann Eisnor is the first to admit that the new economy calls for new leadership. As she recently revealed in a ChannelSeven.com interview, "We need leaders who collaborate rather than dictate, who inspire rather than restrain, and who manage by example rather than through distributing tasks." With these words, she's certainly describing herself. The example she is setting is one of personifying the brand of EI—bold, different, risky, excited.

Eisnor credits EI's success to the team she has been able to assemble. "They are amazing. I learn so much from them every day." At EI, there is plenty of opportunity to learn, given that a large portion of each day is devoted to brainstorming and, simply enough, talking to one another. The forty employees who make up Eisnor's team come from all walks of life. Some come from other agencies; others come from the music industry or directly from a retail environment. Some have business experience, others don't. What they share is a creative energy, similar vision, and an understanding of the Internet medium.

"We don't hire for a given position," explains Eisnor. "We hire based on the question, 'do we like this person?' If we do, we find a role for them that will best leverage their strengths. If you hire someone and put them in a position that they're good at, doing what they love doing, then you have a fully leveraged team. That's the most efficient—and most fun—way to work." This hiring strategy is certainly paying off. In an industry where employee turnover is high, EI has never fired an employee. And only one person has quit. "I'm constantly thinking of ways to ensure that our employees feel like they're making a valuable contribution."

Di-Ann Eisnor's creative management style is not confined to within the walls of her office. Managers at EI manage by finding people's strengths and allowing them to flourish. Above all, managers are expected to lead by creative example. Creative thinking is encouraged in other ways, too. "We have programs that invite outsiders to come in and tell us how they go about thinking and making decisions—people like Joost Elffers (author of 48 *Laws of Power*, *Play with your Food*, and *Secret Language of Birthdays*) and Amnon Levav (a university professor who has founded a company dedicated to creative problem-solving). These types of people inspire us to think more creatively." EI staff are regularly encouraged to make ten-minute presentations to their colleagues about something—anything—having to do with the e-economy. This allows them to expand their own thinking into different areas. In addition, employees who have been with EI for two years receive a four-week paid sabbatical in order to pursue their own inspirations.

Eisnor says that one of the reasons for the creative success of EI has to do with the relatively small size of the staff. "People are here because we're building something great. I expect that once we outgrow tribal size (about 100 folks), we may see a little more turnover and a slight cultural shift. We're trying to keep each office small in size (around 15 people) to prevent this."

Di-Ann Eisnor is most pleased with the fact that EI's core focus and philosophy are the same as they were the first day of the company. With her team, Eisnor has been able to create a unique culture, client base, a connection with consumers, and philosophy that drives an aggressive approach to getting things done. It is clear that she continues to enjoy what she is doing. Her energy is infectious. Her vision is focused and clear. "I took a risk when I founded this company, but I'll continue taking it every day as long as I feel what we are doing is relevant. I am the CEO because every company needs an ultimate leader. But I really think of myself as much more a catalyst for the team. And without them, the agency wouldn't exist."

Di-Ann Eisnor is a catalyst. A brand representative. And a leader. She has made me believe that these words are most likely synonymous in the e-economy.

From a "Me" Point of View to a "You" Point of View

How to provide a perfect customer experience every time

• • •

In Chapters 3 and 4, we looked at what you can do as a leader of an e-business to build a powerbrand and to increase productivity and decrease costs by creating partnerships and synergies enabled by the Internet. The ultimate factor in your success, however, will be in how e-business improves customers' experiences with your company. It is not just the goods and services you sell, but whether your customer's experience is positive, distinct, and memorable.

• • •

Michael Gerber had been driving for seven hours and, tired of the highway, decided to stop for the night before venturing on to San Francisco. He found a hotel located in a redwood grove overlooking the Pacific. As he walked into the lobby, the sun was setting and the grove had turned pitch dark. Right away something told him he was in a special place. The lobby was warmly lit. There were stuffed sofas, redwood paneling, and a blazing fieldstone fireplace.

Behind the desk, a woman appeared dressed in a red, white, and green gingham blouse. "Welcome to Venetia," she said with a warm smile. Within two minutes, a bellboy whisked him off to his room. Given that he didn't even have a reservation, he couldn't believe the ease with which this was happening. And the room! It was large, leaving an impression of earthly elegance, with its thick wall-to-wall carpets, four-poster bed, white-on white-duvet, and stone fireplace prepared and waiting for the wooden match that lay in front of it to be struck.

Delighted with his good fortune, he dressed for dinner. The woman at the desk had made a reservation and he walked down a well-lit path through a dark redwood grove to the hotel restaurant. He gave the maître d' his name and was escorted right off to his table, even though others were waiting. (Alas! the reservation counted.) The meal was exquisite and he lingered over a glass of brandy listening to a classical guitarist playing Bach fugues. As Gerber walked back to his room, the cold chilled his spine and he looked forward to lighting the fire. As he opened the door he discovered someone had beaten him to it. On the night table was a card that said, "Welcome to your first stay at Venetia. I hope it has been enjoyable. If there is anything I can do for you day or night, please don't hesitate to call. Kathi."

The following morning he awoke to a strange bubbling sound in the bathroom and arose to check it out. A percolator of coffee, turned on by an automatic timer, was burbling away. A card lying against the pot said: "Your brand of coffee. Enjoy! Kathi." He wondered how in the world the staff could have known that and he remembered in the restaurant someone asking him what kind of coffee he enjoyed, and here it was. Also, underneath the door had been slipped his favorite newspaper, the *New York Times*. (He had been asked about that when he checked in.)

"This was unbelievable," Gerber said of the experience in his book *The E Myth Revisited*. "It wasn't the mint, it wasn't the coffee, it wasn't the newspaper, it was the total client experience." It had happened because someone had heard him every single time he spoke about his desires, needs, and wants, in even the most cursory way. Not only that, the same thing happened every time he returned to the hotel. Furthermore, the *experience* Michael Gerber had as a customer didn't happen by accident, it happened by design.[1]

Every physical detail from the warm reddish paneling to the stuffed sofas and fieldstone fireplace in the lobby had been, if you will, staged to say, "This is the hotel you have been looking for all your life." Every event, from the warm welcome at check-in to being whisked off to his table ahead of others at dinner, from the lit walk to the blaze in his fireplace, had been conceived, carefully planned, and orchestrated to make him feel like the most important person in the world. Every personal touch, the note on the night table from Kathi, the bur-bling coffee in the morning, the *NYT,* was there to provide a positive, unique, and unforgettable experience.

Welcome to the Customer Experience Economy!

It has been said that the entire history of economic progress can be described in terms of four economies: agrarian, goods, services, and experiences. Though economists tend to put experiences in the same category as services, they are actually separate areas.

For example when you buy a Chevy , Ford, or Toyota, you pay for goods. When you buy long distance phone service from AT&T or MCI, you pay a monthly service fee, and when you go to Disneyland, to a movie theatre, or to a special educational Internet event, you pay an admissions charge for this experience.

An entrepreneur in Israel entered into the experience economy with the opening of Cafe Ke'ilu, which, translated into English, means "Cafe Make Believe." The proprietor, Nir Caspi, mentioned to a newspaperman that people come to cafes to be seen and to socialize. Cafe Ke'ilu takes this to the logical extreme. The restaurant serves the customers plates and mugs that are empty and charges them three dollars during the week and six dollars on weekends for the social experience.

As you can see from the story of the Venetia hotel, or for that matter, a visit to Planet Hollywood, Niketown, or to an auction on eBay, even if companies do not actually charge you an admission fee, they will increasingly wrap the sale of goods and services in certain kinds of staged experiences. At the very basic level, they will work increasingly hard to make sure that customers have a pleasant, efficient, hassle-free experience in doing business with them. The name of the game will increasingly be improving the customer's experience.

It's important to point out that, while the economic offerings of the past (farm commodities, goods, and services) existed external to the buyer, experiences are basically personal and internal to the individual who has been engaged by them. The only way you can tell whether a customer is having a good experience is by asking him or her. As Chan Suh, CEO of Agency.com, says, "It's amazing. Given half a chance, most customers will tell you exactly what they want"—exactly the experience they want to have.[2]

A good metric of customer experience on the Internet is what Jakob Neilson calls "Web usability." According to Nielson, the dean of this subject, whom I met at Jay Abraham's Internet Super-Strategy-Setting Summit, "Most people don't have any idea how the customer experiences their site." He asserts first of all that, "Get it in your mind, that your first Web site will probably be a disaster, from both a marketing and customer experience point of view, so do it and get it over with. When you design your second Web site, invite customers in to try it out and ask them what they experience. After you get their feedback, all you have is a list of suggestions. Don't assume even then that you can do it right. Design another iteration of the site and then invite the customers to try it again. Keep doing it until they say that the experience was these three things: *positive, unique, and memorable*."[3]

Today, Every Company Must Make the Journey to the Experience Economy

To succeed in the new economy, you and your company must run the gauntlet from selling goods to selling services and then to selling experiences. You must not only run the gauntlet, but also transform in the process. In fact you must transform three times. See Figure 5.1 on the Three Phases of Creating Customer Satisfaction.

Phase One. Design innovative goods.   The first transformation has to do with doing everything possible to make sure that the goods you are offering are highly innovative products that have the potential to create a new category that you have the potential to define and dominate. Microsoft did this with its Windows 95 platform (even if it was basically copying Macintosh). Palm Pilot created a new category with the PDA and Amazon did this with e-commerce.

Phase Two. Transform your goods into a service.   Most products are indistinguishable commodities. Does it really matter whether you buy a Ford or a

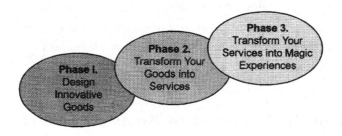

FIGURE 5.1 The Three Phases of Creating Customer Satisfaction

Chevy pickup, a Betty Crocker or Pillsbury cake mix, a Dell or a Gateway laptop? To move from phase one (goods) to phase two (service), you need to transform your product into a service. This will differentiate your brand, as services are harder to compare and will increase revenue. When PC costs fell below a thousand dollars, Gateway announced to customers: "Today you want to do word processing, tomorrow you might want to surf the Internet, the day after, play multiuser games. We will offer you the service of an 'upgradeable computer.'" Today, Microsoft doesn't just want to sell you software; it wants to charge you a monthly fee for customerized software services over the Internet.

Phase Three. Transform your service into a magical experience.   Today, many services are becoming commoditified as well. Does it make any difference whether you use AT&T long distance, MCI Worldcom, or Sprint? Hertz or Avis? This ISP or that one? Companies that want to differentiate their brand and build revenue will increasingly need to run the gauntlet from selling *services* to selling *experiences*. There are many companies that have not made a smooth transition to phase two and thus are unable to move on to phase three. For example, my brother bought a Gateway computer because of the advertising, but it was a nightmare to actually try to upgrade his system.

The companies who want to make the transition to phase three get there by acknowledging the breakdowns in phase two and dealing with them. One of these breakdowns is poor coordination between brick-and-mortar and on-line stores. For example, Landsend.com has worked with Webline to build a customer response system. If you are lost on the site or can't find what you want or if you simply want gift-giving advice, you can click a button and the salesperson will call you right back (if you type in your number). The salesperson can even take charge of the browser and guide you to the most luxurious cashmere sweater, for example.

Who Do You Need to Be as a Leader?

As mentioned before, who you and I are as leaders is the single most important ingredient in designing extraordinary customer experiences. The single most important point is to see yourself as personally responsible for the customer's having a great experience in dealing with your enterprise.

> **See yourself as 100 percent responsible for the customer's having a great experience every time.**

Think of one of your favorite places of doing business in your hometown—a restaurant, a hotel, or shop. I bet the odds are very high that you and everyone else knows that the reason people have great experiences doing business there is because of the proprietor. Now think of a place of doing business in the same town that you hate. Again, no doubt you and everybody else knows that the reason you have an awful customer experience there is because of the thinking and attitude of the proprietor—which is then carried out by everyone else.

Taking responsibility for your customers' having a great experience with your organization means that you are willing to take pride in your company's accomplishments and, at the same time, be willing to honestly acknowledge what isn't working. It takes having a "the-buck-stops-here" attitude and a willingness to shake up the status quo.

For example, Laurie Tucker is the VP of e-commerce at Federal Express. She is also in charge of customers' having a positive experience. After FedEx call centers were assigned to her, she discovered that the customers were contacting the call centers talking about tracking issues that were showing up on their Web browsers, and the people in the call centers didn't have access to the Internet or computers.

She asked her team to put together a five-minute video to show to the board that displayed a split screen with customers talking about Web-related issues and call center reps not having computers. The board members all gasped. The next day, Tucker got the money to provide Internet hookups and computers for the call centers.[4]

See Yourself as Leading the Customer, Not Merely Patronizing Them

The next ingredient of providing great customer experience by design is to lead customers, not pander to them. This means providing them with an experience that surprises and delights them, rather than simply providing them with a commodity that meets their needs. Walt Disney is the consummate example, whose creative genius brought us the magic of movies and theme parks, giving everyone the joyful experience of being a child again.

In Disneyland, the goods (which are the souvenirs) and the services (for example, the rides and restaurants along Main Street), along with the characters of Mickey Mouse, Goofy, and Donald, are all props in the packaging of a total experience. One clear indication of Disney's commitment to creating a great customer experience is that he doesn't charge for each ride. Instead he charges for admission.

To be sure, the idea of marketing experiences has transcended movie theaters and theme parks. We've already mentioned Hard Rock Cafe, and parents are increasingly outsourcing birthdays to Chuck E. Cheese. Nintendo Play Station II is an example of creating a customer experience through advanced graphics.

Another particularly hot area of marketing experiences is cruise ship holidays. For every passenger Richard Fain, CEO of Royal Caribbean Cruise Lines, books on one of his ships, four to five get turned away for lack of a berth. As a result, Fain and Royal Caribbean are on a shipbuilding spree. He believes the most important person on a ship is not the captain, but the designer. He has created a set of design principles for RCCL's newest ships, like the Voyager, and gets directly involved.

For example, he personally designed a topless bathing area so that passengers could feel free and sexy. He designed one of the men's bathrooms, which provides a spectacular ocean view from eleven stories high, beyond the open granite urinal wall, so that customers could feel inspired. He brainstormed a moonlit ice skating rink where couples could feel romantic.

While charging an admission fee marks strong entrants to the experience economy (Planet Hollywood, Hard Rock Cafe, Niketown are examples), not everyone does this. Today's dot-com companies provide an experience that is distinct from what went on in the brick-and-mortar world. This is because interactive technologies tend to foster whole new genres of experiences. You should think of these technologies as paints on your artist's easel with a view toward creating colorful experiences for customers, whether it be using the Internet chat rooms, multi-player games, or virtual reality.

Games are a very hot category for providing positive and unique experiences. Nintendo 64, Sony Play Station I, and Sega Dreamcast all provide super-advanced graphics that have a virtual reality effect. Does it pay off? The market cap of Nintendo alone is worth more than all the movie theaters in every country in the world.

See Yourself as Passionately Caring About Your Customer

One of the biggest errors that people in any company make is falling in love with the wrong thing. They fall in love with their company product or service, when they should fall in love with their clients. Of course, you should passionately care about your company and its products or services, but that should not be your focus. Just providing awesome products or great service, although admirable, is trite.

Falling in love with your customer means you should passionately care about customers and have the genuine desire to want to make a contribution to them. For example, FedEx delivers hundreds of thousands of packages a day with their planes and trucks. The drivers never know if the packages they are carrying contain business contracts, heart valves, car parts, or love letters. Nonetheless, they are trained to see that getting each and every package delivered on time is making an important difference in a person's life.

Falling in love with your customer means having a certain generosity of spirit that influences your thinking and actions. Most people tend to think in terms of "What do I have to do to entice customers to put something in their shopping cart?" Instead, you should say "What do I have to offer that will be of value? What benefit do I have to give?" The Internet allows you to discover this on a one-to-one basis through interactive dialogue. If you listen loudly and empathetically enough to your customers' desires, needs, and frustrations, you will discover what you can do to create great customer experience by design.

Richard Branson has said that the single most important factor in his success is not his showmanship, but rather his customers and employees. "One of the things that has helped me in building our individual companies is that I can separate myself from our products and services and empathize with our customers, based on having a very clear sense of how I would like to be treated if I was in their shoes."

Be a Tinkerer, Systematizer, Enabler

There is a third answer to the leadership question: "Who do I need to be in the matter?" And the answer is that you have to be a tinkerer, systems designer, and modeler. It doesn't matter if you are wonderful to people at your counter if the back office systems in your business don't allow you to deliver the goods.

For example, one day a catalog from Lands' End arrived at our house. I asked my wife, Susan, what she thought of the company, since she has ordered many items for our daughter Eva. She said, "They are great." Lands' End not only has a great children's clothing catalog and makes it easy for you to buy things over the Internet, but all of its back office systems work.

The company acknowledges your order with an e-mail, sends you e-mail updates, and makes it easy for you to return things. She mentioned how she bought children's clothing from another on-line company: "The people were all nice, but it didn't matter, because their back office systems didn't work. They delivered to the wrong address and it was a mess trying to return something."

Do You Have the Mindset to
Design Great Customer Experience?

This section is about making small but high-leverage shifts in viewpoint or focus that will allow you to design great customer experiences and become profoundly more successful in your business. It starts with making a shift in your point of view from your products and services to the needs and wants of your customers.

From a "Me" Point of View to a "You" Point of View

Go into any brick-and-mortar store or restaurant or shop anywhere on the Web and make a simple request of the people in charge for a bit of extra "something." Ask people to empathize and bend the rules and then listen to whether they speak in plain English or technical jargon. You will know in about three seconds, by their automatic response, whether the leader and the entire enterprise operates from a "me" point of view that is egocentric, or a "you" point of view that is customer-centric.

There is a famous episode of the Seinfeld show that illustrates this. It's about a man who runs a gourmet soup kitchen in New York who has a very strong, self-centered point of view and is in love with his own fabulous soup. When Elaine comes into the shop and makes a constructive suggestion, he says in a strong accent, "Very good, very good, no soup for you!" (Laughter). She then rants and raves about his attitude and dubs him a Soup Nazi (laughter). When George tries to intervene on her behalf, the Soup Nazi says, "You, no soup for one year." There is a lesson in this story for all of us, for in one way or another we are all Soup Nazis.

Part of the strategy of preeminence represents a shift from a "me" point of view to a "you" point of view. So few business leaders have this point of view that it will automatically give you an edge or advantage. It is what will make your teammates and employees loyal to you and your organization. It is what will make your customers enthusiastic to do business with your company rather than with your competitors.

Once you begin to come from this point of view, you will always, not just sometimes, stand out in your customers' minds as the best there is. It will naturally lead you to listen to customers and give you an uncanny insight into what they want and what's missing that will make a difference. It will naturally turn customers into friends for life.

The "you" point of view is bankable because human nature is the same. People expect to be talked down to, sold regardless of their needs, and taken advantage of, and when they run into a company that does the opposite, they respond with their hearts, loyalty, and credit cards.

Making the shift from a "me" point of view to a "you" point of view takes focus and discipline. Many people preach this with sincere and honest intentions, but unknowingly don't practice it. As a result of their desire, need, and desperation to make a sale today, they focus their entire energy on the transaction rather than building a customer relationship. Here are some simple things you can do to operate from a "you" point of view on- and off-line.

> *"Succeeding on the Web has everything to do with customers, nothing to do with technology."*
> **Audri Lanford, co-CEO, NETrageous**

1. Focus on customer satisfaction, not gross sales. Chan Suh is the CEO of Agency.com, a company that has arguably designed some of the best Web sites on the Net.[5] He started the company in 1995 on a budget of eighty dollars, while he was employed at Time Warner trying to get the company to start an interactive division. In 1995, British Airways decided to run a contest in search of a Web designer. Over one hundred people from the United States entered the contest and Chan Suh and the budding Agency.com were among the five finalists.

"We were chosen because we had a very clear presentation that said that succeeding on the Web would not be about the technology, but rather about improving the customer's experience," Chan Suh told me. "The emphasis needed to be placed on the customer satisfaction of the existing base, not increasing sales. Many airlines now only focus on gross sales. However, the more you plumb the depths of business in the e-economy, the more you realize that people's having a great experience as customers is the only thing that matters. The price of failure is much more serious than most realize."

For example, let's say it costs you $800 to turn a browser on your airline Web site into a buyer. If you make that customer happy, you earn their business and loyalty. If not, you not only lose that customer's business, you lose the business of other passengers. The rule of thumb is that the customer will tell ten people of their experience. So you will have lost $8,000 worth of business development costs. So how much do you have to make to recover your $8,000? If your business has a 10 percent profit margin, you need to make approximately $80,000 in sales just to make up for one mistake in dealing with customers.

This is why, says Chan Suh, "It's so important to eliminate negative cues to customers." According to a *Fortune* magazine survey, service in the dot-com world stinks. Of the forty-five sites tested, only 60 percent bothered to respond to the customer's e-mail requests. Only 30 percent of the sites had a real-time inventory hookup, fewer than 10 percent had signs that offered guarantees to unsatisfied customers, and only one third of on-line retailers would accept returns from brick-and-mortar stores.[6]

British Airlines was impressed with Chan Suh's way of thinking and invited him and his team to come to London to make a full presentation on a Web-site design. The only problem was that Chan Suh didn't have the money to fly to London and didn't know where to get it. He took a risk and told the folks at British Airways, who found his candor charming and disarming. They decided to send him the tickets and pay all expenses. He and his team went on to win the contest hands down.

Says Chan Suh, "The Holy Grail of Internet brand building is personalization." As we mentioned in the last chapter, Chan Suh and his team have developed a process for creating magical customer experiences that recognizes that people today expect to be treated differently by businesses, particularly on the Internet. They seek dramatic new levels of service: personal, swift, and on demand.

The questions Chan Suh and the design team asked themselves about British Airways were: "How can we help the airline personalize their services for each customer?" and then "How can they take complexity and time out of the process with technology?" The result of their inquiry was a graphically brilliant, well-thought-out Web site that, through different menu choices, allows customers to meet and exceed their own needs, whether they are executives, vacationers, or holiday shoppers.

The Web site also helps people to plan, select, price, book, and confirm their trips by using a customer interaction number to remember each customer and what step in the process he or she is on. Chan Suh stresses three additional points, as ways to generate great customer experience.

Earn the customer's permission, which is derived from earning trust and delivering value. This involves a passive role and refraining from selling until the customers have told you what they want, either through menu choices or surveys.

The active role is to give them information about their wants in language they understand, not technical jargon. A customer may not care if he has a 500-megahertz laptop; he cares if it's lighter and he can do more things with it.

Surprise and delight customers by anticipating their needs. For example, instead of just selling a customer a ticket to New York, you might suggest a special limo that will give them a cook's tour of the city based on their particular interests, some tickets to the theater, or some discount shopping vouchers at their favorite boutique.

Reward customers for their commitment and loyalty. In the past, companies tried to establish their brands by differentiating their products. Today, it's important to think in terms of differentiating your customers. Frequent flier programs for free air miles are a good example. Here's another. In most grocery chains in England, customers bag their own goods. However, when a regular customer comes in and places a credit card in the machine, a bagger shows up to bag the groceries. The store is differentiating its customers and therefore providing a different customer experience.

2. Think about what your company would do differently if it charged admission.   A good way to shift your mindset from the goods and service economy is to think in terms of charging admission. Joe Pine and James Gilmore, authors of *The Experience Economy: Work Is Theatre and Every Business a Stage,* suggest asking yourself and your team the question, "Would we run my business differently if we charged admission?"

This tends to automatically lead people to think in terms of the thematic designing experiences they would like to design for customers. The authors suggest there are four design criteria to follow: *entertainment, education, esthetic, and escape* (like a chat room or adventure). If you can design an experience that does all of these things, you hit a "sweet spot" that has huge appeal for customers. Disneyland's new theme park, Animal Kingdom, is a good example of this.[7]

Many businesses are discovering that they can do more business by adding a thematic wrapper to the sale of goods and services. For example, when you make a reservation in a restaurant and arrive at the right time, you are usually told your table is ready. The maître d' at Rain Forest Cafe, by contrast, says your adventure is about to begin. Another example is the Forum Shop in Las Vegas, a mall that is based on the theme of the ancient Roman marketplace. Every entrance to the mall and every store recreates a Roman theme, and the words "Hail Caesar!" are often heard.

Doing e-business on the Web creates many opportunities to stage experiences, and many of the best sites actually do charge admission—from special educational appearances by authors and celebrities, to the sublime entertainment of your favorite concert, and from the esthetics of private art shows to escapist experiences like erotic chat rooms. Whether or not you are charging admission for people to enter your Web site, ask yourself what you would do to stage high-quality experiences for customers.

One thing that is very important to take into account in designing customer experiences over the Web and elsewhere is that the Web tends to be primarily a visual medium. If you go into a clothing boutique, you not only see the clothes, you feel them, touch them, smell them, and so forth. On the Web, in most cases, you can only see them. Landsend.com does a good job of engaging your senses. From the descriptions of items ("with a silky superfine finish, superior softness and tremendous overall comfort"), to trying on clothes on a 3-D model that looks like you, or chatting live by phone or on-line with someone who can answer your questions—everything heightens people's experiences and thereby promotes sales. Design experiences that include hitting the sweet spot by combining each factor in Figure 5.2.

Action Strategies and Examples

Once you have developed a whole new dynamic mindset consistent with the above, the next step is to begin to design action strategies.

1. Design positive customer experiences and eliminate negative cues. Audri Lanford, co-CEO of NETrageous, a dot-com marketing consulting firm, can rattle off the names of hundreds of Web sites that she frequents.[8] But when you ask her for the place where she has the most positive experience, she mentions Amazon.com. Lanford orders up to $200 a month in books—from e-business to fiction and from marketing management to organizing your closet. Pre-Internet days, she would rarely spend more than twenty-five dollars a month on books.

"Amazon does a lot of things right," says the bright and cheerful Lanford. "First of all, when you look up a book, Amazon gives you recommendations of related titles. The suggestions really come from customers, not from someone in a ware-

Active Participation

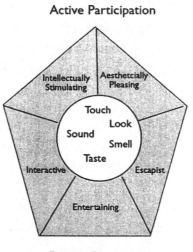

Passive Participation

FIGURE 5.2 Design Experiences That Hit the Sweet Spot by Combining These Factors

house trying to move titles off the shelf. I am amazed at how amazingly excellent the recommendations actually are, and it's rare that they are not."

"Being two clicks away from the order is another plus, and I find that if they have a book that is out of stock, they split the shipment. When the other item comes in, they ship it to you free of charge. Also, if you have sent an e-mail, the chances are you will get a personal response in the next four hours. When you consider how many customers they are doing business with, this is all pretty extraordinary."

One final comment: Poor service is the fastest way to generate negative customer experiences. It's therefore important in establishing a positive customer experience to eliminate breakdowns that send negative cues, such as surly employees, a stain on the carpet of the hotel room floor, a browser or software program that always crashes, or a Web-site shopping basket that won't take your credit card and allow you to check out.

Arrange ways to visit your business, personally or through others, to become aware of any negative cues. Also give customers a way to communicate their dissatisfactions to you—and then listen!

2. Design unique customer experiences that spin heads. To be in a bidding war at an auction on something like Van Gogh's "Daisies," J. D. Salinger's *The*

Catcher in the Rye manuscript, or a Jackie O brooch can be a thrilling, heart-pounding experience. Before eBay, the experience of auctions was reserved for the artsy set, the Saturday afternoon antique crowd, and the rich. EBay changed everything by democratizing auctions and making them available to the rest of us on a twenty-four-hour, seven-day basis.

For some people, the desirable goods and services auctioned at eBay are the point of participating. For the vast majority, however, the point is the experience of being in an on-line, real-time interactive auction and feeling your temperature rise and your cheeks flush as you outbid or get outbid by others. Most offerings are not big-ticket items—things like speedboats, laptop computers or diamonds; they're small-ticket items offered at a nominal price. My son got hooked on eBay selling an old Nintendo Game Boy he got bored with; my niece a Furbee; a friend a baseball glove.

Also, eBay is an excellent example of the shift of the CEO as steward to CEO as entrepreneur. As we said, an entrepreneur not only, through creative disorganization, creates something that never existed, but he or she also changes the social value of the society. Every time you complete an auction event at eBay, the people who participated with you are asked to rate you on such things as your integrity, collaborative attitudes, and actions. People are rated by number of stars and comments, whether they are a buyer or seller. This is no doubt a significant factor in the whole experience.

The interesting thing is that eBay doesn't buy or sell anything. It simply charges a percent royalty on the items sold at auction. You can look at this not just as a charge for goods or services, but as an admission charge for a positive and unique experience.

3. Design an unforgettable experience that keeps them coming back.   In the past, home heating business retailers would have the option of buying their goods from two to three different distributors in their local area. Trying to get companies outside of their area that didn't know them to quote favorable prices was nearly impossible, and the voice mail, letter writing, and faxes involved were highly aggravating.

This left the local home heating companies at the mercy of distributors who understood that they couldn't take their business somewhere else. The result was that the distributors tended to exploit the home heating companies with inflated prices and poor service. The founders of Altra Energy Technologies, a dot-com company in Texas, saw the frustration that the local home heating vendors experienced as an opportunity to make a difference in their industry. They thought of their customers' problem, then thought about how they could use the Internet to solve it.

In essence, Altra came up with a Web-based system by which company leaders like Ed Bingham of Coan Oil in Framingham, Massachusetts, could send an RFP to Altra over the Internet, and within four hours get competitive bids from over 300 different companies, along with differences in grade level. This completely changed Bingham's experience of buying oil. However, what made the experience unforgettable was the panoply of additional services Altra also provided on their site. For example, there are *discussion groups* where the leaders of small home energy companies can discuss marketing strategy, procurement, planning, financing, and people issues. Says Bingham, in a Boston accent, "I'd never been in a chat room before, and before you know it, I was making friends and learning from people all over the country." In addition to discussion groups, there are auctions when distributors try to unload inventory, access to instant on-line credit, and logistics management services with regular e-mail updates that tell customers where their shipments are.

In March 2000, Bingham decided to send an e-mail about a problem with a shipment grade and pricing. It would normally take up to a month to get a response, and then there would be the usual runaround. "My e-mail was answered in less than twenty-four hours. A team descended on my place within forty-eight hours to check the shipment and analyze the problem, and the whole thing was resolved in less than a week. That was an unforgettable experience," he says.[9]

Sponsor a Collaborative Design Workshop on Customer Experience

Holding a collaborative design workshop is one of the fastest ways to come up with ideas to dramatically improve customer experience, as well as to build team alignment on their implementation.

Invite a multi-disciplinary design team. Again, whom you invite is as important as what you talk about. Remember, creative insights come from differences. The key is to invite people from all different areas of your company—the CEO, IT, marketing, product development, logistics, customer service, ethics, and so on. I also strongly suggest inviting some people from other companies in related, as well as unrelated, fields who have "customer experience" design skills. If budgets permit, include some consultants who have expertise in this area and do it every day for a living. Finally, make sure you invite customers. This will insure you have a broad cross-section of different points of view.

Spend some time socializing. Human nature is immutable. As soon as you have people who don't know each other well, or who come from different departments or businesses, you have trust issues. The best way to deal with this is to recognize and disperse them by spending some time socializing.

A more formal exercise is to ask people to introduce themselves and the role they play in the business world and then to explain that role so that other people understand it. "This is what I do as a marketing VP." "This is how I earn a living as a design engineer, or customer service specialist."

Once people have gotten to know each other somewhat, we begin the process of the CollabLab. Here again we follow the three phases of Scan, Focus, and Act to design customer experiences that Wow!

Phase One: Scan to Learn

Spend the first part of the session scanning the environment for examples of companies that provide great customer experience and those that don't. Kick it off by asking people to talk about their best and worst experiences as customers. The discussion should start far afield of your industry, and then move closer to it. For example, here's what Amazon does, or here's what VerticalNet, or Autobytel does.

Now present an example of how someone from your field is using the Web to improve customer experience. This helps to break down the mental models that there is only one right way to run this business. Once you have scanned, see if you can develop five or ten scenarios for improving customer experience in your specific business based on creative, outside-the-box thinking.

Use what Disney calls *Imagineering.* Start by asking: What is the experience that we want to sell customers? When they visit our place of business or come to our Web site, what do we need to do so that they use their credit cards with us and give us their loyalty? This could concern the design of your store, your distribution center, or a game like Play Station II.

For example, you may consider your Web-site design. Brainstorm ideas using the following questions: What theme would we give it? Think of metaphors—space, Egyptian, Las Vegas, university. What would be the look and feel of our business and the Web site that would be consistent with that theme? What would we offer, and how could we make it as easy as possible for customers to get it?

Phase Two: Focus

Once you create the scenarios of different ways to create customer experience by design, the next step is to focus on the ones that are the most creative and the most exciting and that make the most sense. One of the best ways to do this is to spend some time developing a list of four or five solution-specification criteria.

For example, for a business's Web-site design, five criteria might be: (1) States a clear and compelling message, (2) Is easy to connect to and download fast, (3) Strikes an emotional cord, (4) Takes you from easily familiar subjects and menu choices to unfamiliar innovative products and services, and (5) Is easy to navigate; two clicks to order anything.

Once you come up with the solution-specification criteria, go back to the scenarios you came up with and see which scenario or combination of scenarios best fits. If none do, you may want to call a time-out and go back and scan the horizon for more examples.

Phase Three: Act

In this stage, you emphasize to the group that we are going to design, build, and test a rapid prototype of what we have been talking about, rather than plan out what we will do separately later. This becomes an opportunity to talk about the importance of creative collaboration on a daily basis and to give people the experience of being a real design team.

For example, you could ask people to create a mock-up of a Web site, distribution center or product that is designed to give customers a certain kind of experience. Have plenty of materials on hand—magazines with pictures, scissors, tape, poster board, or whatever else is appropriate.

Again, designing and building a physical representation of whatever it is you are creating helps you to not only build shared understanding, but also to test your prototype by showing it to others or seeing how it works. The idea is to come up with something that is directionally right, then iterate. Once you have the prototype, present it to the rest of the group and get their questions and comments.

Ask them to purposely pose "What if?" questions to see if your design holds water. Embrace their feedback and then do another iteration or two until you get it right. As mentioned earlier, each iteration takes half as long and doubles the output of the previous one.

To Reinvent Your Organization, You Must Reinvent Yourself First

Triple-Loop Learning

How do you have to be different?

Write one sentence that describes how you have been as a leader with respect to designing customer experience. For example, "I have been much too product oriented. I have not paid attention to the customer's experience." Write one sentence that describes how you need to be in the future. Discuss with a friend or colleague.

Double-Loop Learning

How do you have to think differently?

Write one sentence that describes your thinking as a leader about designing customer experience. For example, "I have operated from a 'me' point of view, rather

How do you need to *be* different?

- You are what you sell! From goods and services to experiences
- From being condescending to customers to leading them
- From being a CEO, boss, proprietor to being a designer
- From being policy-and-rule bound to being empathetic
- From being a marketer to being a system designer

How do you need to *think* differently?

- From the "me" point of view to the "you" point of view
- From falling in love with your company products, services to being in love with your customers
- From focusing on designing tangibles—products, services—to focusing on designing intangibles—customer experiences
- From thinking in terms of charging for goods or services to thinking in terms of charging for the experience
- From only paying attention to whether the people in your organization are nice to paying attention to whether the back-end systems allow them to deliver

How do you need to *act* differently?

- Create a business design that wraps the delivery goods or services in an experience that is positive, unique, memorable
- Take it one step further and design a business where the products and services are used as a stage or props to produce a certain kind of experience
- Design the system not around superstars, but average people
- Find a way to systematize every aspect of the process so that you get the same, consistent experience every time. Enable with technology
- Find the right measures, use technology to keep track, and adjust your actions according to the feedback you are getting

FIGURE 5.3 A Template for Becoming a Leader Who Creates Great Customer Experiences

than a 'you' point of view in dealing with customers." Write another sentence that describes how your thinking needs to change.

Single-Loop Learning

How do you have to act differently?

Write five new behaviors that you will take on that are consistent with your new ways of being and thinking. Figure 5.3 provides a template for looking at these points.

Interlude

Pehong Chen, CEO of BroadVision

Provide the Perfect
Customer Experience Every Time

Debbie Hendrix picked up the Dell keyboard and slammed it down against her desktop. Hard. Under ordinary circumstances Debbie was a composed young woman, not prone to such outbursts. But she had reached her limit. Make that her "e-limit."

Debbie's a smart woman. She knew her problem was not the computer's fault. She even knew, much to her satisfaction (although it offered little comfort), that the problem wasn't related to a lack of technical skill on her part. The source of her frustration was clearly the mastermind behind the site we will refer to as ToyMind.com. But since a representative from ToyMind.com was nowhere to be found, the keyboard seemed to be the most appropriate, albeit innocent, surrogate for her anger.

Some might consider Debbie to be a typical "soccer mom." She is college educated, works part-time as a travel agent, drives a new SUV, is active in her small town's garden club, and is involved in many activities with her seven-year-old daughter, Madeleine. Typical mom? Yes. Typical shopper? No way. Debbie is savvy when it comes to shopping. In fact, consumers like Debbie are considered by many to be the true "leaders" of the e-economy. They call the shots. They dictate change. And they have the power to make or break a brand like never before.

At first glance, the ToyMind site is impressive. It is relatively easy for shoppers to navigate, and it boasts hundreds of items available, categorized by type of toy, age appropriateness, or general area of interest. The site even offers recommendations for those "difficult-to-buy-for" children—that is, kids who have everything. What makes the site most appealing, however, is its guarantee of offering its items at a significantly lower cost than its competitors. ToyMind.com was a soccer mom's "dream come true." Or so it appeared.

In mid-November, Debbie ordered $104 worth of merchandise for Madeleine. She was quite pleased with herself—not only had she completed her Christmas shopping so early, but she had saved money. Now, all she had to do was wait for the package to arrive a few days later. So she waited. And waited. And waited. She waited so long, in fact, that she actually forgot about placing the order in the first place. But in mid-December, Debbie remembered. She pulled out the confirmation e-mail that ToyMind.com had sent her and went about the process of checking her order. That's when her on-line shopping dream come true turned into a nightmare.

"The first indication that something was wrong came when the ToyMind site wouldn't accept my user name and password. They didn't recognize me as a customer at all. So I sent an e-mail to their customer service support center, letting them know that I had not received my items and that I could not verify my account information on their Web site. In return, I received a standardized form letter that thanked me for my message and suggested that I check my order status on-line at their Web site. It was as if they hadn't even read my note. To make matters worse, they signed their message 'the friendly folks at ToyMind.' That's when I got really frustrated. My next step was to try the customer service telephone number they publicized all over their site. Dozens of times over the next four days, I dialed that number. Instead of connecting to one of the 'friendly folks,' all I got was a busy signal. I could only imagine they were deluged with angry customers, like me, all clamoring for their purchases.

"When I finally got through on day five, the representative was, indeed, friendly. But I didn't want another friend. I just wanted my merchandise! It soon became clear that that wasn't going to happen. Even though the toys were listed as available on their Web site at the time of my order, they were, in fact, on back order. As the icing on the cake, the representative couldn't tell me when I would receive it. Needless to say, I canceled the order."

•   •   •

Debbie Hendrix canceled more than her order with ToyMind on December 17. She also canceled her relationship with them. And that's going to hurt ToyMind more than it hurts her. Consider this. Hendrix spends approximately $1,000 per year on toys for her daughter who, at age seven, has about five years of additional toy wishes bottled up inside her. That's $5,000 worth of toys. And that's $5,000 worth of potential ToyMind business that is now going somewhere else.

I heard Debbie Hendrix's story about the same time I was attending an Internet conference in New York. At the conference, dozens of Internet companies were showing off their latest gizmos and whatchamacallits, obviously building on the notion of creating a unique and memorable customer experience. While wandering among the rock-climbing walls (which, I suppose, promoted the daredevil spirit of adventure), product giveaways and buttons (which drew swarms of people to their booths), and circus performers (which certainly conveyed a "look at me!" marketing approach), I thought about Debbie. All the antics buzzing around me were intended to draw people into their sites and into their worlds. What, if anything, I wondered, would these companies be able to offer their visitors once they were sucked in? Would they understand Debbie's frustration? Were they so focused on attracting new visitors that they would, like ToyMind, ignore her once she became a customer? An image of a Venus flytrap sprang to mind . . . .

As I pondered these things, I rounded a corner and came upon a smaller display area, simple and quiet. In the center of it was a television monitor displaying the image of a man. He was speaking softly, but deliberately, to the handful of people who stood solemnly in the harsh light of the screen. The serenity of the experience stood in stark contrast to the mayhem around me. I moved closer to this select crowd to eavesdrop on what seemed an almost personal experience. It was.

The man on the screen was Pehong Chen, the founder and chairman of Broad-Vision. In hindsight, I am embarrassed that I did not know who Chen was, nor did I know that his company was—and is—on the cutting edge of e-commerce applications. My first impression was that Chen resembled an astute political statesman, albeit younger than most. I was drawn in—not by any "bells and whistles" like those employed by the other vendors—but by Chen's lack of them. It was clear that here was a man with something to say. His message, clear and to the point, was his product.

"In the e-economy, customers have the power," Chen said. "Satisfying each customer's needs is what the new game is all about. And you do that by establishing personal, one-to-one relationships with each of them."

I knew instantly that I wanted to speak to Chen about his pioneering efforts to redefine the way business is conducted in the e-world. He would certainly understand Debbie Hendrix's frustration. He would have some answers.[1]

BroadVision: Customizing the Customer Experience

The Internet provides an unparalleled opportunity for customers to collaborate with sellers in satisfying their needs. It also provides the most efficient and powerful means of customizing a relationship between the two. Amazon.com is able to create personal profiles for each of its millions of customers. When customers return to the site (and they do), they are personally welcomed and then directed to books that, based on their previous buying record, may be of most interest to them. By convincing the buyer that it is easier, more convenient—and, yes, more personal—to shop on-line, Amazon.com is stealing significant market share from traditional retail booksellers.

But it doesn't end with books. Amazon.com is banking on its customers' loyalty to serve as the foundation of a plan to offer music CDs, electronics, and other items. Traditional brick-and-mortar operations are taking notice. They see the threat that on-line businesses pose and are scrambling to establish their own presence on the Web, complete with customer profiles and personalized customer management systems. But personalizing the customer experience is no easy task.

That's where people like Pehong Chen and companies like BroadVision come in. Chen is the maverick who founded BroadVision in 1993. Relative to other multi-million dollar corporations, BroadVision is often considered a young, rambunctious child. In the world of the Internet, however, BroadVision is the granddaddy of the industry—the wise sage that others are trying so hard to emulate. In a half dozen years (barely an eye-blink in S&P 500 terms; a geologic age to Internet start-ups), BroadVision has become the leading worldwide supplier of commerce servers and one-to-one e-business applications for companies wishing to manage their individual customer relationships across an extended enterprise. What that means is that BroadVision makes e-commerce happen.

We've all probably experienced Web sites that have drawn us in, welcomed us, and given us more than we expected—be it service, information, or product. In many of these cases, it's been the BroadVision expertise running behind the scenes that makes the experience so exhilarating. The company's software products reconfigure a business's enterprise/customer relationship so that both buyer and seller get what they need in a deeply personalized way. BroadVision's one-to-one applications are things we, as consumers, don't see that allow businesses to follow their individual customers' preferences and respond to them with personalized content messages so each customer feels unique and valued.

BroadVision has enjoyed tremendous success and will continue to do so because more and more industry leaders are willing to change their mindset. They have to. As Chen points out, "The unit of value for businesses is no longer the number of transactions, but the quality of relationships you can nurture and keep and grow. If you can do that, you get a larger piece of each customer's wallet. And growing each customer you currently have is much more profitable than blindly targeting your products or service to potential new customers."

So how does BroadVision—and its growing number of competitors—deliver this value to clients? By providing the software that makes the interaction easy for the end customer and powerful for the enterprise. On top of this, the company's One-to-One Enterprise software allows its clients to manage all of their business-to-business or business-to-consumer on-line transactions, including ordering, payment, and customer service. And BroadVision can make it all happen very quickly, in as little as seven weeks.

Armed with this knowledge, it was time to talk to Chen.

Pehong Chen: Master of the Universe

Pehong Chen is a pioneer who has grown comfortable in his success. He leads BroadVision's work force of 600 and manages an impressive roster of 400-plus Global 1000 clients. He interacts on a daily basis with industry leaders from around the world, helping them to build their revenue and cut their costs while building powerful and sustainable presences on the Internet. Who, then, does a man like this turn to for advice and inspiration? His mother-in-law. "She is the 'customer' I envision for all of my clients. My goal is to work with companies to create Web sites that will cater to her needs and abilities. I know that if she can do it, anybody can do it."

This unconventional mother-in-law/son-in-law relationship has certainly paid off. BroadVision clients include the biggest names in industry—Fingerhut, Comp USA, Oracle, Hewlett-Packard, Credit Suisse, Ernst & Young, and Wal-Mart, to name a few. The company's revenues in 1999 topped $70 million and its market capitalization stands at $2.5 billion. Business is, to put it mildly, booming.

The reputation of BroadVision's forty-one-year-old chairman, president, and CEO is soaring, as well. Cited by *Business Week* in 1999 as one of the twenty-five most influential people in electronic business and a "master of the universe," Chen is a leader's leader. He is the man industry leaders turn to when they want to create a powerful presence on the Web. His advice to other potential e-leaders is straightforward and dynamic. "Move at lightning speed. Establish your brand. Become the category leader as fast as you can."

To Chen, this is accomplished first and foremost through senior-level buy-in. To be a true leader in the e-economy, you must indicate to your people that you are serious about your on-line strategy. The impact on an organization making the transition to a Web-based environment is huge. It's the leader's responsibility to set the vision and create the organizational structure to make it happen. Secondly, Chen points to the need for the development of e-leaders within organizations. These are the real movers and shakers in an organization who will make things happen. They may or may not be the most senior-level executives in the organization, but they must have full authority to implement the changes required. Finally, you must be willing to move fast. "You've got to move quickly and incrementally, with short-term goals in rapid succession. Don't try to conquer the world. Be willing to experiment and learn from the process. That's the only way to make it."

This type of advice is the philosophy that has allowed Chen to steer BroadVision to its remarkable success. With unprecedented speed and vision, he has redefined how business is conducted and shaped entire industries worldwide via the Internet.

Chen, born in Taiwan in 1957, received his Ph.D. in computer science from the University of California at Berkeley. He began his career as a project manager at the

Olivetti Research Center, where he was in charge of multimedia and user interface development. Already, the seeds of making technological solutions user-friendly were firmly planted. In 1989, with $4,000 and the revolutionary idea that technology could enable consumer interaction and information exchange, he founded Gain Technology, a multimedia software house. Three years later he sold Gain for more than $100 million to Sybase. He stayed with the new company, serving as vice president of multimedia technology with primary responsibility for the company's interactive initiatives. After a short time, he tried to retire. But being the innovator he is, he found that it wasn't the life for him. "After three months, I got restless. I suppose I have a need to create. New technology, new solutions, new companies. It's a great feeling you can't get through any other means."

In 1993, Chen founded BroadVision. "From my experience at Gain and Sybase, I knew that people were looking for ways to conduct interactive business and commerce. The Web seemed the logical place where this explosion would occur, but it was still a great wilderness at that time. Sometimes it seemed pretty lonely out there, in a landscape that appeared to have few opportunities." Fortunately, Chen wouldn't have to wait long for others to appear. Six months after founding BroadVision, the Web was recognized as a potentially powerful business environment. Netscape's browser was introduced. Then came Yahoo! Then E*Trade.

These "first-wave" start-ups found themselves in the same position as Broad-Vision—struggling to define their role in the potential new economy. "We were still developing our solution packages at the time the other players were taking off. It's a shame we missed this first generation of players. They had to build everything they needed themselves, from scratch."

Chen has more than made up for the opportunities that may have been missed with these early players. Today, BroadVision is equipped to work with anyone in e-business in any industry. But using technology to enable consumer interaction and information exchange is not for the faint of heart. BroadVision solutions can cost up to $350,000. Even at that price, there's no shortage of clients willing to pay.

A key to Chen's success is his spirit of innovation, which is driven as much by internal motivation as by external forces. "Everyone and his brother-in-law is in our business now. We can't rest. We have to continue to innovate and make progress or else our competitors will catch up with us very, very quickly. This year, BroadVision's 'battle cry' is, 'It's all about winning. Period.'" That may sound unduly aggressive, but in a cutthroat industry this sort of aggressiveness is required.

According to Chen, a successful organization needs three types of employees. An organization must have many "achievers"—that is, a number of people deeply skilled and capable of achieving goals quickly. In order to accomplish their goals, the achievers must buy into the objectives and have the freedom to work quickly and without bureaucratic restraint. A smaller group of managers make this happen. They "block and tackle" and remove the obstacles so the specialists can move forward at lightning speed. The rarest, but most critical, group of people needed in an e-organization is leaders. Above all else, these people lead by example and guide others to their vision. They are creative and willing to take risks.

Interestingly, leaders may emerge from any and all areas of an organization. In many instances, they will have no one reporting to them. "The real challenge—and at BroadVision, the real fun—lies in balancing the control within a top-down management structure in such a way that leaders are allowed to emerge. For example, there are engineers at BroadVision who are not managers, but they have made invaluable contributions as thought leaders. They are the ones who have identified capabilities we should be exploiting, often against the advice of our marketing people. They are the ones that everyone looks up to, even though no one reports to them."

It is not surprising that Chen, who has established his career on the strength of his ability to conceptualize and enable more effective customer relationships, also works to build relationships within BroadVision. He does this by treating employees as individuals, and by not doing anything that will stifle creativity or information sharing. Establishing an environment that nurtures creativity is a stumbling block for many CEOs—especially those of traditional brick-and-mortar operations. "Whereas the last generation of corporate CEOs was primarily focused on stewardship and management," Chen says, " the new generation of CEOs must be more focused on collaboration and on finding and nurturing leaders within their organizations. Successful leadership is now more closely associated with strong creativity than it is with strong management skills."

Chen certainly encourages creativity and knowledge sharing at BroadVision. As an example, weekly forums provide an opportunity for engineers and others to discuss issues. These forums are broadcast on the company's Intranet for anyone who wants to listen in or respond. Often the ideas generated and discussed lead to further research or white papers.

As for his success in leadership, Chen credits the experienced people with whom he surrounds himself and his own ability to listen to differing views. "It's vital to get feedback from, and explore possibilities with, others. When quick decisions are necessary, as they always are, everyone's perspective is important. The biggest mistake you can make is to look in the mirror for all your answers." Chen will typically consult with a half dozen BroadVision colleagues in making strategic decisions for the firm. The participants in the decision-making process may change depending on the issues being considered, and they can come from all areas and levels of the company.

Chen's passion about creating and nurturing dynamic relationships extends beyond his work with clients or his own employees. He is actively involved with the Committee of 100, an organization comprising 100 leading Chinese Americans from business, education, law, politics, medicine, and other professions. The Committee of 100 was formed in 1989 as a group whose mission is to advance the role of Chinese Americans in the United States and help to influence the thinking about policies between the United States and China. A primary goal of the group is to reflect the diversity of Chinese American leadership in this country and to serve as role models for young Chinese Americans. "It is a tremendous privilege to be involved with the committee. So many diverse talents and perspectives are represented. It's a great learning experience for me, and my involvement with these very successful people makes me a better leader."

If Chen weren't so busy leading BroadVision to its remarkable growth ("My greatest challenge is that there are only twenty-four hours in a single day") he would spend more time, he says, practicing the violin. This may seem to be an uncharacteristically solitary activity for a man so driven by enhancing relationships with others. But Chen considers the violin to be one instrument of many, playing in harmony within an orchestra. Even in his hobby, Chen is committed to his vision of working with others to establish powerful—and in this case, beautiful—relationships.

Leadership That Soars: American Airlines

American Airlines' Web site (www.aa.com), powered by BroadVision, has won numerous awards for its on-line customer management programs. It is the most popular on-line airline site, with 1.7 million site visits each week. It is also the largest personalization effort on the Web today, with the capacity to create custom pages "on the fly" for each of the airline's thirty-five million AAdvantage frequent flier program subscribers.

American realized it needed to revamp its Web presence in 1998, three years after its original launch. At that time the site had already grown to 3,000 pages. It was becoming obvious that customers were anxious to conduct business with the airlines on-line. A primary objective of the redesign was to create a site that recognized each customer individually and, from historical information based on previous AAdvantage activity, quickly generate custom-built Web pages targeting the customer's interests.

The task confronting American Airlines was quite complex. To provide the level of customization that was required, the site had to be integrated with other operating systems, the airline's existing mainframe databases, and the Sabre reservation system. BroadVision had already gained a reputation of accomplishing this type of back-end integration. But BroadVision's real strength lay in its ability to apply mass customization principles to the Web. "We knew the site had to treat individual customers in a holistic way," Pehong Chen says. "It needed to remember everything that I, as a customer, did. And it needed to tie all of my activities together in a neat package."

BroadVision's One-to-One Enterprise solution did just that. Now, when American's frequent fliers log on to the site, they immediately see their accumulated mileage points (as well as notices of when these points will expire). In addition, based on their travel histories and personal information, customers receive targeted offers from American and its marketing partners. The site is, in fact, so sophisticated and so personalized that a customer might receive a special offer on vacation travel (to the type of destination in which the customer has expressed an interest) during the week that his or her daughter is on vacation in her particular school district. Most important, the site is fully transactional and allows customers to review or change their itineraries, reserve seats, and purchase tickets with a credit card—all on-line.

The cost of this site upgrade was not cheap—about $3 million. The returns, however, are already indicating that the investment was a wise one. Record booking days now exceed $1.7 million, and American reports sales of $500 million from on-line bookings in 1999.

The notable success of American is grounded in the relatively simple notion that you can and should provide personalized attention to each of your customers—even when you have millions of them.

From Being a Great E-Tailer to Being a Great Logistician

I n Chapters 4 and 5, we looked at building a brand and providing great customer experiences. Here we will look at the final piece of the puzzle: delivering the goods.

A Buying Imbroglio

It was the season of the Web holiday 2000, the season that was to prove once and for all that the Web was the future of commerce. Everything was supposed to come together. And yet things were falling apart. It was hard to tell one dot-com from the other and difficult to find certain items in stock, to say nothing about returning unwanted items. In early December, I decided to buy my son Morgan, an actor and music aficionado, an MP3 player for the annual round of holiday gift giving. I asked a colleague where I could get one and he routed me to a Web site, which I will call "Playsounds.com." An MP3 player, which allows you to download up to twenty songs directly off the Internet, was right there in living color.

After registering and a few clicks, I had ordered the MP3 player at an attractive price and was told it I would receive it two days later, December 24, by FedEx. December 24 at about three o'clock, I got an e-mail saying my MP3 player was out of stock. It would arrive on the 26th, if that was OK. I ran to local stores, but they were out of stock too. It looked as if my son was not going to get his present on the big day. We waited all day on December 26 for the FedEx truck to arrive with the MP3 player, but it never happened.

I wrote an angry letter to "Playsounds.com," which e-mailed me back profusely apologizing, saying I would receive my player soon and that a customer service rep would contact me in twenty-four hours. I never got the call and the player hadn't arrived a week or so later. "Dad," my son e-mailed me," where's the MP3?" Another e-mail to Playsounds and another twenty-four-hour promised response didn't happen.

Around that time, I took a trip to Europe and met with a client, Philips Electronics, which is a maker of a leading-edge MP3 player. I told people there the story and they told me that MP3 players were going to be standardized like VCRs were decades ago to prevent people from "stealing music off the Internet." They said that in a few months I would be able to take the MP3 player I had ordered and throw it in the wastebasket.

I canceled the order, telling the company that it would have been nice if someone had informed me when I placed the order that it wasn't in stock and that I was ordering a hunk of junk. I was so aggravated by the experience that I told the customer service people, who responded apologetically, that I was going to use them as an example of what *not* to do in this book. Fred, the customer service person I spoke with, wrote me back a letter thanking me, saying he and the company would "really appreciate being included."

A Return Snafu

With your indulgence, I would like to tell you another story regarding the physical movement of goods and information. My brother, as mentioned in the previous chapter, saw the Gateway ads for an "upgradeable computer" and bought one. He decided, however, to send it back for a new model that was released the next week, something that the Internet order department neglected to tell him about. He sent in an order for the new model. No problem. It arrived a week later.

Returning the first computer was another matter. He called customer service and waited on voice-mail hold for twenty minutes. "Oh, you need laptop customer service; you've reached desktop customer service." He waited another twenty minutes on hold to speak to that department. He was then told, "You have to talk to billing." The person readily confided, "Billing is terrible. No one can get through to them. You should try faxing them." He sent them a six-page fax with all the info. A week later there was still no response. He sent two more faxes.

Exasperated, he went to the local outlet with his problem. After all, the ad said, "See us on the Web, call us on our 800 number, or visit our store." The customer service person said, "I am sorry, sir. We can't take this back," you have to call customer service. The store manager was called, "We need to get billing on the phone." After thirty minutes, they got no answer and gave up. The store manager suggested he send a fax. My brother, at that point, handed the store manager the papers and told him, "I am not going to do anything else to return this computer until someone from your company contacts me." The store manager said, "That's a good idea."

The Dark Side of the Internet

We are all familiar with the latest estimate from Forrester Research and the Gartner Group that the Internet will reach $1.3 trillion dollars in sales by the year 2003. Twelve and a half billion dollars was sold over the holidays in 1999 and the average purchase went up to $70 per purchase this year, from $35 the year before.

While the electronic sale of goods still represents only a small fraction of economic activity, the Web at this time in history seems to represent almost unlimited possibilities—not only as a new conveyer belt for goods and services, but as a disrupter of the way things were done in the past.

Yet as Jim Kelly, CEO of UPS, has pointed out, "The Internet has a big dark side that no one likes to talk about." There is a big difference between being able to promise anything and being able to deliver the goods. Kelly says, "Very few e-commerce companies have the means to provide a great customer experience from start to finish right now. We've heard many stories of some Internet retailers who were unable to meet the increased consumer demand, resulting in delays, and this is where UPS makes a difference." He says, "There is no such thing as a virtual package."[1]

The race to the future isn't just about which companies can reserve a domain name and establish an identity on the Web fastest. It's also about which ones can keep up with the pace of growth. The victors will be those who can get all of the products and services to customers swiftly, accurately, and cheaply. The success of the e-commerce revolution depends on an invisible back end that is coordinated, concentrated, and full of detailed hard work.

The Future of Commerce Will Be *Driven* by the Front-End Demand Creators

It's important here to pause and look at the strategic big picture, of how the entire value chain is being reinvented in light of the Web. The Internet allows almost any company, whether it is a manufacturer, distributor, or retailer, to establish a brand and then to offer unlimited shelf space for goods and services of every possible variety. At the same time, this is a big enough job that it leaves lots of room to create partnerships with companies that handle the back end.

Some e-leaders believe that, if you take this vision to the extreme, the world will have four or five e-business portals like Amazon.com, Go.com., Yahoo!, Lycos, and MSN. These portals and others will be the core of the demand chain, as the Sears catalog was in the 1900s. Their role will be to generate greater demand for better products and services. They will create demand by earning the buyer's trust and permission. They will gather and process more and more information about the buyer's tastes, desires, needs habits. Their battle cry will be to "own nothing and sell everything." They will do this by knowing more about their customers than anyone else does, as well as by renting this information out to other retailers for a fee.

Over time, in addition to the portals, a second layer of portable brands that can generate customer intimacy and trust based on their name will play a stronger role on the Web. Examples are Estee Lauder Cosmetics, Virgin brands, and Tommy Hilfiger. Based on the clout of the big, demand-creating portals and portable brands, customers will receive monthly, personalized "deal letters" through personalized Web pages with all kinds of special offerings—everything from Romanian pastrami without fat to L. L. Bean clothes and Volvos for the safety conscious.

The Future of Commerce
Will Be *Sustained* by the
Back-End Innovators and Logisticians

On the supply side of the equation, there will be even more granularized producers. Due to the increased ability to gather customer information, to connect every customer with any and every supplier, and to customerize every order, the level of demand will support greater and greater specialization.

Millions of large and small business owners around the world will provide more and more innovative products and services that are highly granulated to suit customer needs. The result is that the creator of value—the supplier—can get rich by doing one product or service extremely well. An individual who once worked for a company making modems, selling financial services, or cooking pies can now run a business from his or her own home and connect over the Internet.

Then comes the final piece of the puzzle. There is a key role for individuals and companies who can connect everyone on the demand side with everyone on the supply side. This not only includes order processing but also handling the seemingly mundane logistics of getting goods and services from the companies that provide them to the customers who buy them.

The wave of the future will be for demand-side companies to focus on building their brand and generating new customers, larger sales from existing customers, and repeat business while partnering out such functions as order processing and logistics. This is not just a matter of pushing papers across a desk, finding the right supplier, and picking and packing goods in a warehouse quickly. Instead, it's a complex set of interactions that requires networks of people, high technology, and consummate skill.

Who Do You Need to Be as a
Leader to Win the Ground War?

Jim Daniell is the thirty-something CEO of OrderTrust, an e-commerce company in Lowell, Massachusetts, that connects people on the demand creation side of e-commerce with the supply side, and ultimately the customer.[2] Daniell is the chief visionary, or what he calls "strategist of the hump" (overcoming the next challenge). The basic business model is that millions of people are buying things on the Web. OrderTrust doesn't desire to sell any of those things. Nor does OrderTrust want to get rich off anyone's transaction. What OrderTrust does desire is to make a tiny sliver of cash every time someone buys something over the Web, by making sure the correct item is delivered and making sure that the people who sold it get paid.

> It's very difficult to lead in the Internet space where there is so much money being thrown around, and things are moving so fast.

Before saying more about what Jim Daniell and OrderTrust do that allows them to "win the ground war," I want to say something about who Jim Daniell is. He is the kind of leader whose speaking is not full of braggadocio and noble certainties, but rather full of self-disclosure and far-reaching questions.

"It's very hard to lead in the Internet space, because things are moving so fast," says Daniell. "There is so much money being thrown around, it is difficult to not become like King Midas. You are constantly being presented with dilemmas and puzzles that are not easy to figure out."

Daniell says he is often deeply conflicted. "Do I stand by the values I passionately believe in and that I think will lead to the long-term success of the company, or do I drive myself and my employees into the ground?" "Should I take advantage of the huge amounts of cash regularly offered to OrderTrust to do things that fall outside our mission, or stick to the knitting?" "Do I invest millions of dollars in technology so as to be able to provide customers a quantum leap in service, or milk the cash cow that everybody seems to be happy with?"

While Daniell wants his clients' customers to have a great experience in doing transactions over the Internet, his personal experience as a result of this is one of fear. "I am constantly afraid I am going to be blindsided by my own particular perspective or make a decision that will blow up the company." Daniell is in good company; legacy CEOs like Jack Welch and Andy Grove have regularly expressed the same thoughts.

To some, Daniell's reflective stance may lead to questioning whether he knows what he is doing, but to his board and employees, it inspires trust and confidence and ultimately leads to effective action. His willingness to put aside the pretense of having all the answers and to constantly question what he takes for granted seems to make him the perfect leader for the chaotic, fast-changing world of the Internet, where beliefs and assumptions are likely to get you in trouble. Daniell pursues his questions until he hits the insights that lead to pay dirt.

Daniell is the primary architect of OrderTrust's burgeoning business, which provides an end-to-end solution for companies that are good at creating demand but want someone else to handle the supply. He essentially tells customers, "You worry about your brand and your marketing. We'll worry about everything else," or "You fret about where to click the button on your Web page. OrderTrust will take care of everything after the button gets clicked, and charge you a small fee every time that happens."

"I want to be the guy who makes the tips on the shoelaces," says Daniell. "Everything depends on those things, but nobody even notices that they are there." Though this may seem like an insignificant thing, making those shoelaces or, in this case, making sure customers get their orders delivered and clients get paid, requires a lot. It includes expediting orders, finding alternative sources, keeping customers informed, and handling financial settlements.

> **The target is to package virtual inventory so the marketer can sell anything, anytime, and deliver it quickly.**

It requires taking care of one hundred and one mundane details that add up to a difference—taking care of credit card authorizations, routing one order to multiple suppliers, routing status updates from those suppliers to customers, handling order cancellations and product returns, and driving breakthrough software development to keep these services at the leading edge.

Daniell began his career as an entrepreneur of a shoestring software company in Wellesley, Massachusetts, with twelve employees, after earning a Ph.D. in computer science. To accomplish what he has at OrderTrust, he has brought together a team of talented "A" players at the head of his company, orchestrated over 800 strategic alliances, and created a unique management culture that not only encourages leadership and teamwork, but wants people to bring their whole selves to work. (See more on this in Chapter 7.)

When I asked Daniell what kind of leadership attributes it took to "win the ground war," his answer wasn't surprising. "There are two different kinds of people in business: sellers and organizers. Selling means being a good merchant and having good marketing, knowing everything about your customers. It's clear that people can start a business by focusing in on good marketing, but it's not clear they can be successful in only doing that." Success also requires people who are good at operating call centers and logistics systems.

> We offer customers a chance to pay per drink for order fulfillment rather than spend millions of dollars upfront.

The problem has been and continues to be that all of the money that has flowed into the Web has been to build brands that are really marketing-centric. Very little money has flowed to the companies whose job it is to win the ground war. Some order fulfillment companies are good at their own operations, yet their IT systems are often inflexible and it is hard for them to connect with other dot-coms. So there is a chasm between order and delivery, and OrderTrust has filled that chasm. The result is that you, as a consumer, have a better experience because everything works.

The marketing world is about looking at everything from the eyes of the consumer and being focused on the sales event. Marketing requires such qualities as being intuitive, empathic, artistic, colorful. The operations world is different than that. It's more black and white. It's about seeing everything in the process needed to deliver the goods.

Daniell says that if you take a group of marketing and sales people and put them in a room with one hundred people from an organization walking around, the marketers will go up and initiate a conversation about people's goals, aspirations, needs, and desires. If good operations people, by contrast, wind up with the same number of people walking around in a room, their minds will automatically organize them, find out about the tasks they are performing, and see the lines connecting them.

According to Daniell, "The front end of any business is all about creating emotion around the product or service offer. The back end, which we handle, is almost void of emotion. Our Ops team is predominantly ex-military and predominantly humorless, which is something I coach them on. I have a marketing side that is emotional, but there is a part of me that is very dry, like our Ops people, because to be in this business, you have to be driven and very focused."

At this point, readers should have an intuitive sense of what side of the fence they are on. Are you a marketing and demand-creating type or are you more the operations type? If you had to characterize your organization in the same way, which side of the fence would it wind up on? It's important to honestly answer these questions, because it will empower you to determine whether you want to take a do-it-yourself approach to the logistics of your organization or create a strategic partnership.

If you decide that you and your organization are suited both to strategic demand creation and operations excellence, then you need to discover and call forth the kind of leadership qualities that Daniell and OrderTrust embody. If you decide, however, that you are best suited to focusing only on the brand and demand creation, it makes sense for you and your organization to create strategic partnerships with other firms. This in itself will require that you discover and call forth new leadership qualities.

To realize your strategy, you will need to give up the illusion of control and be willing to invest in a long-term partnership with others. You will also need to adopt a spirit of cooperation and an attitude of openness, which are necessary to making any partnership succeed. You will need to share your front-end market strategy with your back-end order fulfillment center (OFC) or logistics partner, so that it can formulate a strategy that will make your operations a competitive weapon. This means sharing once closely guarded information about who your customers are, what they order and when, who your preferred suppliers are, and how to work with them in a way that makes sense.

You will also need the leadership communication skills necessary to build the level of trust needed for long-term alliances, together with negotiation and conflict management capability skills. Finally, you will need to be able to generate an organizational culture where this is all deeply embedded.

What Kind of Mindset Do Leaders Need to Win the Ground War?

Balance a marketing and branding focus with a corresponding focus on order fulfillment and distribution systems.   Think beyond your Web site. As with any e-business, it's important to build your brand and create a strong Web presence. This allows you to attract Web shoppers, just as good merchandising will allow you to convert them into buyers. But many marketing and sales people don't think beyond their Web sites. The result is that they often overreach in terms of what they can offer to customers and are not able to deliver the goods on time and in good condition. Their inability to keep their promises results in brand pollution and lost customers.

It's important, then, for companies to not only have a forum or strategic conversations about their Web site from a marketing perspective, but also from the perspective of operations. Furthermore, in the words of an old blues song, "the right hand has to know what the left hand do." Whenever this is not the case, serious problems arise. For example, L. L. Bean in Freeport, Maine, the nation's largest outdoor e-commerce catalog company, with sales of $1.2 billion, found itself in a distribution dilemma a few years back.

The skyrocketing demand caused by big investments in marketing had taken the people who ran the famous distribution center by surprise. It didn't matter that the OFC had been a compulsory stop for catalog cognoscenti on benchmarking tours throughout the '80s and '90s for companies like Nike, Disney, Gillette, and Chrysler. The problem was that the old big-batch system that sent hundreds of orders to the warehouse every twelve hours to be processed by pickers and packers could not handle the proliferation of items sold or get them out the door fast enough.

"We had to go to our marketing division and say that, without a new facility, we simply could not handle any new product offerings," says Jim Helming, senior manager of operations. "Their product line had expanded to the point where they could no longer accommodate up to 150,000 orders a day for 1.2 million products that often included embroidery, monogramming, and customer tailoring. On top of this, orders on any given day would need to be sent to scores of countries throughout the world. People were literally tripping over each other to get the stuff out the door."

The result was that L. L. Bean established a breakthrough project to reinvent the company's distribution center for the millennium. The project involved the participation of hundreds of Bean's people, including many marketing and sales people, each of whom was assigned to a team that was focused on a specific task. Now it was Bean's turn to benchmark order fulfillment and logistics operations in places like Germany and Scandinavia that used advanced technology. This was followed by many multi-disciplinary brainstorming sessions that included people from all levels and areas of the company.

The net result was that the distribution center was completely reinvented. Bean replaced the big-batch system, at twelve-hour intervals, with something called Wave Pick Technology. Instead of holding orders for twelve hours, the computer now dispatches them directly to the OFC. There, team leaders track the activity level in the warehouse and decide which pickers and packers can handle new orders.

Instead of pickers and packers running all over the warehouse with trucks to gather the orders, individual orders are broken down into different parts—duck boots, tents, woven belt, fly rod, winter pajamas. Pickers, who stay in one part of the warehouse, place each component on a conveyer belt and, with bar code scanners, automatically sort the orders and send them to packing stations where FedEx picks them up. It used to take days to process some orders. Today, orders are processed within twenty-four hours and, in most cases, less than two hours elapse between the time an order comes in over the Web site or phone and the time it's ready for FedEx to deliver it.[3]

The moral of the story is this. Every bit of thinking and effort you make to expand your marketing prowess, whether over the Web or elsewhere, should be balanced by a corresponding effort to create a tightly focused order fulfillment and distribution system. If it's not in the cards for you to do that yourself, either by temperament or resources, you need to find someone else who can do that for you.

Go direct and leverage logistics across the supply chain. According to Richard Owen, CEO of Avantgo.com and former chief of Dell on-line, "From the beginning, we figured we could sell to customers directly without the need for a bricks-and-mortar dealer and without the need for the dealer's markup." Owen explains, "If you can offer a better price, better service, and the latest technology directly to the customer, why would you have to sell through a dealer?"[4]

The answer is, you don't, but you do need to reinvent yourself and create a virtual supply chain that eliminates time, cost, and waste. It's important to keep in mind that in 1990 when the then tiny Dell began to emerge on the scene, industry giants like Compaq used to have eighty days of inventory on hand. By selling directly to customers, the upstart Dell Computer was able to slash the inventory and its costs to almost nothing, while speeding up deliveries to customers.

Think in terms of inventory in motion versus inventory at rest.   Of course, for Dell to do this required a lot of help from its logistics partner, Fred Smith of FedEx, who brainstormed with Dell how to create an electronically connected virtual supply chain that not only eliminated the retailer but the distributor, warehouse, and freight forwarder as well. Says Smith, "The only reason a warehouse exists is as a place to put things so that you know that you've got it. It has no economic value in its own right."

"We understood that if you let everybody know where the order or product (or the components to make it) are, you could eliminate warehouses. That's why information is important to us. It allows our customers to keep custodial control of their products while in transit. They don't need to have inventory stuck some place. Our trucks and planes are really 550 mph warehouses. What we are really doing for our customers is not just transportation, we are doing fast-cycle distribution in lieu of inventory investment for customers."[5]

Turn just-in-time delivery into a competitive marketing weapon.   The Home Depot chain not only serves the do-it-yourself market, but building contractors. It is using e-commerce to transform itself from just being a chain that provides products into a network of services. Small building contractors, which are Home Depot's most valuable customers, are given a password to reach a site that is replete with useful applications. The builder provides details of the job he has to do and the Web site tells him what construction materials he needs, how to schedule his work, and what glitches or holdups he is likely to encounter.

Home Depot is not only able to provide instant confirmation about the availability of products from its suppliers, the Web site will ask whether the customer would like the materials delivered to the construction site and whether they should arrive in one big bundled shipment or just-in-time. Also, if the builder needs a carpenter, electrician, or plumber, and the subs he normally uses are not available, Home Depot will publicly list the particulars of the job on its site and operate as a talent pool and labor exchange.

The builder reaps lots of benefits as a result. He saves time in planning his job, he has access to expert advice, no longer has to over-order materials to make sure he has them, and doesn't have to carry extra stock, as he knows there is plenty in the warehouse. This gives the builder a better chance of competitively bidding on jobs, as well as a better chance of completing jobs on time and under budget.

There are advantages for Home Depot too. Because it operates a virtual value chain between its customers and its suppliers, it doesn't have to carry as much inventory. It also gains a ton of information about its customers and builds intimacy by developing deeper relationships with them in the process of providing services. If it cares to pass customer information onto its suppliers, it can help them to reduce their production, inventory, and capital costs as well.

Sponsor a Collaborative Supply-Chain Design Workshop

While many e-business leaders are entranced with creating growth strategies and companies with meteoric growth potential, few put time or creative thought into how to leverage their supply chain logistics for decisive competitive advantage. Yet, this is precisely what the most successful companies of the last decade or so have done—companies like Wal-Mart, Dell, and FedEx.

Here are some guidelines for sponsoring a Collaborative Supply-Chain Design Workshop.

1. Ask: Who can add value to this collaboration?   Invite the entire top management group, as well as a healthy cross-section of people from both the brand-demand side and the supply side of your organization. Invite logistics experts from companies that represent potential partners—OrderTrust, FedEx, UPS—to participate, as well as representatives from world-class companies that you can learn from—Wal-Mart, Dell, Ikea. In most cases, representatives of these companies will consider it an honor, particularly if you are having your meeting near Disneyland or a world-famous golf course.

2. Spend some time socializing and getting to know each other as human beings.   Another good icebreaker for this step is something I call "*checking in*" and "*checking out.*" Ask people to introduce themselves and say whatever is on their minds so that they can be fully present at the meeting. "Hi, my name is John Jesper. I work at the Order Fulfillment Center at L.L. Bean. I am excited to be here, but there is one thing on my mind. My wife is expecting, so if I get a phone call, I hope you'll understand. Anyway, I'm checking in." Ask people to check out at the end of the day, by saying whatever is on their mind and concluding with the words, "I'm checking out."

3. Quickly review your strategic e-business marketing plan or demand-creation strategy.   You want everyone in the room to be operating in the same world. Talk about what your plans are for building your brand, how you intend to establish a Web identity, and so forth. Also, show what you are planning to do to make sure that the customer has a great quality experience in dealing with your company. Leave thirty to sixty minutes for questions and answers.

4. Review your current supply-chain strategy with an emphasis on where you are now.   It's important in this phase of the design workshop to establish what your supply-chain goals have been to date and your process for delivering on them. Cover one long wall in the room with flip-chart paper. Then map out in detail the entire supply-chain process. Include everything that happens from the time a customer orders something on your Web site or wherever to when it is delivered. Show each link in the supply-chain process, for example: an order is made, it goes to OFC, to a supplier in Singapore, to a freight forwarder, to a warehouse, and so on.

5. Set some breakthrough supply-chain goals.   Some questions to ask when setting breakthrough goals for your supply chain might be: Today we deliver 95 percent of our orders in a week. What would we need to do to deliver them in 36 hours? Or 85 percent of our deliveries contain all the things the customer ordered. How could we increase that to 95 percent? I suggest that you set these goals in a couple of iterations. Set them, take a break, and come back to them again after pondering. The first time your group looks at them, you should be declaring powerful new possibilities. The second and/or third time you look at the goals, look from the point of view of what would be realistic to commit to. At this point, the goals should be challenging but attainable.

6. Identify what's missing that would make a difference.   It may be very useful before getting into the meat of the session to take an outside benchmarking trip, hear a presentation from an outside expert on what other successful companies have done to improve their supply chain, and read some outside articles for ideas. Then go back and look at the supply-chain map that you created. One line of investigation for the group might be to ask: What's working and what's not working? How could we optimize the way it is working today without breaking a sweat?

Then take a second more radical line of questioning. How can we create a more *direct* relationship with customers? What links in the supply chain represent unnecessary complexity and waste and, therefore, could be reduced or eliminated? How could the proper use of e-business technology or information be used to reduce mass, speed up cycle time, and reduce costs?

7. Design short-term, high-leverage breakthrough projects. Select a couple of high-leverage projects that can be accomplished in weeks, not months, that, if implemented, could represent a strategic advantage for your company. For example, in 1995, the FedEx CIO, Dennis Jones, and a few IT guys spent two weeks hammering out some rudimentary software scripts connecting the company's mainframe package-tracking system to the fedex.com Web site. The result was that visitors could pinpoint the exact location of their packages by simply entering a tracking number. This became a huge competitive advantage.

> *"Sam Walton told me that while everybody thought he was a great retailer, he was in reality a great logistician."* Fred Smith, CEO, FedEx

Please make sure you refer to the Collaborative Design Workshop accelerators in Chapter 2.

To Reinvent Your Organization, You Must Reinvent Yourself First

Triple-Loop Learning

How do you need to be different?

Write one sentence that describes who you have been with respect to the back end of your business. For example, "Order fulfillment and logistics are boring." Write

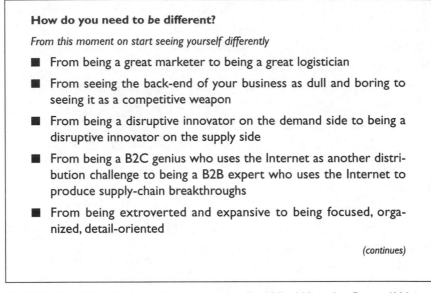

How do you need to *be* different?

From this moment on start seeing yourself differently

- ■ From being a great marketer to being a great logistician
- ■ From seeing the back-end of your business as dull and boring to seeing it as a competitive weapon
- ■ From being a disruptive innovator on the demand side to being a disruptive innovator on the supply side
- ■ From being a B2C genius who uses the Internet as another distribution challenge to being a B2B expert who uses the Internet to produce supply-chain breakthroughs
- ■ From being extroverted and expansive to being focused, organized, detail-oriented

(continues)

FIGURE 6.1 A Template for Becoming a Leader Who Wins the Ground War

one sentence that contains your leadership declaration for the future. For example, "I am going to master fast-cycle logistics."

Double-Loop Learning

How do you need to think differently?

Write one sentence that describes your mindset around logistics. "We can handle this ourselves, we have a fine warehouse." Write one sentence that describes a new mindset that is consistent with your leadership declaration.

Single-Loop Learning

How do you need to act differently?

Write one sentence that describes your current behavior concerning the supply-chain aspects of your business. Write one sentence that describes behavior you will abandon or adopt. Figure 6.1 is a template that will guide you in this exercise.

(continued)

How do you need to *think* differently?

From this moment on start thinking differently

- From thinking that your strategy of preeminence should be based on "big sales volumes" to thinking that it should be based on "winning the ground war"

- From thinking that what you can sell is limited to your warehouse to thinking that, through a virtual supply chain that runs at Net speed, you can sell anything to anyone, anyplace

- From thinking that your business can only make money on the demand creation side selling B2C to thinking your business can make money on the supply side selling B2B

- From seeing inventory at rest in your warehouse (tying up working capital) to seeing inventory in motion—i.e., fast cycle production and distribution, freeing up working capital

- From seeing the back-end of your business as something you need to do "inside" (hence an obstacle to getting started in e-business) to seeing it as something that can be outsourced

How do you need to *act* differently?

From this moment on start acting differently

- Look at how you can use the Internet to produce breakthroughs in order fulfillment, production cycles, inventory management, logistics, accounts receivable

- Create 2 to 3 breakthrough projects to streamline your e-commerce supply chain based on the above

- Look for ways to use information to dramatically speed up your company's flow of goods, and to reduce costs and waste

- Create a direct electronic connection to improve interoperability between yourself and your most important business partners on the supply side of your business

- Improve your ability to be a good partner whether you are on the demand creation side of the e-commerce puzzle or the supply side

FIGURE 6.1 A Template for Becoming a Leader Who Wins the Ground War

Interlude

David Roussain, EVP of FedEx E-Commerce

Win the Ground War!

Nickie Ballentine cautiously ascends the spiral staircase of the gritty-turned-urbane loft space, turns on the fifth step and raises her fluted glass to the thirty bright faces looking up at her. This is the moment she, and they, have been waiting for. In five minutes, at 12:01 a.m., Eastern Standard Time, cafebadaboom.com will "go live."

"We have built an amazing thing," she begins. "We have sacrificed months of our lives, months from our families and friends, months of our sanity—all for this moment. Some people think we're crazy. You've probably heard, as I have, people question the very premise of our work. 'Who in the world is going to buy place mats and salt and pepper shakers on-line?'" Her audience laughs in agreement. "My answer to them is, 'lots of people.' Today is our moment of truth. Thanks to all of you for helping us get to this exciting point."

As the applause subsides, she makes her way to a PC on which the home page of www.cafebadaboom.com is displayed. "Thirty seconds," Henry barks from the back of the room. Nickie holds her breath. She imagines her colleagues are doing the same. If they can get a few hundred orders placed the first day, she will be able to prove to her investors—not to mention her husband and family—that she knew what she was talking about. "But," she wonders, "have we done enough to generate demand? Are the print and television advertising going to be distinguishable in the marketplace? Will the coupons for free merchandise lure anyone in?"

Nickie crosses her fingers, something she hasn't done since elementary school. The Web has made her superstitious again. At 12:03 it happens. The first order is placed—for a copper-bottomed saucepan. Nickie smiles. "At least one person knows we're out here," she says quietly. Her colleagues are laughing around her, straining in for a better look at the screen.

The first order is followed quickly by numbers two, three, and four. Then there is a pause. The crowd around the PC grows quiet. Ten seconds pass. Twenty. Twenty-five. Silence. Then it happens. Unexpected. Unrehearsed. And, most important, unmanageable. Hundreds of orders pour in, simultaneously. The counters that have been set up to register the number of hits and orders spin in an unrecognizable blur. The crowd around Nickie erupts in cheers.

Nickie, however, is not cheering. She stares at the figures rolling by—300, 400, 450, 500. Cafebadaboom.com has sold more merchandise in ten minutes than Nickie thought would be sold in a day. This is a huge problem. One she should have foreseen. At this rate, her supply chain will collapse. She has the inventory in stock. She simply doesn't have the systems in place to fulfill this number of orders.

It's a problem she never dreamed of. But she should have.

●   ●   ●

We've all heard of Internet start-ups that have found themselves in Nickie Ballentine's predicament—facing a huge customer demand and unable to deliver. It is common for new e-commerce leaders to focus on the tactics that will generate interest in their Internet products and services. It is equally common for them to pay much less attention to the issues impacting the supply side of the equation. Perhaps these leaders believe that supply-chain management is a tool that can be applied or modified once a certain level of demand is realized. Not so. By then, it's too late. As Nickie will sadly learn, there's nothing that will drive a customer from your site faster than a broken promise.

Supply-chain management and customer fulfillment entail everything that occurs from the time a consumer clicks on an order button to the moment that the merchandise is delivered to his or her door. This includes many elements that are transparent to the consumer—inventory management, logistics planning, warehousing, credit card security, and so forth—as well as elements that are more visible, such as the delivery of the actual merchandise on a timely basis. Ensuring that demand can be met requires much more than product transportation and delivery systems. It requires, above all, the ability to manage huge amounts of information about your customers, suppliers, and distributors to ensure optimal customer service.

While the race seems to be about which new companies can get their domain name and brand identity on the Web fastest, that's only half the battle. The real winners will be those who can manage their growth and supply products to consumers accurately, swiftly, and economically. This is the part of business that many people relegate to the back burner. Unfortunately, it's typically a costly and irreversible decision.

Comprehensive supply-chain expertise, grounded in complex information management systems, is being offered today by what might appear to be an unlikely source—Federal Express. That's right. FedEx, the company that most of us trust to move our packages anywhere in the world overnight—absolutely, positively. What fewer of us realize is how FedEx is repositioning itself as the end-to-end provider of supply-chain management for e-business enterprises. Nickie could certainly have benefited from a partnership with FedEx. Perhaps you could, too.

Absolutely, Positively FedEx

I have a confession to make. While FedEx is a groundbreaking company that's making exciting and innovative inroads in the dot-com supply-chain area, I have another, more personal, reason for including them in this book. Simply put, I love this company.

Silly, I know. I mean, I come into contact with hundreds of inspiring companies each year. I help many other creative businesses put themselves on the map by positioning a radical new idea or product that will change the way we conduct business. And I'm constantly meeting leaders who propose that they are launching "the next big thing." Yet, among all of these wonderful organizations, FedEx remains one of my favorites.

Part of the reason comes from the admiration I have always felt for FedEx founder and CEO Fred Smith. Smith singlehandedly invented the overnight package delivery business in the early 1970s and has grown FedEx into a $17 billion company that now operates the world's second largest airplane fleet and handles 1.2 billion customer transactions per year. He's obviously doing something right.

One of the things he's done right is generate trust between customers and the company. I believe that FedEx will get my packages where they need to go—absolutely and positively. So do millions of other customers. This trust is grounded not so much in the complex information, tracking, and transportation systems that underlie much of the company's work (but remain fairly transparent to the average customer), but in the personal attention I receive from FedEx employees. They understand the importance of the packages I am sending and receiving.

Finally, my affection for this company is rooted in a personal anecdote that occurred many years ago. I was in California when I received a long-overdue payment. Naturally, I was ecstatic, but there was a problem. I was in LA. My business and my employees who were anxiously awaiting the payment were in Boston. This was before the time of electronic wire transfers and certainly before the time of ATMs. I needed to get the check to my office immediately, yet I wasn't returning to Boston until the following week. By then, Boston Electric would probably have shut out the lights. As I was pondering what to do, I noticed a FedEx truck coming toward me. What the hell? I thought. I flagged the driver over and, much to my surprise, in a matter of moments, he had helped me with my situation. FedEx would deliver the check directly to my bank by 10 the following morning. We would be able to pay our employees—and the phone company, the landlord, and a whole host of people—by tomorrow afternoon. I am still grateful for that FedEx driver who came to my aid and for the company that instilled that philosophy and work ethic in its drivers. On that dusty street in Santa Monica, FedEx made a customer for life.

So, as I recognized the importance of companies being able to win the ground war in the new economy, I naturally thought of FedEx. I did not know, but was soon to learn through several conversations with David Roussain, the executive vice president of e-commerce, that FedEx is much more than a package-delivery business. It is positioning itself as the leading provider of integrated supply-chain solutions for its clients. FedEx is not only winning the ground war for itself, but for hundreds of small and mid-sized companies that are recognizing the value and expertise FedEx brings to the supply table.[1]

According to Laurie Tucker, senior vice president of e-commerce and customer service at FedEx, "This company has always listened to the customer. Now, it's about anticipating the customer."[2] What FedEx is anticipating is a need for supply-chain and logistics consulting services that FedEx is uniquely positioned to offer. Granted, the back-end mechanisms may be less glamorous than the front-end Web designs, but they are critical to the success of an organization. FedEx is counting on the emerging dot-coms to recognize this. "This is absolutely the way the world is going to work," says Fred Smith. "If we aren't successful in this area, we're not going to be successful at all."[3]

Identifying the Battles

To fully understand FedEx's position in the e-commerce ground war, one must appreciate the company's brief, but revolutionary, history. Particularly telling has been the company's ability to predict consumer demand and transform itself to be able to meet that demand.

In the late 1960s, information technology emerged as an important enabler for a wide array of businesses. In fact, mainframe computer systems were replacing thousands of employees in positions that required fast calculations and information processing. Fred Smith, a Yale University student, realized that business's emerging reliance on computers would translate into a reliance on express transportation of replacement parts. After all, reasoned Smith, businesses couldn't afford to stock all of the expensive parts they might need. At the same time, businesses couldn't afford to have data processing come to a grinding halt while parts were shipped via slow, conventional freight services. The time was right, he thought, for the formation of an express delivery and transportation business.

Few people agreed with him. His initial college paper proposing the idea of the new company earned only a "C" from his professor. Undaunted, in 1971 he set out to establish the Federal Express Corporation, but he had difficulty obtaining financing. Finally, in April 1973, with 389 employees, the Federal Express Corporation was operational. It delivered fewer than 200 packages per night.

From these humble beginnings, however, FedEx grew rapidly. Within ten years, the company was an American household name and had reached $1 billion in revenues. The company expanded its operations in the 1980s to the European and Asian markets. By the end of the '80s, FedEx was providing service to more than 100 nations. In this way, customers were driving the company's success. By responding to customer needs—wherever they were located—FedEx spread its brand *"when it absolutely, positively has to get there overnight"* throughout the world. FedEx had single-handedly created (and won) the first revolution—the invention of overnight shipping anywhere in the world. As former U.S. Senator Howard Baker has said, "Fred Smith is the only man I have known who created an entire industry."

A large part of the company's success was due to an ambitious initiative undertaken in 1979, when the company created its powerful internal computer network called COSMOS. The system not only enabled FedEx employees to get real-time status reports on the exact location of a shipment, it also made the information available to customers who called a toll-free number. This level of "just-in-time" customer service was unheard of in the shipping industry and heralded additional advances, such as the company's high-speed scanning technology and hand-held tracking computers. With its transportation network secured, FedEx looked toward its information architecture to exploit the second revolution in the company's brief history.

In the mid-1980s, Fred Smith extended the information architecture of COSMOS to provide real-time shipment information directly to the customer on-line. Given the success of COSMOS as an internal information network, Smith recognized the potential savings and efficiencies that could be garnered if customers could order shipping services electronically. So FedEx engineered it.

In 1987, the company developed FedEx PowerShip, a stand-alone terminal that was given to FedEx's best customers and linked directly to the company's COSMOS system. For the first time, customers could place their own shipping orders electronically and print airbills. And for the first time, customers could manage their shipping services electronically. This advancement was important, not only in that it dramatically improved customer service and efficiency, but also because it marked one of the world's earliest e-commerce applications.

In 1994, FedEx built on this program with FedEx Ship, which brought the power of electronic transactions to front-office personnel with desktop computers. Any user could ship, print airbills, track, and report deliveries with ease. During this same year, FedEx launched www.fedex.com. The site, which offered general information about the company and shipping rates, also gained significant press attention because it offered something very few sites did at the time—real functionality. The site actually *did* something by offering real-time tracking through its COSMOS system. Shortly thereafter, fedex.com was improved to allow users to complete and print shipping labels over the Internet.

This marked a new era for the Internet and the World Wide Web. As former Netscape CEO (and former FedEx CIO and COO) Jim Barksdale said, "It was the first outward and visible demonstration of a practical, productive use of the Internet by a real business for a real business purpose."[4] It is ironic that a company formed to support the emerging information technology industry would, within twenty years, be leading that same industry. It continues to do so today, as it launches its third revolution—delivering fully integrated customer-driven supply-chain systems.

This third revolution is grounded in the explosion of e-business opportunities, which are no longer constrained by geography or limited consumer choice. Internet traffic doubles every one hundred days, and a 70 percent annual growth rate is predicted for Internet access and hosting over the next five years. As more customers turn to the Web, they gain greater access to merchants all over the world. Coupled with greater access to international merchants is the trend in business toward "fast-cycle" logistics. Businesses have recognized that in order to maximize productivity, they must maximize the velocity of movement of goods through their supply chains. They must meet customer demand without increasing overhead. This means they must eliminate inefficiencies. However, to take advantage of these global and cost-saving opportunities, merchants will require sophisticated information management and delivery systems to ensure customer satisfaction. That's where FedEx is positioning itself today.

Today, FedEx e-commerce solutions are enabling customers to expand their market reach and customer service capabilities while minimizing their investments in inventory and infrastructure. These solutions, illustrated in Figure 6.1, allow businesses to integrate FedEx's transportation and information systems with their own.[5] Let's go back to Nickie Ballentine and cafebadaboom.com to see how such an integrated system might have worked.

Cafebadaboom.com is a Web site that allows customers to place orders. By using FedEx-supplied coding, the order would be transmitted directly through a

Complete Solutions

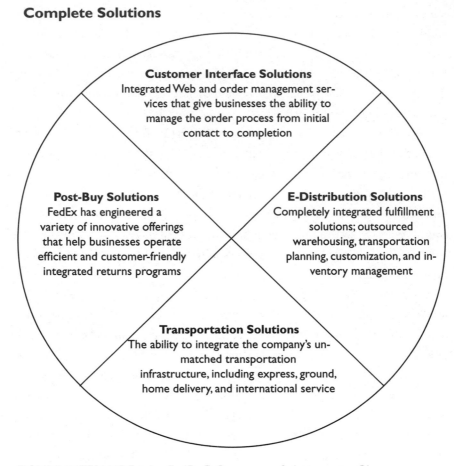

FIGURE INTERLUDE 6.1   FedEx E-Commerce Solutions at a Glance

FedEx server to a FedEx warehouse where a just-in-time stock of products is maintained. That's right. FedEx would own and manage the cafebadaboom warehouse. Once an order is placed, FedEx would send a confirmation to the company and to the customer, and the product would be shipped that day. If the customer needed to return any cafebadaboom merchandise, he or she would contact FedEx NetReturn System, which would in turn notify cafebadaboom of the pending return. FedEx would then send a courier to retrieve the product and return it to the warehouse. In this way, all of the fulfillment headaches would have been handled by FedEx, an organization used to the complications involved in managing a supply chain. Ballentine could have stayed focused on generating even more demand from her customers.

Through its e-commerce offerings, FedEx is positioning itself as a leader in information—as well as in package distribution. The real revolution occurring in the world of information management can be seen in companies like Dell, Proflowers, Garden.com, and Acer, all of whom benefit from fully integrated supply-chain management systems that meet their specific needs. According to Tom Peters, author of *In Search of Excellence,* "It's been a distribution revolution, and FedEx has led the way." In helping its clients re-engineer their supply chains, FedEx has had to ramp up its own information management systems over the years. In fact, many people don't realize that FedEx has built the third largest private computer network in the world or that it operates the most extensive client-server network in the world, handling more than 100 million information requests each day.

FedEx is no longer the simple transport company of thirty years ago. It is one of the largest, most successful information and supply-chain management companies in the world. It has engineered its successes by focusing on customer needs and providing end-to-end supply and distribution management systems that best meet those needs. The company's philosophy has been generally simple: *Identify a customer need and figure out a way to deliver a solution.*

Sometimes, however, even a leader like FedEx needs help from other leaders in recognizing customer frustrations and possible solutions. Enter David Roussain.

Leading the Revolution(s)

David Roussain knows a thing or two about leading change—in his own life and within the companies for which he's worked. Armed with a degree in mechanical engineering and a years-long interest in cars, Roussain joined Goodyear Canada where he remained for a year and a half. "I realized I was just building what others told me to build. That wasn't for me. I wanted to get into a business where I could decide what to build." In 1987, he formed his own company, Applications Software, which wrote industrial process software for several clients, including Goodyear. Within seven years, Applications Software had the dominant presence in its southern Ontario market. "I had achieved everything I wanted to achieve with the company, and I was ready for a change." This readiness for change led Roussain to Hewlett-Packard in 1994.

As business planning manager for HP's $8.2 billion North American retail business, Roussain became quite familiar with high-volume, high-velocity products and the importance of efficient supply-chain management. "In any given month," remembers Roussain, "we would move more than a million inkjets, laserjets and scanners through the supply chain into the retail channel and out to the customers. When you're talking about a million units per month, and each of those units has to be associated with a perfect customer experience . . . well, you can imagine the complexities involved with that." Indeed. Roussain offered an example of a miscalculated sales forecast that resulted in 800,000 printers being stockpiled in HP warehouses. "To give you an idea of how many printers that is," Roussain explains, "consider that end-to-end, these boxes would stretch for sixty miles. They would fill twenty-two jumbo jets. They could be used to build a wall around the HP factory that was four miles long, two rows deep and ten rows high. Obviously, getting your forecast right and having inventory management in place is a very important thing. The moral of this story is that the more flexible and responsive your supply chain is, the better off you're going to be."

In 1997, Roussain was promoted to direct HP's e-commerce strategy and simultaneously develop the HP Shopping Village, which provides on-line sales of HP products. In this capacity, he led a team of sixty-five people that created the Web site's presentation layer, as well as all the back-end support systems, including logistics, distribution, procurement, inventory management, accounting, and billing. A goal of the new Web site was to provide an easy and convenient channel through which the growing number of home-office workers and smaller dot-com organizations could receive the same quality of service and order fulfillment as HP's institutional customers, who typically ordered HP products in bulk. This would shift HP's business model considerably—from fulfilling a manageable number of large orders to fulfilling a very large number of small orders. Related to this were the goals of reducing refurbished and new product inventories and increasing sales.

To help him develop the most appropriate solution, Roussain pulled together a high-level team comprising eight people with different areas of responsibility. The team first created the vision for HPShoppingVillage.com and then worked with their respective teams to build the solution. Roussain realized that partnering with an expert in product distribution would provide HP the supply-chain systems it required. He approached FedEx for this role for a number of reasons. "We chose FedEx because we knew that customer service was going to be a major part of our value proposition. FedEx certainly had an advantage in dealing with customers, based on its solid reputation. We knew that FedEx could get our product to the customer. They were also masters at high-velocity fulfillment of many smaller orders."

But Roussain saw the potential for a relationship with FedEx that would go well beyond shipping products to customers. "FedEx had mastered several components of distribution that were very appealing to us. They were experts in warehousing, in shipping, and in information management. They had successfully integrated these single components into the distribution systems of many large clients. Yet, we knew of no case in which FedEx had bundled its services in these discrete areas for a client." That didn't deter Roussain from approaching FedEx with the idea of integrating and managing HP's entire warehousing, inventory, and shipping operations.

Surprisingly, Roussain had to convince FedEx that it would be able to provide a comprehensive e-commerce solution for HP. "In this solution, FedEx evolved with us. They had never done anything like this before and were a bit skeptical that they could carry it off." But carry it off they did. The HP/FedEx solution involved both companies working together—and with BroadVision (see interlude after Chapter 5)—to create the front-end Web site. FedEx then established a warehouse and inventory system in Memphis, which was linked electronically to the BroadVision-supported HP Web site.

Because of this integration, when customers place an order through the HP Web site, product availability is immediately verified. "This is critical," says Roussain, "because you need to have real-time visibility to understand what is happening in the warehouse. If, for example, you're out of stock, you cannot charge a customer's credit card. FedEx's integrated system allowed us to know what was in stock at any given moment and, therefore, better serve our customers. The tools that FedEx has for this are not commonly available. They gave us a distinct advantage."

FedEx was also selected to manage the implementation of the integrated solution, which included the components just mentioned and also the call center, all logistics functions, and a critical returns program. The HP/FedEx solution is represented graphically in Figure 6.2.[6]

The results of this partnership have been impressive. HPShoppingVillage.com has become one of the Web's largest consumer retail sites since its 1998 launch and has experienced revenue growth of 500 percent annually. It has been ranked number one in retail revenue, number seven in overall revenue and number three in the best PC "product sites" category by *PC Computing* magazine. The time it takes to process returned items has dropped from fifteen days to two, and the overall per-unit cost of returns has decreased 80 percent, from $100 to just $20.

Naturally, HP is delighted with these results. FedEx, however, is even more delighted. With Roussain's insistence, the company was pushed toward offering a truly comprehensive, integrated e-business solution. Roussain made FedEx realize that it was well positioned for an entirely new—and potentially lucrative—business segment. Is it any surprise that FedEx asked Roussain to join its team and lead its e-commerce strategy development?

The New Revolutionary

Roussain was a natural choice. He was, after all, familiar with the needs of FedEx customers. He had been one of them. And what he wanted while at HP was what he believed many other customers would want in the future—an integrated solution that leveraged FedEx's distribution and supply-chain strengths.

"It's a logical extension of service for FedEx," says Roussain. "We developed discrete customer automation devices in the mid–'80s that provided electronic connectivity. Full integration through the Internet was the next step." Ironically, FedEx had already achieved this next step. It simply hadn't realized it. "FedEx had the capability to implement electronic integration with clients for some time. We had been doing it with clients, but in piecemeal fashion. Because of this, many people at FedEx didn't realize how valuable this integration capability would be to clients. I knew that companies—particularly dot-com start-ups—were looking for managed solutions that integrated order fulfillment and shipping."

Roussain saw medium and small businesses and emerging dot-coms as a vitally important new market segment for FedEx. FedEx has, for years, promoted the importance of business-to-business (B2B) opportunities. This is the trend that ana-

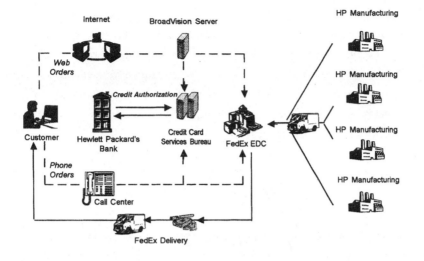

FIGURE INTERLUDE 6.2   HPshoppingvillage.com Ordering and Distribution Process

lysts are most interested in, and that is one of the reasons that B2B services make up such a large segment (99 percent) of FedEx's current offerings. However, the business-to-consumer (B2C) market is poised to explode, and if David Roussain has anything to say about it, this will become the company's primary revenue source. In fact, the company is already making inroads here with the development of FedEx Home, which provides retailers a cost-effective means of providing residential shipping. "The distinct strategy here is to move away from bulk-order shipping from manufacturers to the retail market, where we can provide a targeted distribution solution that is manageable and disciplined and leads to better margins."

Roussain's role, then, was not only to make FedEx's integrated service offering stand out in the marketplace, but also to convince the internal audiences at FedEx of the value that was at their fingertips. This would prove to be a significant challenge. "As a change agent, my primary responsibility was to bring visibility to what's important in the marketplace. What was difficult at FedEx was that the company already had all of the components needed to integrate e-commerce and supply-chain solutions. We weren't creating anything new. Rather, we had to reposition what we already had in a new, highly valuable language and structure."

Roussain likens his experience at FedEx to that of a ship captain, trying to turn an aircraft carrier to face the market demand. It is a position that he finds challenging, yet comfortable. "Both HP and FedEx are networked companies that employ large numbers of people. If you try to create change from the outside, it is typically a long and painful process involving lots of negotiating and influencing." What, then, is Roussain's approach to driving change? "First and foremost," he explains, "is the need to create the truth."

Creating the Truth

Roussain has realized that in e-business, players want solutions that integrate into their organizations. They are no longer satisfied with a solution that simply hooks into their business, like the automated customer devices that FedEx distributed in the '80s. This shift is driving an entirely new value proposition in the marketplace. And, in order to succeed, FedEx's employees must buy in.

"I realized early on that I couldn't just say, 'Here's a great idea, and this is what we're going to do.' That would never work, because FedEx has been a single-product company for thirty years. Every employee and every marketing piece of the company was aligned to the notion that *we pick up packages and drop them off the next day*." That alignment and clarity of focus are what led to the company's profoundly successful value proposition. Every function of the company was designed to optimize the delivery of its single product.

This strong value proposition, however, proved to a double-edged sword. On the one hand, employees were fiercely loyal to the company. On the other, they were so focused on delivering a quality product that they had difficulty understanding the role of an expanding value chain. Roussain continues, "When I tried to explain to my colleagues the emerging customer needs and how FedEx could position itself to satisfy those needs, I was met with cynicism. Not only did my colleagues not believe that customers were demanding integrated services, they felt that FedEx couldn't deliver—even though we had been doing it for years. Initially, people said candidly, 'we can't do that.'"

Roussain drew on his experience at HP and implemented a collaborative approach to try to convince his coworkers of his idea. While this approach led his colleagues to agree that the idea might be sound, they still resisted. "It's not that the people at FedEx are not innovative. It's just that they had been aligned for so long to a singular value proposition that they could not help but ask questions like, 'how will your idea reduce my packaging costs?' or 'how will this idea make my shipping occur more quickly?' I would explain to them that this integrated suite of e-commerce solutions had nothing to do with *moving the package*. It had to do with integrating our services with the customer so he could *move the package*." After four months of, as Roussain describes it, "banging my head against the wall," he realized a completely different approach was required.

The approach that Roussain utilized is elegantly simple. It involved writing down the "truth." As David explains, "We needed to come to a common understanding and move away from all the reasons that an integrated capability might not be feasible. We needed to articulate what we believed in and what we wanted to do." Roussain assigned a team of eight people from various areas within FedEx to draft what has become known as the "FedEx Manifesto."

The seventeen-page document describes the history of revolutions at FedEx and explains how the market is shifting. It also identifies the new opportunities for value creation and the new solutions that can be applied to these new values. The document does not say anything dramatically different from what Roussain had been espousing for a number of months, yet, according to him, "By writing it down, they believed it." The manifesto also served a greater purpose. "I no longer needed to go around internally preaching about the benefits of an integrated e-commerce strategy. I could give my colleagues a comprehensive document that would serve as a foundation for discussion. It put us all on the same page."

Some may think that the manifesto is just a fancy word for a new business plan. Not so, according to Roussain. "This is much more powerful than a business plan because it tells the story of the business, the story of what the business believes, and how it's going to accomplish its goals. Business plans, on the other hand, lack passion and vision and are entrenched in MBA terminology. They are, in effect, just cumbersome financial documents."

Roussain is now a firm believer in the use of a written manifesto. "I've learned that if you put a dedicated team together to crunch out a manifesto, they come out of it with an absolutely coordinated vision for what they're trying to achieve. Once they have that, it's much easier to communicate the ideas to other executives we might need to influence. It serves as a guide to keep us on course and focused. Drafting the manifesto was the fastest way to bring a very complex issue to a critical point of decisionmaking." The manifesto has paid off. One by one, groups that need to be aligned to the new vision of e-business at FedEx (for example, marketing and sales, advertising, ground operations, the electronics group) are coming around.

Lessons from a Revolutionary

David Roussain has learned a lot about leadership in his year and a half at FedEx (and during his five-year stint at HP). The first lesson has to do with collaboration. "Collaboration is so much more than getting people together. It involves a real art to lead a meaningful discussion." Roussain's "art" of collaboration was made more difficult by the makeup of the people whom he needed to influence. "At HP and at FedEx, I needed to lead intensive sessions with very powerful and very innovative people. The obvious benefit of this is that these people are the ones who can get things done. I have complete confidence in their abilities. The downside, if you want to call it that, is that you cannot lead these people. In other words, you cannot tell them what to do."

The manifesto, which outlined a shared point of view, certainly helped Roussain architect his collaborative solutions. It provided a benchmark around which he could rally his troops. "If we ever started losing focus, we could always refer back to the manifesto—back to our vision." In addition to the manifesto, Roussain learned the importance of the white board. "I found that a good leader needs to be able to draw concepts out for a group that further focuses people on the same idea in the same way. I found that even though you may have a roomful of smart people discussing issues, you really need a visual reference to bring it to life. Even though we might be saying the same words, the meaning we assign to them may be very different—especially when you're dealing with new spaces like e-business."

Roussain's second lesson has to do with trust. This is especially important for a company like FedEx, which has built its value proposition with customers around the same notion—customers can trust FedEx to do what it promised it would do. Similarly, Roussain needed to establish a trusting relationship between himself, his team, and others in the organization who needed to buy in. Most important, he needed to develop a universal trust in the "truth" as outlined in the manifesto.

Interestingly enough, Roussain established this environment of trust by constantly raising the bar with his colleagues. "I always know that the individuals involved in a process are genuinely good people. Yet, I need to be tough with them by constantly raising the bar on expectations. The challenge is doing so without making them feel as if they are being personally criticized." His collaborative approach involves bringing together groups of people who will then go back to their functional areas and work on a specific project.

Roussain does not accept poor quality work. In fact, he doesn't always accept good quality work either. "You have to always push people and ask them if they've thought of this or that in solving a particular problem." Some may consider this approach demeaning to the work of his groups. Roussain disagrees. "By pushing back and striving to raise the bar, I'm telling them that I really believe in the 'truth.' I'm affirming that I believe in the importance of the work they are doing. I've heard people say, 'David has a complete and vested interest in this—and in us to do it. He believes in our abilities, even though we haven't done a good enough job, and believes that this is vitally important.' If you raise the bar in a visionary way, you can influence a group by showing that you believe in the general direction and that you will support them. By seeing a leader's commitment, the team begins thinking, 'This must be a worthy project.' That builds trust."

Above all, as a leader of a collaborative effort, you have to be prepared at certain times to take the lead. When push comes to shove and decisions need to be made quickly, a leader must be able to put a "stake in the sand" and propose a clear action-plan for moving forward. According to Roussain, "With something like e-business solutions, you have to be able to move fast. You have to be able to make decisions quickly. This is where collaboration becomes an 'art.' When you have very powerful people working with you, you need to give them the freedom to do the job you know they can do. But you've also got to give them the structure and discipline to keep them focused."

After speaking with Roussain, I have no doubt that he is the one to achieve this collaborative balance of forceful leadership and collaborative freedom. In the near future, I expect to see the third revolution of FedEx come into its own. I predict the company will become known for much more than superb delivery services. Customers wanting to focus their attentions on generating demand will trust FedEx to integrate all of their supply and distribution processes within a system that works efficiently and reliably—*absolutely, positively.*

7

From Being a Manager/Technician to Being a Coach/Mentor

The new economy favors the e-leader with a fresh perspective who is a pacesetter and first-mover, who can come up with nonconformist strategies, and who can innovate and deliver products to market at the speed of the Internet. In essence, this means we are talking about someone whose thinking and attitudes are not hardwired by twenty years of experience in a given industry.

Yet therein lies the rub. This very lack of experience, while being a strength on the one hand, can lead to pie-in-the-sky business plans, unthought-out decisions, and reactive behavior. E-leaders in every quarter are tackling this question of leadership development.

The answer they have come up with? Finding capitalist coaches and mentors, anyone from professors who invest in their business while providing words of wisdom on the side to the partners in VC firms who see that their job is to make extraordinary leaders, not just money.

The August 2000 issue of *Red Herring* magazine had a cover picture of a Stanford Business School professor, Audri MacLean, forty-eight, and twenty-four-year-old Erin Turn, CEO and founder of the on-line music gateway Gigabeat.

"When you try to come up to speed on all fronts and you are still in your twenties or thirties," says MacLean, "you need to build a set of advisers."

After Turn raised $6.5 million, she approached MacLean, her former teacher who had twenty years of experience in the computer and communications industry, and said, "Do you really think this will work?" The two formed a close relationship, with MacClean acting as a "capital mentor."

OK, so you have a great e-Business idea. Who is your mentor?

"When you are as young as I am," says Turn, "you bring a fresh perspective, and you don't bring the baggage that someone else in a traditional industry might bring. At the same time, you have to recognize that there are things you know and don't know. You find the people who can be mentors, are those who have done things you haven't done before."

While Turn and her cohorts are confident that they know music on the Net and the demands of the space they are intending to dominate, where they falter is in knowing the how to create a powerful strategy that is scalable, as well as the ins and outs of business on a day-to-day basis.

Says MacLean, who not only decided to be a mentor but an "angel" investor in Gigabeat and had the experience and financial freedom to do it, "I know of at least a dozen people who are doing this. We can offer these young entrepreneurs a pragmatic perspective. They are starved to know if their idea is feasible and if they can carry it forward."[1]

One of the toughest things for the newcomers to figure out is whom to trust and whom to bring on board to build the company, as well as whom to find to mentor them. Once they do that, they can engage in day-to-day conversations with a mentor in which whole new levels of experience can quickly be communicated around bothersome issues. For the mentors, there is not only the possibility of financial reward but, more importantly, the psychic reward of knowing that they have made a difference.

A mentor can provide input on a day-in, day-out basis around real-business issues that would take years to learn from experience or business school.

Seasoned CEOs Seek
Coaches and Mentors, Too

The harder you dig into the roots of the new economy, the more you will see a pattern. Almost all of the Net billionaires (and millionaires) consciously and intentionally created mentors. For example, Marc Andreessen, co-founder of Netscape and now Loudcloud, a virtual assembly line for sophisticated Web sites, attributes much of his success at Netscape to the mentoring he received from its co-founder, John Chambers, who cut his teeth in business at Silicon Graphics, a company he started. Andreessen thinks of Chambers every day in his present role in guiding the company to make wise business decisions.

> Scott McNealy challenged Welch to a golf match. Welch thought it was about "competing." For McNealy, it was all about "mentoring."

Yet we are not only talking about CEOs of start-ups finding coaches and mentors, we are also talking about leaders of veteran companies. The cover of *Fortune* magazine in March 2000 showed Scott McNealy, CEO of Sun Microsystems, with his arm affectionately around the shoulder of the somewhat shorter Jack Welch, CEO of GE, both smiling to the gills.

The picture illustrates that McNealy—known for his almost arrogant pride in what he has accomplished and the irreverence with which he regularly challenges the computing status quo—has clearly subordinated a bit of his ego to acquire some words of wisdom from Welch. What you see is a picture of proud humility that he could have created this relationship in the first place and of reverential respect. In fact, McNealy unabashedly admits to being a "Jack groupie."

How the relationship started is an interesting story. Both CEOs are avid golfers. In fact, *Golf* magazine in 1998 rated McNealy the number one CEO golfer and Jack Welch number 2. When the issue came out, McNealy saw it as an opportunity to build a relationship. He sent the highly competitive Welch a message by phone and challenged him to a match "to find out who is really number one."

Welch fired back an e-mail in about two minutes, saying "You're on." For McNealy the whole thing was a ruse to get some mentoring time with Welch. McNealy was one of the first e-leaders and began talking about the network computer and an e-mail-based collaborative company as far back as the 1980s. Over a decade or two, he transformed Sun from a start-up to a $12 billion company.

What he wanted was to learn from Welch the lessons that are required to run a really "big" company. He had all kinds of questions: How do you develop a culture of leaders and leadership? How do you avoid becoming a bureaucracy? How do you apply something like "Six Sigma" quality?

Welch won the golf match, but McNealy won a windfall of wisdom. Still Welch may have gotten the best of the bargain. He enrolled McNealy, whom he refers to as "off the wall sometimes," on GE's board and asked him to mentor Welch in return on some e-business issues. The two talk to each other on a very regular basis.

Now that we have taken a look at how leaders at the top get the coaching and mentoring that they need to succeed, let's look at the issue of leadership development on a broader level, as it applies to the topic at hand.

Does Your Company Have a Leadership Supply Gap?

Sandy Ogg, Motorola's vice president of organization development, told me a story that captures the essence of what every business today is going through with regard to what McKinsey & Co. calls the "war on talent." Ogg, the CEO, and the top management team of a $15 billion business unit at Motorola had just spent two days in an intense brainstorming session on how to redesign their organization to take advantage of the growth opportunities of the e-economy.

"We live in extraordinary times," said Ogg. "We are living in times in which the world is literally reinventing itself. To be a part of it requires lots of leadership talent." Ogg explained, "We had all the senior executives sitting around the table with the organizational architecture—the employee boxes we needed to fill. The CEO asked, 'Who can go in this box?' The executives around the table looked at each other and back at the CEO. 'There's only one person who can fit in this box, it's Charlie.' Everyone's head nodded in agreement."

Ogg continued, "The CEO looked around the table again. 'Who could fit in this box?' The heads turned and looked at each other again. Someone said, 'The best person to fit in that box would be Charlie.' The CEO looked a little frustrated.

'OK, then who do we have who could fit in that box over there?' Someone said, 'I got to tell you, there is only one person, Charlie.'"

"At this point," said Ogg, "there was a brilliant flash of the obvious. Everyone realized we only had one Charlie."

He went on to explain, "Motorola lives at the interface between the Internet and mobile handheld communications, which means we are poised for tremendous growth opportunities for the future. We are poised to be able to take advantage of tremendous opportunities. The issue is that we need leaders to be able to do this." He explained, "Unfortunately, every Charlie we have on our staff today has at least two to three messages from search firms looking to hire them away."

"In effect," he said, "we have a very big leadership demand and a very small leadership supply. In other words, we have a leadership supply gap."[2]

Today every company of any consequence is asking the same question. From Ford Motor Company to Autobytel, from GE to Cisco Systems, and from Microsoft to PepsiCo, it's the same issue. The burning question is how do we impact the mounting leadership supply gap with enough power and velocity to be able to seize the strategic opportunities in front of us before the window closes? How do we produce leaders fast enough to still be in the theater when the curtain opens?

Filling the Leadership Supply Gap: Talent Acquisition or Talent Development?

As background here, it's important to point out that in 1998 Mckinsey & Company published an article called "The Talent Wars." This landmark article, based on research of 6,000 managers and executives, said that the most important strategic resource in the future would not be strategy or capital. Rather, it would be talent.

Business leaders received this article as the sounding of the tone calling them to battle. It wouldn't just be a battle with the typical Fortune 500, but thousands of Internet firms flushed with venture capital, stock options, and entrepreneurial opportunities that made the idea of working in any big company sound dreary and confining by contrast. Dave Anderson, president of the Americas for Heidrick

& Struggles, the world's largest search firm and the firm that placed Lou Gerstner at IBM and Mike Armstrong at AT&T, estimated that Silicon Valley at the time of this writing had openings for 750 CEOs.

Dave Arnold, managing partner at Heidrick & Struggles, tells an anecdote to illustrate just how tight the talent acquisition market really is.[3] The former CEO of EDS was at a meeting one day having a very intense conversation with his board. He said, "I am going to be looking for a new EVP of HR. Do you guys have any ideas?" At that point, one member of the board shot back, "Well, I don't have any ideas, but if anybody does," and he got out a piece of paper, "I'd be interested in them, too." And everybody laughed. It turned out that each of the ten other board members had the exact same need.

Winning the talent war will require an extraordinary effort. Says Arnold, "Those companies that will survive in the future will embrace the unthinkable on how to attract and keep talent. CEOs, wedded to the old ways of getting the best superstars, will be left in the dust by their more creative and nimble competitors."

At the same time, companies need to focus a lot more on development. They have to break the grip of the paradigm that says leadership acquisition is the one right way to create a powerful future for your firm. The new paradigm will be that senior leaders, not just rank and file, need to be developed from the inside and not just through sending people off to executive education at business schools but through executive coaching in the context of challenging assignments. Executive coaching will be an exploding new field for at least the next ten years.

Filling the Leadership Supply Gap Will Require Creating a Culture of Coaches and Coaching

While executive coaches, given their depth and breadth of experience with leaders in many companies and many situations, have a meaningful role to play in developing leaders, it's axiomatic that they can never replace the person in the corner office as people developers. The first thing for most executives to realize is that, if you are a leader, you are a coach and teacher, not a manager or technician.

What Kind of Leader Do You Need to Be in the Matter?
A Leader Who Develops Other Leaders

In the 1980s, Roger Enrico was a rising star in PepsiCo. By demonstrating flair for marketing and the ability to get results, he climbed the ranks. He liked doing things in his own way and taking bold risks, even if he fell out of favor. In 1983, when Enrico's boss, John Sculley, left to become CEO of Apple Computer, Enrico became chief executive of PepsiCo's U.S. business.[4] In 1996, after a long apprenticeship with PepsiCo chairman Donald Kendall, Enrico became CEO of PepsiCo. Things started well enough. Friends and colleagues sent good wishes. Others wrote notes; a few even sent flowers. One Pepsi bottler in Turkey took a different tack to get Enrico off on the right foot and sacrificed a sheep.

Enrico was to need these good luck charms. Within a few months of the sheep's demise, the head of Pepsi's international division quit, a Venezuelan bottler defected to Coke, another bottler almost went bankrupt, and Pepsi took a half billion-dollar write-off. Enrico remarks, "That turncoat in Venezuela had been part of Pepsi for forty-five years. In the process, he had become a billionaire. Suddenly, they were whistling on their way to the bank, painting ugly red logos on what used to be Pepsi trucks."

Enrico led a strategic review effort, which started with assessing the company's strengths and weaknesses. When Enrico took over, the company's brands were fundamentally strong and had a cash flow most CEOs would die for, but the company was not focused on growth. This resulted in a strategy called the "Power of One," which in essence was, "If customers buy a Pepsi, let's make it easy for them to buy one of the company's salty snack foods." Enrico also focused the company by selling some of Pepsi's restaurant businesses like Pizza Hut and Taco Bell and leading the acquisition of Tropicana. Most importantly, he got personally and methodically involved in a leadership development effort that has had a significant impact on the whole company.

Actually Enrico began coaching and teaching leadership a few years earlier, after suffering a heart attack and doing some soul-searching about who he wanted to be in life. When he decided he wanted to be a teacher, and perhaps do it at a university, PepsiCo Chairman John Calloway suggested that after his sabbatical, "Why don't you do it here?" As evidence for how much Enrico is willing to personally invest himself in education, as well as what a man of the people he is, last year he donated his entire salary of $1 million to set up college scholarships for the children of line workers in PepsiCo. So far 150 people have enrolled in college as a result.

Enrico's master class for high potential leaders, as it has become known, is based on personally and methodically coaching people on both leadership and business challenges over the course of a year. Each class is limited to nine people and so far 120 people, virtually all of PepsiCo's senior management, have participated. At the kick-off session, where he is often dressed in jeans and a plaid shirt, he provokes participants into seeing themselves as leaders versus cogs in the wheel. "Nobody in this room can look at the company's problems and blame the turkeys at the top. You're now one of them."

Each of the thirty or so people who attend the class participate in an introductory session in which Enrico lays down his five basic beliefs about leadership and the participants present a high potential business-building idea or project. Enrico's leadership development method involves coaching people on their "business-building idea" over the course of the year. The nature of the course is one where both Enrico and participants share not just their goals, but also their vulnerabilities by acknowledging uncertainties about their plans and by freely talking about mistakes.

For example, Enrico tells the class that in the 1980s, as a rising Pepsi star, he had trouble with authority and liked doing his own thing. This resulted in his committing a major faux pas. He invited hundreds of the company's bottlers to a lavish black-tie dinner in Manhattan at the Waldorf-Astoria and neglected to invite Donald Kendall, the chairman. Needless to say, Kendall was not pleased.

The inevitable dressing down was followed by an invitation by Kendall for Enrico to visit him once a week. This began a mentorship that was quite extraordinary and resulted in a rare bond. Enrico says Kendall occupies an office two floors above his own. "I ask his advice on many things. In fact, I rarely make a move without doing so." Comments like these help set the stage for participants in Enrico's class to welcome his coaching and mentoring and to have an attitude of learning.

Five Leadership Premises

Enrico's approach to coaching is based on five premises that can apply to both on-line or off-line businesses.

1.   *Inspire people with a noble cause.*

"Every leader has to supply the people in their company with a noble cause," Enrico says. "As far as I can tell in business, there are only three noble causes; kicking your competitor's butt, giving customers something better, and making your company a great place to work."

2.   *Communicate with your whole body and soul.*

If you're trying to inspire people, e-mail just doesn't do the job. "In my mind there is no substitute for face-to-face, eyeball-to-eyeball contact. You have to communicate with your body and soul if you want people to see what you see, feel what you feel." Enrico, who once wanted to be an actor, believes that great leadership and marketing is pure theater. Mouthing the right words is not enough. If words were enough, we would all understand Shakespeare a lot better. It takes a great actor, a real person to make Shakespeare come alive.

3.   *Stay focused on what you're good at.*

Leadership that has a sustainable impact takes focus. Enrico tells people that whatever you have going for you in the way of resources, get them centered on what you and your organization do best. Though going off on a tangent into a new opportunity may look appealing, it is often like trying to win the lottery.

4.   *Get results.*

Enrico believes that producing extraordinary results is what allows your business to grow and your people to develop. He coaches people in the program to see that achieving extraordinary results in an honest way is everything. "Business people often confuse activity with results, process with outcome, motion with production," Enrico says. He tells people, "Keep in mind what Mark Twain said, 'Thunder is impressive, but it's lightning that does the work.'"

5.   *Learning.*

The final leadership point concerns learning, truly understanding yourself and your business. This not only means knowing the strategic big picture, but also the details. To me, the notion that senior executives can't be bothered with the details of their business is crazy. Michael Eisner, for example, works on the design of rides at Disney World and has input into all of Disney's films. To do this, he has to learn about the details.

Coming out of the mouth of most CEOs, Enrico's leadership principles, no matter how simple or profound, might be mistaken for pablum; but coming out of Enrico's, it's somehow different. One reason is that he uses these leadership principles to coach and teach people in his master class on their business-building ideas or projects. He is constantly asking questions and listening attentively for whether people have a noble cause, are focused, and are result-oriented. If not, he intervenes.

Furthermore, the coaching doesn't just take place in one grueling three-day session, which is the typical case, but rather over a year. Every participant is invited to call him at any time without the knowledge of his or her boss, just as Kendall once encouraged him to do. "It was a remarkable experience," says Beth Struckell, who refined her strategy for the newly acquired Crackerjack Cheese. "It's as if Roger becomes your personal coach and mentor, leading you in the right direction on both leadership and business challenges."

It's not all business, but play as well. One day he will take a group horseback riding, finding metaphors to coach and mentor them on. The next day he will take them fly fishing in the mountains of Montana. Evenings are spent singing songs, like Frank Sinatra's "My Way" and "American Pie". The sambuca flows freely.

The program finishes with a three-day workshop in which everyone shares the insights and lessons of the year. Enrico believes that as CEO, coaching and teaching are an important part of his job, as well as a payback for the time he spent with Kendall. "Besides," says Enrico, "it's a heck of a lot of fun to be with young people who are really making things happen."

Creating the Right
Leadership-Development Mindset

After studying and teaching leadership for almost three decades, I would like to say something about what I consider to be the first principle of leadership development, as it is especially relevant to e-business and e-leaders. First, as mentioned in the introduction, no leader ever sets out with the idea of becoming a leader. He or she sets out with the idea of accomplishing something that is beyond and out of the ordinary.

That being the case, leadership arises from taking a stand that a difference can be made in your industry or business or for your customer or from a commitment to launch a new business, or to become the preeminent force in your field. Leadership does not arise from leadership characteristics and traits, your position, leading-edge leadership development programs, 360-degree feedback, corporate competency models, or abstract training programs (though these can play a supporting role).

The fact that we are perhaps seeing much more leadership today from the nifty fifty dot-coms than we have perhaps seen from the Fortune 500 in decades is testimony to the fact that leadership arises when an individual takes a stand that a difference can be made and has the courage to pursue it through their speaking, listening, and actions.

When someone like Jeff Bezos is written up as *Time* magazine's Man of the Year, or Steve Case of AOL and Jerry Wang of Yahoo! grab the headlines for their mergers and market caps, it is hard to imagine that only a short time ago these people were standing at the gate of the Fortune 500 with their ideas and plans only to be summarily rejected. Jeff Bezos was rejected by Barnes & Noble; Steve Case was rejected in his job application to Time Warner; Jerry Wang by a venture capital firm for having such a ridiculous name as Yahoo!

Today we see these people as leaders. But who was Steven Case before the first person subscribed to AOL? Who was Jeff Bezos before the first person bought a book from Amazon.com? Who was Jerry Wang before someone looked up a news story on Yahoo!? I suspect that they were ordinary people, like you and me, who saw an opportunity to make a difference and dared to take a stand.

Furthermore, it's my experience that, when individuals take a stand, and their speaking, listening, and actions begin to be consistent with that stand, something extraordinary happens in which who they are today is transformed into who they need to be to meet their particular leadership challenges. It is in this context that people begin to discover and express their own natural leadership ability. It is also in this context that they discover the particular leadership attributes and skills that they will need to develop. It's at this point, and this point only, that formal leadership development programs begin to make sense.

In other words, leadership development can only occur when an individual sees an opportunity to make a difference and dares to take a stand. If you are trying to spur leadership development in a corporation, understand that it occurs by giving talented people the space to express their personal vision, goals, and ideas, not through formal programs, 360-degree feedback, or leadership competency analysis. Instead of seeing it as your job to develop leaders, see it as your job to create the space for talented people to make a creatively productive contribution that will require them to take the lead.

Today, as every industry reinvents itself, there is an incredible window of opportunity for talented people to come up with new wealth-creating business ideas. In about four years, that window of opportunity will close forever. There has never been a more strategic, urgent or important time in the history of business to focus on the development of leaders who can step into those opportunities and make a difference. There needs to be a process in every organization that allows the senior managers to focus on hiring new talent and developing leaders already in the company.

Once that kind of nascent leadership space has been created, and a game-changer process installed, more formalized leadership development programs can begin in earnest. We have already seen from the story of Roger Enrico that a key bedrock of any leadership development campaign is a leader's developing other leaders. Now let's explore the other dimensions of the mindset needed to develop leaders consciously and intentionally. Be ready to question everything you take for granted about leadership development.

Link Strategy and Development— Your Preeminent Competitive Advantage

I want to make an assertion here. Leadership development needs to be seen as a strategic necessity, not just a nice idea. CEOs and executives, whether they are in big companies or dot-coms, need to recognize that leadership development is the only way companies will be able to take advantage of the strategic opportunities that are being generated by the new economy. For that idea to be made real, rather than just a polite slogan, every potential leader must have a personal leadership mission that is strategically important and operationally essential.

I strongly advocate, based on years of coaching and teaching almost 30,000 leaders, and years of field research, that your leadership development program begins with the CEO and the top management team's developing a strategy of preeminence. (For the company to develop leaders, it must first assume the mantle of leadership.)

To understand what I am talking about, just think about the legendary leaders of our day, Jack Welch of GE, Andy Grove of Intel, Roberto Goizueta of Coca-Cola, Scott McNealy of Sun Micro, John Chambers of Cisco, Jeff Bezos of Amazon, Steve Case of AOL. Each of them built his organization based on a strategy of preeminence. Not a single one built his organization based on the premise of being a worthy competitor. And consequently, each of them is known for developing a culture of leaders and leadership.

In coaching executives to develop a *strategy of preeminence* for their business, I have discovered that, just in asking people "What is your strategy of preeminence?", you inaugurate a process in which people begin to break through the prevailing paradigms that are limiting their businesses and to excel beyond them. In answering this question many e-leaders have been able to see something that no one in the industry ever saw before and to craft a strategy that allowed them to launch a preemptive strike and reinvent their industry.

Several other things happen when executives begin to craft a strategy of preeminence in such a way that allows them to maximize their assets and minimize their weaknesses. The first is that they begin to get in touch with their own greatness, or what James Champy calls their "arc of ambition."[5] You will find yourself feeling inspired and empowered as your strategy of preeminence takes shape, with the sense that you will be able to master the possibilities and challenges in front of you. At the same time, the experience may be humbling, not only putting you in touch with your strengths, but also showing you how you need to develop as a leader to meet the challenge.

Finally, whether you are a CEO or a business leader, you realize that you cannot do it on your own, that to fulfill your strategy of preeminence you will need other leaders and a culture of leadership, a culture that is internally collaborative and externally competitive. This sets the stage for defining both the key strategic roles and responsibilities and the talent pools of people with leadership potential to realize them. (Remember the Charlie story!)

Each person on the CEO's immediate staff and beyond it should look at the strategy of preeminence and ask him- or herself, "What can I do to forward this?" Specifically, "What is my greatest leadership challenge?" "What is my greatest business challenge?" Finally, as a synthesis of the two: "What is my personal leadership mission?" In other words, what am I going to do to assume the mantle of leadership in my business, function, or team? As soon as the leadership mission is clarified, people need to look in the mirror and recognize that who they need to be to deliver on their commitment is probably different from who they are today. This often leads to declaring their strengths and their development gaps in a personal development plan.

I want to emphasize that my view is to focus leadership development on those who have the greatest leadership potential and who have the necessary background, mindset, and skillset to fulfill the most strategic roles in the enterprise, regardless of their position today. This could include people in the top management group, experienced business leaders, or new business leaders (or the people who report to them), or high potentials who may be found anywhere and at any level of the organization. While it is true that today's companies need leadership at all levels, you need a place to start.

At PepsiCo, for example, Roger Enrico's master class started with only nine people. At Philips, (a client) Jo Pieters, the de facto leader of executive development, has focused the program on six business unit CEOs and the 120 people in the company who report to them. (There are other programs for top potentials and high potentials.) At Royal Bank in Canada, Frank McCauley of HR says, "We focus our leadership development efforts on top talent." He explains, "Those who can impact the strategic future of the company," and he adds, "It's not based on elitism, but merit."[6]

In 1997, Ford was starting down a similar path. Noel Tichy of the University of Michigan designed a leadership program called Capstone to develop those executives who had the potential to move up to the top. The theme was that each year Ford would invite thirty-six of its brightest stars to visit Dearborn for a week of classes. Those executives, grouped in teams of six (each including members from diverse areas of the company) would be assigned a strategic group project by Jacques Nasser, the CEO, himself. Six months later, the teams would report back to the CEO on their findings.

People Don't Develop as Leaders From the Classroom But From Challenging Experiences

One of the key strategic issues that both old legacy firms and the new Internet companies face is developing the quantity and quality of leadership to cope with rapid growth. Noel Tichy, who in part designed GE's leadership renewal effort, says, "As far as leadership goes, Jack Welch was ahead of his time. But he had time. In today's world, he would have to do what he did ten times faster."[7]

Jeff Taylor, CEO of Monster.com, told me that his company is growing at almost 100 percent a year. It is hiring dozens of people every week, just to keep up with the dizzying growth. Though Monster.com has made a substantial commitment to leadership development programs, Taylor says that the speed of growth is moving much faster than it takes to move up the development curve. The net result, according to Taylor, is that trying to do development through the typical classroom approach doesn't seem to fit the speed at which the new economy moves. Taylor's preferred approach is to develop people through job changes. Some of his people have had at least eight job changes in the last three years.[8]

This seems to fit the new emerging paradigm of leadership development, which says that leaders develop not in the classroom, but through challenging experiences. According to Morgan McCall of the University of California, in his book *High Flyers*, out of thousands of leaders he surveyed, the vast majority said they developed as leaders primarily through stretch assignments.[9] While classroom experiences may have provided some value, it was small in comparison to the value of the stretch assignment, such as first leadership assignment or a posting to foreign office.

As it's not always possible to develop leaders by assigning them to new jobs, many leadership gurus (and I am one) are looking for innovative ways to develop leaders by creating challenging experiences by design. One of my favorites is John Burdette of a company called Orxestra in Toronto, Canada.[10] Burdette was the lead design consultant for CEO Sergio Marchionne of the AlGroup (formerly known as Allusuisse), who wanted to put together an ambitious leadership development effort for his company. Marchionne's view was that, in a commodity business, the one thing that can give you a competitive edge is leadership. So John Burdette developed the entire leadership program around a poem:

> *Come to the edge.*
> *They came and they were afraid.*
> *Come to the edge he said.*
> *He pushed.*
> *And they flew.*

John Burdette and Thomas Moll, of AlGroup corporate HR, designed a series of leadership forums in which not only were strategic issues and stretch assignments discussed, but also each leader was brought to the edge through various kinds of challenging experiences. Burdette points out that there is a difference between such things as play as learning, the typical ropes course, and learning as play, where metaphorical learning experiences are cooked up to meet a specific leadership challenge.

In one program, where the theme was coming to the edge and letting go, Burdette and company had people jumping off a cliff with a bungee cord. In another, where Burdette was teaching executives courage in the face of fear, he took a team to Spain where each engaged in a bullfight. In another program, where the leadership challenge was teamwork and grace under pressure, he had a group of middle managers moving blindly through a room with hoses trying to put out a blistering fire that flashed up to 5,000 degrees.

As mentioned in the introduction, Burdette believes there are four leadership dimensions to consider: head, heart, hand, and spirit. Most leadership programs develop the head (knowledge) and the hand (skills). He says that, while teaching leaders things like brand building and supply-chain management is important, it's "not the difference that makes the difference." What makes someone stand out as a leader is the development of the other two dimensions—heart (passionately caring) and spirit (the ability to inspire).

When Burdette found himself trying to explain this rather esoteric theory to a dozen or so rather stiff Swiss executives who were way too much in their heads and hands (they were engineers), he was met with initial resistance. So he stopped in mid-sentence, realizing that everything he was saying was going right over their heads. In order to foster what he calls "whole-body learning" or in this case "spirit" and "heart," he made arrangements for the entire group to be enrolled in a "tap dancing class." It was just what the doctor ordered. The impact was so transformational on the managers that their wives couldn't believe what was happening to them and asked to be able to enroll in the class as well.

Leadership Renewal Programs That Include Action Learning Lead to Accelerated Experiential Development

Action learning is proving to be another highly effective approach to leadership development and is particularly suited to the fast-paced e-economy. In action learning people are selected to participate in what I call "business impact projects" that provide some of the same development opportunities of a stretch assignment without people having to leave their jobs. Some of the companies that are having great success with this approach are Ford Motor Company, Eriksson, and Philips Corporation.

Following Ford's Capstone Leadership Experience for executives, Ford Motor Company decided to put 2,500 leaders a year through a series of challenge programs called the Experienced Business Leader and The New Business Leader. The programs start with a leadership development boot camp. "How many of you feel comfortable being here?" asks Janine Bay, head of Ford's vehicle customization program, to a group of high potential business leaders. About 50 percent were out of their comfort zone. "OK. Well, I hope to change that this week. I want all of you to be uncomfortable. Because if you're comfortable, you can't really be a revolutionary, can you?"[11]

Ford's program doesn't allow participants to backslide after the initial mindset shift that happens in the first week. For one thing, the core canon of all the programs is action learning. Thirty days before their weeklong workshop, new business leader trainees get an assignment. They must each identify and develop a "Quantum Idea Project" (QIP) that will transform Ford into a more consumer-driven, shareholder value-driven company. They must then present that idea to their peers and instructors on the first day of the workshop. After that, they have three months to get the project rolling. At Eriksson, participants in a similar program choose something called a business impact project, which is designed to *make* or *save* the company money.

"The value of learning by doing is great," says Stew Friedman, director of the Ford leadership program. "People learn more when they're the ones who are pulling in the ideas, the people, and the resources." Every Ford leadership project must also require participants to negotiate the entirety of Ford, "up and out" of their roles and divisions. Every project must force participants to encounter the rest of Ford—and the rest of Ford to encounter them.[12]

One of the interesting things about the Ford new business leaders program is that participants are trained to be "total leaders." They are not only expected to have a teachable vision that they can put out on a ten-second elevator ride where they bump into the EVP of finance and to inspire teamwork and collaboration, but also to coach and teach others.

For example, Nancy Gioia is a chief program engineer at Ford. She heads a team of engineers, designers, marketers, and purchasing managers who work on the Ford Thunderbird. A graduate of Capstone, Gioia has been with the company for almost eighteen years. But Gioia has an even more important job: She's a mentor to participants in the experienced leader and new business leader challenge programs.

On the first morning of a recent new business leader session, she huddled with a bunch of participants to review their Quantum Idea Projects and to offer coaching and feedback. "Where do you want to stretch to?" she asked, stating the transformational impact of stretch goals, not only on remaking the company, but on remaking yourself as a leader. "Pick one or two challenging things that you want to learn, because those things will usually prove to be the most rewarding experiences. Keep pushing yourself. Start to explore areas outside of your silo.

"Ask yourself, what does it take to be transformational? Is what you're doing not only transforming the company but also transforming you as a leader? Understand what it is that you want to get out of this. Anybody can write up a business plan. You need to put your plan into action. That's what transformation is about. Lots of people and things have the potential to slow you down. Don't let them."[13]

To Sallie Hightower, a development leader of Conoco University, "One of the most important, but often overlooked things about action learning groups is not to use them just for people in a project to come back together to review their progress, but to come back together to look at themselves."[14] For example, asking questions like: How am I developing as a leader? What are the one or two personal (corporate) leadership competencies that show up as missing? How am I making progress with respect to the things that show up on my 360-degree feedback? Where am I stuck or ineffective? How will I deal with this?

The Powerful New Role of Executive Coaching

Let's summarize. Leadership development starts with the CEO's, or business leader's developing a strategy of preeminence. Then every business leader in the company develops a *personal leadership mission* based on achieving that strategy, which begins to highlight their development needs and gaps. The development of these leaders is then accelerated through various kinds of adverse and diverse experiences. (Obviously, if your effort involves more than a few people, there needs to be an organizational process that supports this.)

Now we are ready to introduce the final piece of the puzzle, which has to do with the role of executive and managerial coaching. This is a role that my colleagues and I have a great deal of experience with and, while not wishing to appear self-serving, I would be remiss if I didn't share this with you.

It's one thing to have a personal leadership mission based on a stretch goal or to develop people through challenging experiences, but it's entirely another thing to ensure that people grow and learn in the process. To draw an analogy, you can take an intermediate skier and put them on an expert ski slope with ice and moguls or an intermediate golfer and put them on a championship golf course with lots of bunkers and tight fairways, but will they really grow and learn as a result? The greater likelihood is that they will not grow or learn, but merely survive the challenging experience.

However, I have discovered in working with thousands of executives and decisionmakers that the combination of the challenging experience plus masterful coaching is unbeatable. A masterful coach whom people experience as both challenging and supportive, and who possesses the necessary insights, knowledge, and skills to further one's learning, can dramatically accelerate the process of development. I have witnessed this both at the executive levels of management and also at the grassroots level.

One of the issues is that, while coaches can make a huge difference in supporting leaders in realizing their leadership mission and in developing at the same time, most companies do not have a culture of coaching. In fact, my company surveyed over 5,000 managers in Fortune 500 and dot-com companies and discovered that close to 85 percent said that over the course of a ten-, fifteen-, or twenty-year career, they received little or no coaching. Sixty-five percent said that they provided little or no coaching to their direct reports. Ninety-two percent said that they would like to increase these skills and thought they were highly important.

> *"To have an executive coaching has become a badge of honor for CEOs and top executives."*
> **The Financial Times**

The most effective way to generate a culture of coaching in support of leadership development is not to enroll everyone in coaching courses. Rather, it is to provide people at the top of the organization with an executive coach in the context of shaping and realizing their personal leadership mission based on a strategy of preeminence. According to my colleague Michel Renaud, this sets the stage for seeding a culture of coaching into an organization through a series of cascades.[15]

Renaud says, "The people who make the best coaches are the people who have had a powerful experience of coaching over a period of time (usually a year or more) that has impacted their strategic vision and values, and at the same time optimized their performance and development. These people naturally develop through experience the skills to coach both experienced and new business leaders, and with a minimum of training can be extremely successful in doing so."

For global corporations, executive coaching may be the only way to develop executives in a way that is business connected. For smaller dot-coms, executive coaching may be the only way to maintain any correlation between the speed of growth and the pace of development. As Jeff Taylor of Monster.com told me, "The company is growing so fast that I may have to put another senior management team over my existing one to get the necessary depth of experience." Executive coaching focused on real-world goals and accelerated experiential development may be the way to avoid the repercussions that such a move would make.

Jo Pieters, head of executive development at Philips, believes that coaching, whether in sports, the performing arts, or business, is the best and only way to get people to the next level.[16] He cites the example of Earl Woods, Tiger Woods's father, who contacted a master golf coach, Butch Harmon, and asked him to take Tiger to the next level. That was in 1998, after Tiger had already won the Masters at the age of twenty-three and was coming in a close second or third in many other tournaments. After Woods spent a year rebuilding his golf swing with Harmon, he won something like seven tournaments in a row.

Jo Peiters and I co-designed and implemented an executive-development-through-coaching program that would take the Philips leadership group to the next level, tapping into my Masterful Coaching World Network of executive coaches. The program was designed to support Philips's strategic goals of excellence through innovation, as well as to support its BEST program—"Business Excellence Through Speed and Teamwork"—and, most importantly, its ambitious e-commerce efforts.

Pieters decided to focus this program on the top management group of 120. (This was a subset of the Philips leadership group of 750 that would eventually embrace the program through a series of cascades.) According to Pieters, "We realized that if we were to meet our goal of being a world-class company in every respect, we needed to have world-class leaders especially at the top."

Pieters and his HR colleagues, Hilde Paul and Thomas Stassen, first broke the leadership down into four levels as noted in Figure 7.1. The idea was to use the program "Leadership Through Coaching" to move as many people as possible from levels II and III to level IV or the world-class level, a very high gradient and one in which most Global 2000s are lucky to have a handful of people, and most dot-coms one or two at most.

Stages	Level I.	Level II.	Level III.	Level IV.
Primary Roles	Learner, Assists others	Individual contributor, Technical skill	Leading, Managing, Coaching, Bridging	Legendary leader, Pathfinder
Capability	Performs under supervision,"directed creativity"	Establishes distinctive competence	Linking global and local goals, Drive for results, Coaching	Changing the game or direction of major part of industry
Relationship	Dependence on leaders	Independence from leaders	Assuming responsibility for others	Assuming total organizational responsibility

FIGURE 7.1   Masterful Coaching Takes People to the Next Level

Phase One. 360-Degree Feedback.   Pieters felt that the way to get there wasn't necessarily executive development programs at schools like IMD and INSEAD or internal leadership training programs, but to provide each and every person in the top management group some 360-degree feedback based on where they stood at that moment. The basis for the feedback was a set of corporate leadership competencies that were cleverly embedded within the four levels of leadership.

Phase Two. Provide World-Class Executive Coaches.   Pieters contacted us. He wanted the executives to gain the insights that only a world-class executive coach can provide, while at the same time honoring the implicit coaching relationship between the CEOs and their direct reports. The role of the coach was to jump-start the whole process. There were three initial coaching sessions.

Coaching Session One. Establish a coaching relationship with each executive based on Philips's strategy of preeminence to build a *Performance Excellence Scorecard* (PES) as a basis for coaching him or her to accomplish what he or she needs to accomplish.

Coaching Session Two. The coaches review the 360-degree feedback with the executives in a way that helps them gain insight into their strengths and development gaps. They then develop a *Personal Development Plan* (PDP). The underlying purpose is to engage the executives in authentic coaching conversations that can help them to take the blinders off, allowing them to see themselves as others see them.

Coaching Session Three. This session was designed as a follow-up around three simple questions. What happened? What's missing? What's next? The idea is to support each person in forwarding both personal discovery and action with respect to both their PES and the PDP. It is also an opportunity to plan next steps in plotting the course of the coaching relationship.

Phase Three. Leaders Developing Leaders.   The design of this phase involves leaders' developing other leaders through their coaching and mentoring. This required some training in both team learning and collaboration, as well as teaching the managers my one-to-one masterful coaching method. See Figure 7.2. (For more details, see *Masterful Coaching Fieldbook* [San Francisco: Jossey Bass, 1999].)

The design of Phase Three also included the idea of each executive's sponsoring a business impact project with experienced business leaders or designated high potentials.

I can't overemphasize that the role of the CEO or manager is primary and the role of the outside coach supplemental. With that in mind many company leaders, including dot-coms, are coming up with innovative approaches to leadership development through coaching.

Candice Carpenter is the CEO of iVillage.com, one of the hottest women's sites on the Internet. Carpenter realized early that, despite creative and aggressive recruitment practices, she needed to focus time and attention on developing her best people. At the same time, realizing that she was working at Internet speed with little discretionary time available, she decided on a course of action that involved personally and methodically coaching one person every four to six months. She

---

Five Step Masterful Coaching Method

Step 1. Develop a Personal Leadership Mission

Step 2. Develop a Teachable Point of View *(for shifting mindset and behavior so as to achieve the mission)*

Step 3. Set *Stretch* Goals Collaboratively

Step 4. Forward the Action Through Small, Doable Breakthrough Projects

Step 5. Provide Feedback and Learning

FIGURE 7.2   The Masterful Coaching Method

would approach a highflier and ask them, "Are you ready to develop faster?" If the answer was yes, her response was likely to be, "Buckle your seatbelt and let's go."

Yet, coaching does not only take the form of a top-down or a senior-junior kind of thing. In 1999, Jack Welch realized he needed to do something to become e-savvy. As a result, he hired a thirty-one-year-old high-potential leader to be his personal e-mentor. Welch met intensively with this person for months, which impacted his strategic thinking and gave him a broad working knowledge of the Internet. At the same time, his mentor also developed at an accelerated rate through her regular contact with the CEO.

Welch got so much out of the relationship that he mandated that the 350 or so top executives at GE also find an e-mentor, whom they in turn would mentor on other issues. This is a good example of how coaching can work top-down as well as bottom-up.

Sponsor a Special Collaborative Leadership Development Strategy Workshop

Invite people from top management, from experienced business leader groups, from new business leader groups, from corporate HR, from training, as well as outside consultants.

Ask people before coming to the session to read this chapter, my book *Masterful Coaching Fieldbook* (1999), and other current leadership books and articles. I suggest *On Becoming a Leader* by Warren Bennis and *The Leadership Engine* by Noel Tichy. *Fast Company* magazine also has some good articles. Go to Fastcompany.com to see articles on Shell's Grassroots Leadership Program and Grassroots Leadership at Ford Motor.

Phase One: Scan to Learn

Review the organizing principles and examples mentioned here. Also scan the horizon for other companies that have put together highly successful leadership programs, both in the traditional past and on the dot-com horizon. Create a reasonably long list of leadership development approaches that you might be able to use for your company.

Phase Two: Focus

Collectively decide the most important solution-specification criteria for your company's leadership development needs. Create four or five different or distinctive criteria. For example: to develop leaders at a pace congruent with fast-paced business growth; to develop the executive level in your organization; and to mass-produce leaders at all levels.

Phase Three: Act

Take a look at all the different leadership development strategies you have developed in the Scan phase and see if you can match them to your leadership development criteria from the Focus phase. If it doesn't all immediately fall into some kind of logical order, see if you can find some way to combine or recombine the different elements in a way that makes sense for your organization. You should be working toward designing a leadership development model. Once you come up with one, work toward maximizing it. If you get stuck, go back and scan the horizon for some more alternatives.

After you develop the model, decide on next steps for execution and implementation. Think in terms of exploiting the existing readiness for a leadership development program, rather than in terms of creating new readiness. Sometimes taking small doable steps and succeeding creates the opening for a more ambitious program and a widening circle of successes.

To Reinvent Your Organization, You Must Reinvent Yourself First

Let's look at the triple-loop learning approach to developing yourself as a leader who is coach/mentor to the people in your organization. It will take reflecting on how you have approached leadership development in the past and how you must approach it in the future.

Triple-Loop Learning

How do you need to be different?

Write one sentence that describes who you have been around leadership development to date. (For example, a "distant supporter" or "delegator.") Write one sentence that describes who you need to be in the future.

Double-Loop Learning

How do you need to think differently?

Write one sentence that describes what your mindset has been around leadership development. For example, "Leadership development is HR's job or the job of consultants." Write one sentence that describes what your new mindset is going to be.

Single-Loop Learning

How do you need to act differently?

Write one sentence that describes your behavior around leadership development, and another that describes how your behavior needs to change. Figure 7.3 is a template that will guide you in this exercise.

How do you need to *be* different?

- From seeing that your leadership comes from your position to seeing that leadership arises from the stand that you take

- From seeing yourself as the executive (the CEO) in the corner office, removed from recruiting, to seeing yourself as the chief talent officer

- From seeing yourself as a top performer to seeing yourself as a top performer and people developer

- From seeing yourself as a manager and technician to seeing yourself as a coach/mentor

- From seeing yourself as moving too fast or being too busy to focus on leadership development to seeing it as your highest priority

How do you need to *think* differently?

- From thinking that things like strategy or getting venture capital are your most important priorities to thinking that winning the talent war is

- From thinking that leadership development is something that is "a good idea" to seeing it as a strategic priority of the highest order

- From thinking that leadership development is about studying traits to thinking that it's about "breakthrough results and breakthroughs for people"

- From thinking in terms of developing leaders in the classroom to thinking in terms of developing leaders through challenging experiences

- From thinking of leadership development in terms of executive MBAs or training to thinking of it in terms of business-connected coaching

- Concoct a strategy of preeminence with your senior team that will give you a competitive edge or advantage

- In view of this strategy, schedule a meeting with your top management group to discuss whether you have a leadership supply gap and how to fill it

- Develop a creative, inventive, and out-of-the-box recruitment strategy

(continues)

FIGURE 7.3   Template for Becoming a Leader Who is a Coach/Teacher

(continued)

How do you need to *act* differently?

■ Make sure everyone on the SMG has stretch goals and a Personal Development Plan

■ Next do the same for Experienced Business Leaders and high potentials

FIGURE 7.3   Template for Becoming a Leader Who is a Coach/Teacher

Jeff Taylor, CEO of Monster.com

Recruit the Person,
Not the Position

"Where are we?"

This is the question Kevin Laracey, CEO of edocs Inc., asks his leadership team every Monday morning. He's not asking about rate of sales or secured investment capital or strategic planning. Those topics will be addressed later. What Kevin is questioning is the status of his start-up's most important initiative—recruitment.

"We signed Anderson and McIlvane on Friday," offers Shannon.

Kevin smiles and nods, scribbling in his notebook. "Good, good." Kevin is familiar with the resumes and knows that these two programmers will bring great skills to the fast-growing Web design team. "What about O'Brien and Kilroy?"

Marge steps forward as the bearer of bad news. "We lost both of them last Thursday."

Kevin frowns, still scribbling. Their failure to sign O'Brien, who was being considered for a top marketing spot, and Kilroy, whom Kevin had handpicked as the best choice for a finance role, is bad news. "What did you offer them?"

"Everything I could think of," admits Marge. "Stock options. Unlimited personal days. Parking spaces. The health club membership. The fruit baskets. The Lava Lamps. I even upped the signing bonus to $10,000 for each of them."

"What do we think went wrong here?"

"I think they had other—better—offers." Then Marge adds quietly, "And I think there was an issue with timing."

Kevin has worked with Marge long enough to know that when she lowers her voice and drops eye contact, she is about to say something that makes her uncomfortable. "What do you mean?" he asks gently.

"Kevin," she begins, "I think we could have had a chance here, especially with Kilroy, but we were a little too slow in getting our offer together."

"Why is that?" Kevin hears the others shift in their chairs.

"Because you were in Miami on Tuesday, Tucson on Wednesday, and Minneapolis on Thursday."

"So?"

"Kevin, you're the only one who has the authority to sign the offer letters. By the time you got back on Friday, these guys had been snapped up."

Kevin sits back in his chair and ponders the irony of it all. The purpose of his travels during the last week had been to interview potential job candidates. "Have any of you," he glances around the room at the other ten managers, "noticed this sort of problem before?"

One by one, heads start bobbing around him. Kevin shudders at the thought of the talent that has probably slipped through his company's fingers. He looks back at Marge. "Thank you for bringing this to my attention. I had no idea my schedule would ever be a stumbling block to the hiring practice." He looks back to the larger group, "I tell you what. Let's change the way this system works right now."

•   •   •

While the vignette above is based loosely on thirty-four-year-old Kevin Laracey, whose company sells electronic bill payment software, similar scenarios are playing out in executive suites all across the e-business landscape. The key issue for hundreds, if not thousands, of new companies is acquiring the talent necessary to drive success.

Fortunately for Laracey, he learned the importance of talent acquisition early. Given the rapid growth of edocs in 1999, he realized that he was running into a resource shortage that would impact the company's ability to grow. Now, in addition to the fruit baskets and Lava Lamps (yes, Lava Lamps), Laracey has equipped his recruitment team (which, by the way, is larger than his marketing team) with a powerful tool: control. Recruiters now have the authority to interrupt him with impunity, whenever they feel it necessary, to get the signatures they need to get the offers out the door. Laracey remembers being interrupted twice during one meeting with potential investors last fall. "I said, 'Please excuse me. It's hiring. We've got to do that.'" The investors' response to the intrusions? "Somewhere between being amused and impressed." In addition, Laracey now allows two of his colleagues to sign offers for his direct reports if he is unavailable.

Laracey founded edocs Inc. in 1997 in a spare bedroom and has grown the company into a multi-million dollar business. Within one year, he raised $22 million in venture capital and secured more than twenty large corporate accounts. That's when his role shifted from CEO to "recruiter in chief." Robert Davoli, edocs chairman and partner of one of the company's leading investment firms, remembers, "My message to Kevin was, 'you're now in the hiring business.'"[1] Laracey now spends two-thirds of his time looking for new talent, an effort that he undertakes with the same ferocity he used to attract initial investors and clients. It's all or nothing for Laracey. As he puts it, "You grow fast or you die."

Richard Owen, former vice president for Dell Online and newly appointed CEO of AvantGo, a company that delivers mobile Internet services, agrees. "A challenge for us, as for so many other companies, is recruiting. We thought we might need twenty to thirty new people this year. It looks like we'll need over a hundred." The challenge is not just in finding the right people for AvantGo, as up-and-coming leader in the wireless market, but in implementing the cultural mind shift that needs to occur as AvantGo transforms from a small business to a big one. "We are asking ourselves, 'What will this company look like when we have 1,000 employees?' and 'How will we secure the talent we need to make it happen?'"[2]

These are the right questions to ask. As a leader in the e-economy, you're used to thinking big—about your market share, your strategy, your business model. You just need to be sure you're thinking about how you're going to deliver on your goals. That means you've got to think about attracting the talent to make it all happen. But one thing to consider: Your business strategy will most likely change, over a period of months, if not weeks. How do you attract talent when the needs for your organization are constantly shifting? The answer lies in not hiring for a specific position because, let's face it, that position may not be around in three months. Rather, you should do what so many leaders profiled in this book have learned. That is, you should recruit the person who has the potential to wear many hats and bring skills to bear on a number of areas—existing or potential—of your organization. The days of filling a slot in an organizational chart are over.

Bracing for the Attack

Getting the right people on board is a big deal. Not just for a company needing employees, but for the leader needing troops to carry out his or her vision. After all, as Richard Owen says, "As a leader, the most enduring change you can make, the greatest impact you can have, the legacy you will leave behind, is through your people. You're not going to make a difference in the company. The people you hire are. The only difference you will make is by attracting and choosing the right people."

Recruiting. For the longest time, this word described the tactic used by fraternities, cults or, more commonly, the armed forces to gain membership in their organizations. No longer. In the past ten years or so, the word "recruit" has sidled its way into the lexicon of corporate America, along with the military metaphor we've heard so much about—*the war for talent*. To prepare for the war, HR departments now have dedicated *recruiters*, and new-hires are referred to as *recruits*. This militaristic vocabulary shift makes sense, when you consider that commerce has always been a battleground in which fortunes are won or lost and entire economies thrive or crash. Let's not overlook the fact, too, that mergers and acquisitions can be as cutthroat as any military campaign.

In the new economy, capital is plentiful, ideas for business are generated overnight, and knowledge workers are willing to change jobs just as quickly. Competition for smart knowledge workers who are technologically literate, globally astute, and understanding of dot-com operations is fierce. It will only get worse as e-businesses realize that the spoils of corporate war are that much richer—and the losses that much more devastating.

As we said earlier, the study conducted by McKinsey & Company indicated that the demand for talent—particularly among knowledge workers—will continue to rise, while the supply will continue to fall. Talent, in fact, is predicted to be the most important resource for companies over the next twenty years. According to Ed Michaels, a McKinsey director involved in the study, "All that matters is talent. Talent wins."[3]

The demographics are compelling. Let's assume the U.S. economy grows at 3 to 4 percent per year for the next fifteen years. With this increase, we can estimate that 25 percent more thirty-five- to forty-five-year-olds will be needed in the workforce. Yet, over that same period, the number of people in this age group will actually decline by 15 percent. You don't need to be a statistician to see that this spells trouble. This shortage is going to affect all industries all over the world. It will, however, have the greatest impact on high-tech businesses, where the real need for knowledge workers is focused. Many of these businesses, like edocs Inc., recognize the threat and are implementing innovative methods to retain their current employees and, perhaps more importantly, recruit new ones. Others, unfortunately, are not.

Where do the dot-coms fit into all this? They are squarely at the forefront. They are generating the strongest demand for talent, and making traditional businesses (and their e-competition) nervous. For example, in the Silicon Valley alone, there were 270 openings for CEOs at emerging companies. The number of openings at the lower levels is in the thousands.

While these companies can't usually offer exorbitant salaries, they can offer the new form of reimbursement—stock options. Armed with dreams of Dell- and Gates-like success, the dot-coms are positioning themselves as the marauding troops massing on the hilltops ready to attack the fortresses of traditional big business. And before you know it, they will be riding into the sunset with your best programmers, marketers, and finance and legal types stuffed neatly into their saddlebags.

OK, I may be too dramatic here. The dot-coms, after all, don't have to launch fireballs over your corporate walls to get your people. A red-hot package of stock options, coupled with an informal work environment and an occasional Lava Lamp seem to be doing the trick. Is that all? Maybe. But I think there is something else—something much more subtle and powerful than that—going on. What I think dot-coms are offering is the opportunity for people to make a real difference in an industry and in their lives.

As Michaels points out, "People at start-ups . . . have a chance to be very connected to the top of the company. They can play a key role and make a difference to the whole institution—all at an earlier age." Whatever the reason, workers are leaving their current positions in record numbers for a lucrative piece of the dot-com pie. They are doing so without looking back, confident that they will land on their feet, even if it means hopping from job to job for a while. Michaels continues, "A highly talented thirty-year-old is confident that even if he or she goes bust on a small-company venture, there will be another job out there."[4]

He's right. For the foreseeable future, the dot-coms will be fighting for talent. Who will win? It's too early to tell, but we're already seeing many forward-thinking executives spreading out their battle plans and determining their strategies. Leaders like Kevin Laracey of edocs, Jim Daniell of OrderTrust, Richard Owen of Avantgo.com, and Jeff Taylor of Monster.com. These men have innovative yet practical ideas for how to recruit the troops they need, and one of them just may have unveiled the not-so-secret weapon that will change the recruitment battle lines for good.

"When I Grow Up . . . "

Do you ever think back to when you were a kid, wondering what your life would look like at the grim old age of thirty-five? I remember most of my friends wanted to be doctors or lawyers—if for no other reason than those were the professions that seemed most lucrative at the time. In the media, those were the careers that were most emblematic of success. Certainly, none of my friends were thinking about being an e-commerce leader. I'm not sure why I was a bit different, but I didn't buy into the dream of practicing medicine or law. In fact, I didn't really have any idea of what I wanted to do as an adult—other than knowing that I wanted to make a difference. Pretty lofty thoughts for a ten-year-old.

This became clearer to me when I graduated from college and started looking for work. At the time, the majority of available positions were for engineers, COBAL architects, and systems programmers. I didn't see myself in any of that. So I ended up working for a book distribution company. It seemed like an ideal fit. I enjoyed books and knew that they added value to people's lives. I was going to help the process of putting valuable information into the hands of thousands of people.

What I was soon to learn, however, was that the business of book distribution is not about improving a customer's quality of life, but about sales. Period. That's when I realized my mistake. I had been looking at job opportunities from "the outside in." I had approached my job search by assessing the skills that I could bring to a potential job. What I should have been doing was assessing what the job might bring to my life that would allow me to further unlock my potential and contribute to my growth as a whole person. At the age of twenty-two, I had finally fully realized that each of us has the right to expect more from a job than a paycheck.

Jeff Taylor, the thirty-nine-year-old CEO of Monster.com, obviously understands that, too. It's apparent in the company's advertising (the now-famous "when I grow up I want to be a yes man" ad), which illustrates in a powerful (and sad) way the permeating belief that so many of us consider jobs to be just that—simply a way to pay the bills. Speaking to Taylor or any of his 1,000 employees, it is apparent that he has built a company that is sending a clear message that we have the right to aspire to personal greatness and to dream big.[5]

Jeff Taylor, a former DJ and ad executive, remembers reading an article that described the potential for the emerging Internet space. This was 1993, about the same time the World Wide Web and MOSAIC, the original Web browser, were invented. While the Web was being used primarily as a tool to exchange information among academicians, students, and the military, Taylor believed it had tremendous potential for commerce.

At that time, Taylor was heading a relatively successful recruitment-advertising agency in Boston, Adion Inc., which devoted much of its efforts to positioning job ads in the *Boston Globe*. "I had this philosophy at the agency that what our clients paid us for was a big idea, and everything else was just in support of that idea, to get it done. One of our clients said they wanted a monster idea. That's where the name Monster came from."

He had the name, but not much else. Then, at four one morning, his monster idea came to him in his sleep. "I woke up and scribbled down the idea of a Monster Bulletin Board, in which people seeking work could be matched to potential employers on the World Wide Web at a greatly reduced cost. This was a 'monster' idea and naming it that was a way of letting people know this was a monumentally creative idea."

Initially, his monster idea fell on deaf ears. His wife and colleagues felt the idea was premature. No one was using the Internet at that point. This was before Yahoo!, Amazon, and the other household-name Internet companies had even been formed. Taylor's friends also questioned the name "monster," which didn't seem serious enough for the audience Taylor was hoping to attract. Despite his detractors, Taylor moved ahead. He took $65,000 in profits at Adion and found twenty-three Boston-based companies willing to allow him to post their ads on the Internet. "The first six months were pretty bleak," recalls Taylor. "We weren't getting the volume of visitors we were expecting. More troubling were the letters I was receiving. People were calling me a communist and a fascist for polluting and commercializing the Internet." Yet Taylor believed in his idea. He felt he could offer all of us something that had been missing from our lives—a new understanding and appreciation of job opportunities and, above all, options. He wasn't ready to back down.

About this time, Taylor's wife gave him a copy of *Into Thin Air*, Jon Krakauer's bestseller that chronicles a Mount Everest climbing disaster. The book had a powerful impact on Taylor. It reinforced his strong personal conviction that the human spirit could achieve goals that appear insurmountable. "I knew if I worked hard enough, Monster would succeed." Taylor devoted almost all of his time to the new venture and hired a PR specialist to publicize the site. Nine stories ran across the Associated Press and Reuters news wires. This was the break he was looking for. He received an avalanche of calls and letters from around the world. Taylor had been right—there was an emerging demand for the type of recruitment service he was offering. One organization that recognized Taylor might be on to something was TMP Worldwide, which bought Monster in 1995, retaining Taylor as CEO. TMP Worldwide, an interactive company known for its suite of global career solutions, had the resources necessary to promote the site and the infrastructure, market penetration, and national clout to support it.

Today, Monster.com is the Internet's leading career hub and is turning the art of recruitment on its head. It offers services for everyone—from college interns to what Taylor refers to as "elderprenuers"—and allows its 4.7 million registered members a personalized career operating system that allows them to look for jobs, post and edit their resumes, and set up sophisticated job searches to match their employment needs. The site also offers career content, chats with other jobseekers, message boards, and general networking information. The site boasts 2.5 million visitors from twenty countries per month, posts 250,000 jobs, and stores more than 2 million resumes in its database. Its recently launched Talent Market is the first real-time, auction-style marketplace for 100,000 (and growing) free agents and contractors. The company has been profitable for five straight quarters—a legendary success in the Internet economy. In 2000, the company is expected to have sales upwards of $120 million.

It is perhaps ironic that the CEO of the leading job site—one who understands perhaps better than anyone else what it takes to attract and retain talent—is facing the same talent shortage as everyone else. But he is. Monster's growth is typical of the industry, more than doubling in size every year. For example, the company entered 1999 with 170 employees. At the beginning of 2000, the number of employees was 650 and it was expected to reach 1,100 by year's end. Taylor estimates that Monster adds fifteen new people to the payroll each day. It's a far cry from the handful of people at Adion six years ago.

"My greatest challenge as CEO," says Taylor, "is developing and securing talent to keep up with the pace of the growing business. In the old economy, the pace of a company's growth tended to complement the pace of growth in people. Now it's reversed. In the past, you could track someone's career in a company—from the mailroom to the boardroom. During that time, a leader had time to develop his or her people for the long haul. That's not the case today. We don't have the luxury of time to develop our people."

Despite the speed with which Taylor needs to bring new talent into the Monster fold, he understands the importance of developing his existing staff. Monster, for example, offers its employees four trainings per year, including a week-long training when they join. "This may not sound like a lot," says Taylor, "but look around and you won't find anyone else doing that." He also encourages employees to develop by shifting their roles and applying their talents to new areas within the organization. Many of his staff have been with him for six years, yet have held seven or more positions within the company. They are able to make these transitions because of who they are as people. Taylor doesn't bring people on board to fulfill a specific role. Rather, he attracts people who have the potential to excel in a variety of positions to meet the changing needs of Monster. How do you know, when interviewing a candidate, whether they will be able to assume a variety of responsibilities—especially when you don't know what the future responsibilities will be? According to Taylor, the greatest skill a recruit can bring to the table is one that can't necessarily be gleaned from a resume or learned from experience. It is passion.

Recruiting for Passion

One of Taylor's strengths as a leader is his ability to focus on the individual needs of his employees. Taylor understands that people have individual passions, and he nurtures those whenever and however he can. Case in point: Michele Pearl, vice president and general manager for Monster's new economy executive services. While assigned to a project to build Monster's European infrastructure in the United Kingdom, Pearl became pregnant with her second child. "I went to Jeff right away and told him that my husband and I wanted to return to the states. Yet my project wasn't complete. Jeff understood what I needed and together we worked out a plan that would satisfy the needs of the project and would allow me to return to the U.S. I've worked with Jeff off and on for twelve years, and he's always been this sort of leader. He has always had a remarkable capacity to take care of his people in the here and now while simultaneously looking to the future needs of the business. I think he's one of very few entrepreneurs who can balance these things."

Another entrepreneur who shares this balanced view of individual needs versus long-term company success is Jim Daniell of OrderTrust. He knows that successful recruiting requires a willingness to spend more money and provide more stock options than his competition does. But he also knows what Jeff Taylor knows—that you've got to be able to ignite the personal dreams and understand the individual needs of the job candidate. "As a leader today, you have to realize that everybody wants to be somebody when they grow up. It's part of my role as a leader to help them realize their aspirations."

Notice the similarity between Daniell's vision of leadership and the branding that has launched Monster.com to its success? Daniell is concerned, as is Monster, with the voice of the child: *"When I grow up I want to be a yes-man"*. Both realize that people are looking to bring their whole selves to work. As leaders, Daniell and Taylor need to create environments in which that is possible.

One way that Daniell promotes this sort of culture at OrderTrust is by recruiting people who have higher callings. "When I interview candidates, I will ask them about their social values, their commitment to charitable organizations, and their involvement with the less fortunate." As a result, he has built around him a team of 130 people who work for the school system, build homes for Habitat for Humanity, or are involved in a number of other helping organizations. The company, too, has developed a culture of giving back to the community.

Daniell says that it's a challenge in the fast-paced world of e-business to build a special culture that appreciates the importance of individual commitment and values. "I tell people that we all have a higher calling, we all want to be something when we grow up, we all have a duty to our families and communities. The job should support all of that." Some new recruits find this sort of personalized attention a bit startling. Daniell makes the transition easier by using the Socratic method of inquiry—asking questions to help steer his employees onto a path of personal fulfillment and effective decisionmaking. "When I ask people to talk about their dreams, many will say they want to leave a legacy. They may aspire to be a great marketer or a pathbreaking engineer. And I say to them, 'OK, but that's not what you're doing. What can we do to help you tap into the passion of what you want to become?'"

Daniell is affectionately known by his colleagues as "Hurricane Jim." His style is often compared to the scenario played out in the Maxell ad campaign, in which music blasts at high decibels, blowing back the hair of the person in the armchair. Daniell is the music. His employees are sitting in the armchair, braced against the power of his drive, commitment, and passion. Richard Owen of AvantGo has a similar, albeit more soft-spoken style. "One of the things I look for when hiring new talent is drive. Everybody is going to define success in his or her own terms and be driven by different ambitions. That's great, because it creates a dynamic organization. Ambitions change, and that's fine. But, as a leader in this organization, you've got to be able to nurture these ambitions. You've also got to be able to articulate your ideas and inspire others to understand your point of view."

Obviously, one of the most effective ways a CEO can communicate his or her vision of personal triumph, drive, and aspiration is through direct dialogue. As companies like OrderTrust and Monster.com grow, however, that gets harder to do. Monster has realized that it can't always rely on Jeff Taylor to rally the troops around the flag of personal fulfillment. As a result, Taylor's focus on individual expression and personal aspirations is now formalized at the heart of Monster's culture. The company has spent a great deal of time articulating its four core values, several of which drive this message of personal growth. *Share the passion* encourages employees to be their best, be creative, and pursue opportunities to grow their talents. Employees are also encouraged to *express big ideas*—to continuously innovate, anticipate market needs, and learn—and *share a great experience* with customers, clients, visitors, shareholders, and employees. Everyone involved with

Monster understands that the company is doing something radically new and exciting. This spirit of excitement runs through every relationship in the organization. Finally, employees are encouraged (and expected) to *make an impact*. No one at Monster takes his or her job lightly. They realize that they are involved in a revolution of the human spirit, promoting the idea that everyone has the right to a fulfilling work life.

These values are more than lip service. In fact, these values permeate every aspect of Monster's culture. More important, these values are what attract new talent to the company. According to Michele Pearl, "People tend to look at Monster in one of two ways. Some consider us only a database for jobs and resumes. Others realize that we're changing the world. These are the people we attract as employees. And these are the people who are attracted by our mission and by our culture, which is embodied by Jeff and the hundreds of other people who work here. Sure, people are attracted to dot-coms by large salaries and stock options, but we offer something more—the ability to be part of something truly monumental." Monster's relative stability in an unstable market doesn't hurt, either. "We're seeing a lot of angst out there among employees of traditional brick-and-mortar organizations," continues Pearl. "They feel they are missing an opportunity in e-business, and that's making them nervous. But at the same time, they are hesitant to make a jump to a new start-up that might go belly-up in a year. We've got a track record of success and an established brand. Many people are attracted by that sort of security."

Living the Brand

Having a great brand, however, is often not enough. Savvy job seekers know that a lot of CEOs are saying what they feel prospects want to hear. These job changers are looking for a company that *lives* its values and its brand. This should be palpable throughout the organization and driven directly from the CEO's office.

How does a CEO live the company brand? We've already mentioned that Jack Welch, Di-Ann Eisnor, and Richard Branson are shining examples of this. So, too, is Jeff Taylor. Who else would try something as monstrous as accepting a challenge by Virgin's Richard Branson to water-ski while being pulled by a blimp?

(Virgin owns two blimps that Monster uses for advertising, so the challenge makes sense.) What Taylor didn't realize was the skill of his competitor. Branson, well known for daring stunts, had already won the world record in this competition by being pulled for a mile and a half.

Taylor, however, saw the opportunity to align Monster with the powerful Virgin name and decided to throw caution to the wind. "I had only been on water skis twice in my life," remembers Taylor. "I knew Richard held a record of some type for being pulled on skis by a blimp, but I figured he went for 500 feet or so. I had no idea what I was getting into. But I genuinely thought, 'Once I get up on the skis, how tough could it be?'" Michele Pearl is quick to add with a laugh, "When we realized that Richard Branson had previously skied for more than a mile, we were pretty anxious for Jeff. But he told us that for the publicity, he was willing to have the blimp just drag him through the water for a mile if need be." Luckily, it didn't come to that. Taylor not only got up on his skis, but he won the competition—completing an astounding three and three-tenth smiles (even boldly waving with one hand as he crossed the finish line). "It all comes down to a CEO being willing to take risks and create a buzz about the company," Taylor says. He is certainly willing to do both.

The blimp example is just one way that Monster has created buzz about its service. The successful ad campaign is another. An exciting workspace is a third. The company has recently renovated a 75,000 square-foot brick mill (with an additional 55,000 square feet being annexed) and has outfitted it with huge windows, open spaces, bright colors, and, of course, monsters. "Employees are so excited by the space, they bring their families and friends in to see it," says Taylor. "And there's been more than one case when a visitor said, 'Wow! I love this place. How can I get a job here?'"[6]

A fourth way the company creates buzz is through employee word-of-mouth. It's not something Taylor has had to train his people to do. They do it naturally. "I know that people like talking to their friends about their jobs and about Monster.com. They're proud of the company. And they're excited about their roles in changing the world. They pass that enthusiasm and excitement on to their friends and relatives." In fact, a large percentage of new recruits to Monster.com are introduced to the company by people who work there. A few others, naturally, come to the company through the Monster Board.

Releasing the Human Spirit

In my consulting practice over the years, I have run across hundreds, if not thousands, of employees who were indifferent or even *resigned* about their jobs. There was no passion, no alignment to the company's purpose, no commitment to a higher purpose, and perhaps most unsettling, no sense of *choice*. And with no choice in their careers, people have felt that they aren't making a difference. What I have found is that by giving employees choice in their actions, their roles, and their functions, you can challenge the prevailing culture of resignation.

This is the secret weapon that Monster.com is rolling onto the battlefield. People are craving choice. Monster.com, by radically transforming the process of looking for a career, is changing the climate of resignation to one of opportunity. With companies like Monster.com, and hundreds of other emerging organizations that put a premium on individual satisfaction, people are realizing that they can work for a company that allows them to live their values.

Of course, recruitment will always involve an eye toward competitive pay, stock options, signing bonuses and, perhaps, even a Lava Lamp or two. But there are more fundamental things you can do as a leader to attract the right kind of people. These things lie in the way you express your passion, your commitment to your mission, your belief that you can (and are) making a real difference in the world, and your respect for individual aspirations. Once you offer this of yourself, job candidates will come flocking to your door. I guarantee it.

As Monster articulates in its core value statement, everyone has the right to a fulfilling work life. People shouldn't be chained to a job that diminishes their human spirit. Rather, they should find positions that will allow them to define and achieve their personal levels of excellence. That's why the Monster.com ad rang such a chord with me when I first saw it two years ago. Jeff Taylor recognizes the importance of providing an environment that releases the human spirit—not only for the 1,100 employees at the company, but also for the hundreds of thousands of job seekers looking for a better life.

So the next time you find yourself signing an invoice for new Lava Lamps, you may want to think again. Why not give your new employees something of real, long-lasting value? Why not give them the freedom they crave to make a difference for themselves, and for your company?

Notes

Introduction

1. Seth Godin, Permission Marketing: Turning Strangers into Fiends and Friends into Customers, (New York, Simon & Schuster, 1999) and Seth Godin, "Unleash Your Ideavirus," Fast Company, August 2000, issue 37, page 115

2. Gary Hamel, Leading the Revolution (Boston, Harvard Business Press, 2000)

3. Kevin Kelly, New Rules for a New Economy, (New York: Viking Press, 1998)

4. Charles Fishman, "The War for Talent," Fast Company, August 1998, pg 104

5. I am appreciative of Andres Gomez, who has worked with thousands of people in intensive transformational seminars on the distinctions of transformational coaching for this diagram on creating the possible future that is not just an extension of the past.

6. I would like to acknowledge Tracy Goss for her work in executive reinvention. The three declarations she outlines for creating the impossible are truly powerful. See her book, The Last Word on Power: Executive Re-Invention for Leaders Who Must Make the Impossible Happen, (New York, Currency Doubleday), 1995

Chapter 1

1. From a speech by Lou Gerstner at the second international Harvard Conference on Internet and Society in Cambridge, Massachusetts, May 27, 1998.

2. Patricia Sellers, "The Big Score," Fortune, February 7, 2000, p. 138.

3. Harriet Rubin, Soloing, Realizing Your Life's Ambition (New York: Harper Business, 1999).

4. Michael Gerber, The E Myth Revisited (New York: Harper Business, 1995).

5. David Kirkpatrick, "The New Face of Microsoft," Fortune, February 7, 2000, p. 92.

6. Constance Gustke, "Back to the Future," Worth, February 2000, p. 41.

7. Michael Lewis, The New New Thing: A Silicon Valley Story (New York: W. W. Norton & Co., 2000).

8. Gary Hamel, "Bringing Silicon Valley Inside," Harvard Business Review, September 1999.

9. Again I am appreciative of the work that Tracy Goss has done in the field of executive reinvention; see also Tracy Goss, *The Last Word on Power: Executive Re-Invention for Leaders Who Must Make the Impossible Happen* (New York: Currency Doubleday, 1995).

Interlude I

1. I am appreciative of conversations with Tony Tjan and Bill Seibel of Zefer about their company.

2. Jim Biolos, "Career Models for the 21st Century," *Harvard Management Update*, May 1997.

3. Elliot Zaret, "Charting the Digital Path," MSNBC Business Web Site, August 12, 1999.

4. Ibid.

5. Jim Biolos, "Career Models for the 21st Century," *Harvard Management Update*, May 1997.

Chapter 2

1. Katharine Mieszkowski, "WebSight—Let Your Customers Lead," *Fast Company*, April 2000, p. 210.

2. I am appreciative of conversations with Jim Lanford, co-founder of NETrageous. See netrageous.com

3. I especially want to thank my friend and colleague Jay Abraham, a marketing guru who coined the phrase "strategy of preeminence", for his contribution to the thinking behind this book.

4. Peter Burrows, "Personal Computers: Are the Glory Days Over?", *Business Week Online*, February 14, 2000.

5. Thanks to Ken Kaplan, founder of *SellBigOnline Newsletter* sellbigonline.com, for conversations on building an e-business.

6. Again, I am grateful for conversations with Tony Tjan, co-founder of Zefer.

7. Katharine Mieszkowski, "WebSight—Let Your Customers Lead," *Fast Company*, April 2000, p. 210.

8. I appreciate conversations with Keith Fox, marketing vice president from Cisco Systems.

9. Jonathan Rosenoer, Douglas Armstrong, J. Russell Gates, *The Clickable Corporation* (New York: Free Press, 1999).

10. I am appreciative of conversations with Laurie Tucker, senior vice president of e-commerce at FedEx.

11. This is reprinted with permission from Jonathan Rosenoer, Douglas Armstrong, J. Russell Gates, *The Clickable Corporation* (New York: Free Press, 1999).

12. Jathon Sapsford, "Deal & Deal Makers: J. P. Morgan Tries Not to Be E-History—Venerable Firm," *Wall Street Journal*, March 9, 2000.

13. The "Scan, Focus, Act" model was developed by Jim Channon, Frank Burns, and Linda Nelson and is the copyright of Metasystems Design Group 1983. We first heard about the model from the people at MG Taylor Corporation in Cambridge, Massachusetts.

Interlude 2

1. I am very appreciative of conversations with Kevin McCallum about his unique process of customer interaction for product development.

Chapter 3

1. Michael Schrage, *No More Teams, Mastering the Art of Creative Collaboration* (New Yor: Currency Doubleday, 1989).

2. Thomas J. Neff & James M. Citrin, *Lessons from the Top, The Search for America's Best Business Leaders* (New York: Currency Doubleday, 1999).

3. Ronald A. Heifetz, *Leadership Without Easy Answers* (Belknap Press, 1994).

4. I am grateful for the time spent in conversation with Joan Holmes, the director of the Hunger Project.

5. I am appreciative of conversations with Roger Ackerman, CEO of Corning Incorporated.

6. David Kirkpatrick, "The New Face of Microsoft," *Fortune,* February 7, 2000, p. 92.

7. Dee Hock, *Birth of a Chaordic Age* (San Francisco: Berrett-Koehler, 1999) p. 191.

8. Quoted to me from a friend, Hieni Zugg from Ciba Geigy in Switzerland.

9. Kathleen Eisenhardt, D. Charles Galunic, "Coevolving: At Last, a Way to Make Synergies Work," *Harvard Business Review,* January–February 2000.

10. Ibid.

11. I appreciate conversations with John Seely Brown, Chief Scientist of Xerox research center (PARC).

12. Steven Prokesch, "Unleashing the Power of Learning: An Interview with British Petroleum's John Browne," *journal name*, Sept–Oct 97.

Interlude 3

1. I am grateful to Avram Miller for the time he gave for conversations about the work that he is doing.

2. "Who's Fast 2000," *Fast Company*, December 1999, p. 150.

3. Katharine Mieszkowski, "Digital Competition—Avram Miller," *Fast Company,* December 1999, p. 156.

4. Ibid.

5. Ibid.

6. Ibid.

Chapter 4

1. I am appreciative of conversations with Chan Suh of Agency.com.

2. I am thankful for time spent in conversations with Al Ries; see Laura and Al Ries, *The 22 Immutable Laws of Branding* (New York: HarperCollins, 1998).

3. Seth Godin, *Permission Marketing: Turning Strangers into Friends and Friends into Customers* (New York: Simon & Schuster, 1999) and Seth Godin, "Unleash Your Ideavirus," *Fast Company*, August 2000, p. 115.

4. Again, thanks to Keith Fox of Cisco Systems.

5. Seth Godin, *Permission Marketing: Turning Strangers into Friends and Friends into Customers* (New York: Simon & Schuster, 1999) and Don Peppers and Martha Rogers, *One to One Future: Building Relationships One Customer at a Time* (New York: Currency Doubleday, 1997).

Interlude 4

1. I am appreciative of conversations with Di-Ann Eisnor about her in-the-street marketing.

Chapter 5

1. Michael Gerber, *The E Myth Revisited* (New York: Harper Business, 1995).

2. I am grateful for conversations with Chan Suh, CEO of Agency.com, about his company.

3. I heard Jakob Neilsen speak at Jay Abraham's Billion Dollar Internet Strategy Setting Super Summit in January 2000. See Jakob Neilsen, *Designing Websites with Authority: Secrets of an Information Architect* (New York: New Riders, 1999).

4. Again, thanks to Laurie Tucker of Federal Express e-commerce.

5. Again, a special thanks to Chan Suh of Agency.com.

6. Jodi Mardesich, "The Web is No Shopper's Paradise," *Fortune,* November 8, 1999, p. 190.

7. B. Joseph Pine and James Gilmore, *The Experience Economy: Work Is Theatre and Every Business a Stage* (Cambridge, Massachusetts: Harvard Business School Press, 1999).

8. Again, appreciation to Audri Lanford, co-CEO of NETrageous, for sharing her knowledge of customer experiences on the Web.

9. Thanks to conversations with Ed Bingham of Coan Oil.

Interlude 5

1. I am appreciative of the time spent with Pehong Chen finding out more about BroadVision.

Chapter 6

1. From a speech by Jim Kelly, CEO of UPS, on February 9, 2000, to a Georgia-Pacific chairman's meeting in Fort Meyers, Florida.

2. I am appreciative of the time Jim Daniell, CEO of OrderTrust, an e-commerce company in Lowell, Massachusetts, spent with me.

3. Kate Kane, "LL Bean Delivers the Goods," *Fast Company,* August 1997, p. 104.

4. I am grateful for conversations with Richard Owen, CEO of Avantgo.com and former chief of Dell on-line.

5. Thomas J. Neff & James M. Citrin, *Lessons from the Top, The Search for America's Best Business Leaders* (New York: Currency Doubleday, 1999).

Interlude 6

1. I appreciate conversations with David Roussain of FedEx on the innovative, business-building ideas he has implemented at FedEx.

2. Scott Kirsner, "Digital Competition—Laurie A. Tucker," *Fast Company*, December 1999.

3. *Wall Street Journal Interactive*, "Ante Up! Big Gambles in the New Economy: Overnight Everything Changed for FedEx," November 4, 1999.

4. *Internet Week Online*, October 25, 1999.

5. This figure was taken from the FedEx Manifesto written by David Roussain and his top group.

6. This figure was taken from a FedEx e-business case study presentation by David Roussain.

Chapter 7

1. Michael Copeland, "Me and My Mentor," *Red Herring*, August 2000, p. 172.

2. The "Charlie story" was told to me by Sandy Ogg, vice president of organization development at Motorola.

3. I am appreciative of conversations with Dave Arnold, managing partner at Heidrick and Struggles.

4. The story of Roger Enrico comes from two articles: John Byrne, "PepsiCo's New Formula," *Business Week*, April 10, 2000, and Noel Tichy, Christopher Derose, and reporter Anne Faircloth, "Roger Enrico's Master Class," *Fortune*, November 25, 1997.

5. James Champy and Nitin Nohria, *The Arc of Ambition: Defining the Leadership Adventure* (Cambridge, Massachusetts: Perseus Books, 2000).

6. I am appreciative of conversations with Frank McCauley of the Royal Bank in Canada.

7. Keith Hammonds, "Grassroots Leadership—Ford Motor Company," *Fast Company*, April 2000.

8. I am appreciative of conversations with Jeff Taylor, CEO and founder of Monster. com.

9. Morgan W. McCall Jr., *High Flyers, Developing the Next Generation of Leaders* (Cambridge, Massachusetts: Harvard Business School Press, 1997).

10. I am thankful of conversations with my colleague, John Burdette of Orxestra in Toronto, Canada, about the subject of leadership development and the role of the "head, hand, heart and spirit" in developing leaders.

11. Keith Hammonds, "Grassroots Leadership—Ford Motor Company," *Fast Company*, April 2000.

12. Ibid.

13. Ibid.

14. Thanks to Sallie Hightower, a development leader of Conoco University.

15. I am appreciative of conversations on the subject of coaching and leadership development with my friend and colleague, Michel Renaud of Renaud Pemberton International in Montreal.

16. I would like to acknowledge the working relationship with Jo Pieters and the opportunity to work with him in creating a world-class leadership development program.

Interlude 7

1. "An E-Company CEO is Also the Recruiter-in-Chief," *Wall Street Journal*, November 9, 1999.

2. I would like to acknowledge Richard Owen, AvantGo.com, for the time spent in conversation about how he leads his company.

3. Charles Fishman, "The War for Talent," *Fast Company*, August 1998, p. 104.

4. Ibid.

5. Again, appreciation to Jeff Taylor, CEO of Monster.com.

6. Lisa Chadderdon, "Monster World," *Fast Company*, January 1999.

Index

About "Me," the Author

The Internet is a personal medium,
so let's get personal.

I live in Brookline, Massachusetts, with my wife, Susan, and five children. My passion is inspiring, empowering, and enabling people to make a difference in their world. My personal passions are superb ethnic food, adventure travel, golf, skiing, sailing, mountain climbing.

I began my career doing leadership coaching programs with a transformational twist that were designed to produce a breakthrough for people and a breakthrough in results. These high-impact programs were done on a global basis, with local centers in various parts of the world.

Thirty thousand people later, I got interested in the question of organizational transformation. As a result, I began to do intensive work for Global 2000 clients in the area of leadership renewal, culture change, marketing, supply chain, and other issues.

This resulted in my books (besides this book) *Mastering the Art of Creative Collaboration*, *Masterful Coaching*, and the *Masterful Coaching Fieldbook*. These books have created unparalleled opportunity, not only to express my ideas, but also to meet many fascinating and intriguing people—world leaders, CEOs, scientists, artists, students, and front-line employees.

About My Work—Masterful Coaching

The fastest route to becoming an e-leader and creating an e-business.

I am the founder and co-CEO of Masterful Coaching, Inc., and a speaker for the Washington Speaker's Bureau. We call ourselves the world leader in executive coaching, not because of the size or geographic spread of our handpicked Masterful Coaching World Network, but because we are changing the conversation about executive coaching in the world.

We believe that masterful coaching can only take place in the context of inspiring our clients to be the source of a powerful new future, not merely reacting to events; to create what's possible rather than what's predictable; to accomplish what they really need to accomplish, not just to psychologize.

Our one-year coaching programs start with asking executives to stand in the future that they want to create to declare ambitious aspirations for themselves and their organizations and to declare that fulfilling those aspirations is "the game" they are playing in life. This involves asking clients to step into the *reinvention paradigm*.

We coach clients to stretch their definition of their business, to recognize discontinuities brought on by the e-economy, and to leverage their strengths. At the same time, we coach clients to stretch their definition of themselves to break the grip and excel beyond old patterns that limit their creativity and effectiveness.

As no leader is an island, most of the work we do involves inspiring much higher levels of collaboration through a process I have developed called the CollabLab—*an accelerated solutions environment*. This process is applied to issues such as e-business strategy, brand marketing, virtual supply chain, human capital, and corporate culture.

The principal offices of Masterful Coaching, Inc., are in Brookline, Massachusetts, with satellite offices in Montreal, London, Brussels, Hong Kong, and Cuernavaca, Mexico. Please visit our Web site MasterfulCoaching.com. I also very much enjoy interacting with people who have read my books. My preferred means of communication is e-mail and I invite you to contact me at Robert.Hargrove@MasterfulCoaching.com.